Proper Noun Speller

Compiled by Jean Emerich

QuikRef Publishing
Los Angeles, California

PROPER NOUN SPELLER

Published by: QuikRef Publishing
                 4391 Sunset Blvd., Suite 531
                 Los Angeles, CA 90029

Printed in the United States
Fourth Printing

Copyright © 1990 by QuikRef Publishing

ISBN: 0-944494-11-0
SAN: 243-6302

Library of Congress Cataloging in Publication Data.

Emerich, Jean, 1933-
    Proper noun speller.

    Summary: A reference work for the correct spelling
of over 15,000 proper nouns or names.

    1. Spellers. [1. Names, Personal.   2. Names]
I. Title.
PE1146.E53   1989   428.1   89-10977
ISBN 0-944494-10-2
ISBN 0-944494-11-0 (pbk.)

FOREWORD

The purpose of the *Proper Noun Speller* is to serve as a convenient reference for the correct spelling of proper nouns (names). This first edition offers a list of over 15,000 entries, compiled from over 2,800 reference sources.

Proper nouns include: names of people, organizations and their members, titles of people, brand names, trademarks or service marks, publications, literary, dramatic and musical works, paintings, sculpture and other artistic works, places, geographic divisions, districts, regions, locales, rivers, lakes, mountains, oceans, ships, airplanes, space vehicles, nationalities, races, tribes, languages, historical periods, events, names for Deity and sacred works, days, months, holidays, councils and congresses, specific judicial courts, treaties and laws, geological eras, periods, epochs, prehistoric divisions, constellations, planets, stars, and specific scientific terms.

USING THE PROPER NOUN SPELLER

Spelling Variations. Because of country origins, or phonetic translations, some personal names may have more than one correct spelling. These variations are shown as follows:

> Carl Maria von Weber, also Karl

Similarities. To avoid confusion where spelling of two separate entries is similar, or the same, a brief description, or location, follows such entries:

> Cannon™ linens   Pittsburg, CA
> Canon™ electronics   Pittsburgh, PA

> Engelbert Humperdinck (contemporary singer)
> Engelbert Humperdinck (Ger. composer)

Pronunciation Marks. Nouns listed in the *Proper Noun Speller* are the Anglicized version. Pronunciation marks are thus limited to those proper nouns in which such marks are considered to be integral to the correctness of the spelling:

> Häagen-Dazs, ice cream

Personal Names. For easier reference, listings for persons living, dead, or fictional, are shown in two ways: 1) first name first, 2) last name first:

> Michelangelo Buonarroti
> Buonarroti, Michelangelo

Additionally, individuals known by a pseudonym are listed in the following manner:

> Mark Twain (pseud. Samuel Clemens)
> Twain, Mark (pseud. Samuel Clemens)
> Clemens, Samuel (aka Mark Twain)

Trademarks. The ™ symbol is used to indicate all trademarks and brand names, including those registered:

Kleenex ™

Titles. Personal titles considered to be of permanent nature— royalty, religion, or educational—are shown in the following way:

Sir Lawrence Olivier
Olivier, Sir Lawrence

Personal titles considered to be of a temporary nature, such as political, whether past—if that title is considered an integral part of the person's public image—or current, are shown in the following way:

Yitzhak Shamir, P.M.
Shamir, Yitzhak, P.M.

Italicized Nouns. Titles of books, magazines, newspapers, plays, movies, paintings and sculpture, long musical compositions, very long poems, ships, planes, spacecraft, as well as foreign words which are not yet Anglicized, indication of names of plaintiff and defendant in legal citations, the New Latin names of genera, species, subspecies and varieties in botanical and zoological nomenclature, but not phyla, classes, orders, and families are normally italicized:

Proper Noun Speller

Note: If you are printing by hand, or using a typewriter, these nouns may be identified by underlining them.

Hyphenating Proper Nouns. While the practice of hyphenating is far from standard, to reduce chances of confusion, it is best to avoid splitting any one single word of a proper noun. If splitting cannot be avoided, the following rules should be observed:

Nouns of one syllable should not be divided.

Nouns of more than one syllable should be divided only

between syllables.

Persons with titles should not be divided so that the title is left alone on one line, with the balance of the name on the next.

Acronyms: A separate section of acronyms follows the main section.

ABBREVIATIONS USED
IN THE PROPER NOUN SPELLER

Adm.	Admiral	Grc.	Greece
Afr.	Africa	Guat.	Guatemala
AK	Alaska	H.M.S.	His (Her) Majesty's
AL	Alabama		Ship
Alb.	Alberta, Can.	HI	Hawaii
AR	Arkansas	Hung.	Hungary
Assoc.	Association	IA	Iowa
Aus.	Austria	ID	Idaho
Austl.	Australia	IL	Illinois
AZ	Arizona	IN	Indiana
B.C.	British Columbia,	Inc.	Incorporation
	Canada	Ire.	Ireland
Bel.	Belgium	Is.	Islands
Br.	British	Isl.	Island
CA	California	It.	Italy
Can.	Canada	Jap.	Japan
Capt.	Captain	Jew.	Jewish
Chanc.	Chancellor	KS	Kansas
Ch.	China	KY	Kentucky
chem.sym.	chemical symbol	L.A.	Los Angeles
CO	Colorado	LA	Louisiana
Co.	Company	Lt.	Lieutenant
Co.	County	MA	Massachusetts
Col.	Colonel	Man.	Manitoba, Can.
Com.	Commander	MD	Maryland
CT	Connecticut	ME	Maine
Czech.	Czechoslovakia	Mex.	Mexico
DC	District of	MI	Michigan
	Columbia	MN	Minnesota
DE	Delaware	MO	Missouri
Den.	Denmark	Mor.	Morocco
Dept.	Department	MS	Mississippi
dist.	district	MT	Montana
E. Ger.	East Germany	Mtn.	Mount, mountain
Eg.	Egypt	Mts.	Mountains
Eng.	England	myth	mythology
Eur.	Europe	N. Ire.	Northern Ireland
Fed.	Federation	Nat. Fr.	National Forest
Fin.	Finland	Nat. Mon.	National Monument
FL	Florida	Nat. Pk.	National Park
Fr.	France	Neth.	Netherlands
GA	Georgia	N.A.	North America
Gen.	General	NC	North Carolina
Gov.	Governor	ND	North Dakota

NE	Nebraska	Scot.	Scotland
NH	New Hampshire	SD	South Dakota
NJ	New Jersey	Secy.	Secretary
NM	New Mexico	Sen.	Senator
NV	Nevada	Sp.	Spain
NY	New York	Swe.	Sweden
NYC	New York City	Switz.	Switzerland
N.Z.	New Zealand	TN	Tennessee
OH	Ohio	Tur.	Turkey
OK	Oklahoma	TX	Texas
Ont.	Ontario, Can.	U.A.E.	United Arab
OR	Oregon		Emirates
Organ.	Organization	Un.	United
P.R.	Puerto Rico	Univ.	University
PA	Pennsylvania	UK	United Kingdom
Phil.	Philippines	US	United States
P.M.	Prime Minister	USS	United States Ship
Port.	Portugal	USSR	Union of Soviet
Pres.	President		Socialist Republics
Pr.Ed.Is.	Prince Edward	UN	United Nations
	Island	UT	Utah
prov.	province	V.P.	Vice President
Que.	Québec, Can.	VA	Virginia
reg.	region	V.I.	Virgin Islands
rep.	republic	VT	Vermont
Rep.	Representative	W. Ger.	West Germany
Rev.	Reverend	WA	Washington
RI	Rhode Island	WI	Wisconsin
S.A.	South America	W.I.	West Indies
Sask.	Saskatchewan, Can.	WV	West Virginia
SC	South Carolina	WY	Wyoming

A & W™ Rootbeer
A-bomb
A-frame
A-horizon
A-line
A-Team
A. A. Milne (*Winnie-the-Pooh*)
A. C. Nielsen Co.
A. E. Hotchner
A. E. Housman
A. E. van Vogt
A. J. Cronin (Archibald)
A. J. Foyt
A.l.™ Steak Sauce
A.R.M.™
Aachen, W. Ger.
Aalborg, Denmark
Aamco Transmissions™
Aare River, or Aar
Aarhus, Denmark
Aaron Bros. Art Marts
Aaron Burr, V.P.
Aaron Copland
Aaron Spelling
Aaron, Henry 'Hank'
AB Newsamerica Satellite Newsnet
Abaddon (the Devil)
Abbado, Claudio
Abbas I
Abbassid dynasty
Abbe, Cleveland
Abbeville Press
Abbeville, Fr.
Abbevillian, Fr.
Abbey Road
Abbey Theatre (Ireland)

Abbie Hoffman
Abbot, Charles Greeley
Abbott and Costello
Abbott, Bud
Abbott, George
Abbott, Lyman
ABC After School Special
ABC Information Radio
ABC News
ABC Radio Network News
ABC-TV
Abdul, Paula
Abdul-Jabbar, Kareem (Lew Alcindor)
Abdullah, King of Jordan
Abe Burrows
Abe Kobo
Abel (son Adam & Eve)
Abel Janszoon Tasman
Abelard, Peter, or Pierre
Abercrombie & Fitch
Aberdeen (Black) Angus cattle
Aberdeen Proving Ground, MD
Aberdeen, Scotland
Aberdeen, SD
Abernathy, Ralph
Abidjan, Ivory Coast
Abigail, Adams
Abigail Van Buren ('Dear Abby')
Abilene, KS, TX
ABM missile
Abner Doubleday
Abner, Li'l
ABO system
Abominable Snowman
Aboriginal Science Fiction
Abracadabra, Lady
Abraham Lincoln, Pres.
Abraham, Plains of
Abraham's bosom, in
Abruzzi region, Italy
Abscam scandle
Absinthe
Absoft™ software
Absolut™ vodka
Abstract Expressionism
Abu Dhabi, U.A.E.
Abyssinia
Abyssinian cat

Abzug, Bella
Ac (chem. sym. actinium)
AC/DC (electrical current)
AC/DC (rock group)
Academy Awards
Academy of St. Martin-in-the-Fields
Acadia Nat. Park
Acadia, Nova Scotia
Acadian
Acapulco, Mex.
Acarigua, Venezuela
Accra, Ghana
Ace™ bandage
Achates (in *Aeneid*)
Achernar (star)
Acheron River ('river of woe')
Acheson, Dean, Secy. State
Achille Lauro
Achilles (Trojan hero)
Achilles' heel
Achilles' tendon
Ackroyd, David
Acoma pueblo
Aconcagua Mtn.
Acrilan™
Acropolis, Athens
Act™ floride
act of God
Actifed™
Acts of the Apostles, or the Acts
Acuff, Roy
Acura™ cars
Acura Integra™
Acutrim™
Adak Naval Air Station, AK
Adam and Eve
Adam Ant
Adam Clayton Powel, Jr.
Adam 12 TV show
Adam's apple
Adam's needle
Adams, Abigail
Adams, Ansel
Adams, John, Pres. (2nd)
Adams, John Quincy, Pres. (6th)
Adams, Maude
Adams, Samuel
Adar (Jew. mo.)

Adar Sheni (Jew.)
Addams Family, The
Addams, Charles
Addams, Jane
Adderly, Cannonball
Addis Ababa, Ethiopia
Addison's disease
Addressograph™
Adelaide, Australia
Adele Astaire
Adelina, Patti
Aden, Gulf of
Aden, South Yemen
Adenauer, Konrad, Chancellor
Adidas™ activewear
Adirondack Mts., or the Adirondacks
Adlai E. Stevenson, Jr., Gov.
Adlai E. Stevenson, Sr., V.P.
Adlai E. Stevenson, III, Sen.
Adler, Felix
Adler, Larry
Adler, Luther
Adler, Stella
Admetus, king of Thessaly
Admiral of the Fleet
Admiralty mile
Admission Day
Adnan Khashoggi
Adolf Eichmann
Adolf Hitler
Adolfo™
Adolph Coors Co.
Adolph Zukor
Adolphe Menjou
Adonis
Adrenalin™
Adriaen van Ostade
Adriamycin™
Adrian Boult, Sir
Adriatic Sea, or the Adriatic
Adrien Arpel
Adrienne Vittadini
Advent
Advent Sunday
Adventist (doctrine)
Adventists, Seventh-Day
Adversary (the Devil)
Advertising Age

Advil™ pain reliever
Adweek magazine
Aegean civilization
Aegean Is.
Aegean Sea
Aegeus, king of Athens
Aegir (Norse god)
Aeneas (a Trojan)
Aeneid
Aeolian harp
Aer Lingus
Aeroflot airline
Aeromexico
Aerosmith
Aeschylus
Aesop's fables
Affenpinscher, or affenpinscher
Affonso de Albuquerque
Afghan hound
Afghan people
Afghanistan
Africa
African violet
Africanism
Africanist
Afrikaans (language)
Afrikander cattle
Afrikaner (speaks Afrikaans)
Afrin™ nasal spray
Afro hairstyle
Afro-American
After Five™ clothes
Ag (chem. sym. silver)
Aga Khan (a title)
Agam, Yaacov
Agamemnon
Agana, Guam
Agassi, Andre
Agassiz, Louis
Agatha Christie, Dame
Agathocles
Age of Aquarius
Age of Enlightenment
Agee, James
Agent Orange
Agesilaus II
Agfa™ film
Agincourt, France

Agnes De Mille
Agnes Moorehead
Agnes Nixon
Agnes, Saint
Agnew, David Hayes
Agnew, Spiro T., V.P.
Agnon, Shmuel
Agnus Dei (holy lamb)
Agostino Carracci
Agra, India
Agricola, Gnaeus
Agriculture, U.S. Dept. of
Agrippa, Herod
Agrippa, Marcus Vipsanius
Agrippina, the Elder
Agrippina, the Younger
Agua Caliente Race Track
Aguascalientes, Mexico
Aguecheek, Sir Andrew
Aguinaldo, Emillo
Agulhas Cape, Afr.
Agulhas current
Ah-H Bra™ bra
Ahab, Captain
Ahaji Shagari, Pres.
Aherne, Brian
Ahmad Jamal
Ahmad Rashad
Ahmanson Theater, L.A.
Ahmed (Turkish sultans)
Ahmed, Kazi Zafar, P.M.
Ahmedabad, India, or Ahmadabad
Ahtena Indians
Ahura Mazda
Ahvaz, Iran, or Ahwaz
Aida (Verdi)
AIDS
AIDS-related complex
Aiello, Danny
Aikawa, Jap.
Aiken, Conrad
Aiken, Joan
Aikido, or aikido
Ailey, Alvin, Jr.
Aim™ toothpaste
Aimee Semple McPherson
Ainsworth, William Harrison
Air America™

Air Cal™
Air Express™
Air Force Cross
Air Force Magazine
Air Force One (Pres. plane)
Air Force Times
Air France™
Air-India™
Air Malta™
Air Medal
Air Paraguay™
Air Supply
Airedale (dog)
Airwalk™ shoes
Airwick™ air freshner
Airwolf
Aisha (chief wife of Mohammed)
Aisne River (France)
Aiwa™ cassette
Aix-en-Provence, Fr.
Aix-la-Chapelle, Fr.
Ajaccio, Corsica
Ajax (Trojan)
Ajax™ cleanser
AK-47 assault rifle
Akai™ stereo
Akbar, the Great
Akeley, Carl Ethan
Akhenaten, or Akhenaton, or
  Ikhnaton
Akiba ben Joseph
Akihito, Emperor
Akim Tamiroff
Akira Kurosawa
Akita (dog)
Akita, Jap.
Akkadian people
Akron Beacon Journal
Akron, OH
Akvavit™
Al (chem. sym. aluminum)
Al Capp
Al Jarreau
Al Jizah, Egypt, or Giza
Al Jolson
Al Joyner
Al Michaels
Al Pacino

Al Unser
al-Fayumi, Saadia ben Joseph
Al-Mansurah, Eg., or El Mansura
al Sadat, Anwar, Pres., or Anwar
  Sadat
Alabama (AL)
Aladdin (magic lamp)
Alameda Naval Air Station
Alameda, CA
Alamine™
Alamo™ car rental
Alamo, the
Alamogordo, NM
Alan Alda
Alan Arkin
Alan Funt
Alan Ladd
Alan Jay Lerner
Alan Parsons
Alan Rachins
Alan Shepard, Astronaut
Alan Thicke
Alar™ pesticide
Alarcón, Pedro Antonio
Alaric (Visigoth king)
Alaska (AK)
Alaska Airlines™
Alaska Highway, or Alaskan
Alaska Peninsula
Alaska Range
Alaska Standard Time
Alaska, baked
Alaskan malamute
Alaskan purchase, or Seward's folly
Alba, Duke of, also Alva
Alba, Italy
Alban Berg
Albania
Albany Congress
Albany, GA, NY
Albee, Edward
Albemarle, Earl of
Alben Barkley, V.P.
Alberghetti, Anna Maria
Albers, Josef
Albert Brooks
Albert Camus
Albert Dekker

Albert Einstein
Albert Finney
Albert Gleizes
Albert McCleery
Albert Michelson
Albert Nipon
Albert Bruce Sabin
Albert Schweitzer, Dr.
Albert Speer
Albert, Prince
Alberta, prov., Can.
Alberto Giacometti
Alberto™ haircare
Alberto Santos-Dumont
Alberto VO5™
Albertsons, store
Albertus Magnus, Saint, also Saint
   Albert the Great
Albrecht Dürer
Albright, Ivan
Albright, William
Albuquerque Journal
Albuquerque Living
Albuquerque, Affonso de
Albuquerque, NM
Alcaeus (Greek poet)
Alcan Highway
Alcatraz Island
Alcatraz prison ('The Rock')
Alcatraz, Birdman of
Alcestis (Gr. myth)
Alcibiades
Alcindor, Lew (Kareem Abdul-Jabbar)
ALCOA Aluminum Co. of America
Alcoholics Anonymous
Alcoran (The Koran)
Alcott, Amos
Alcott, Amy
Alcott, Louisa May
Alcuin, or Albinus (Eng. scholar)
Alcyone (Gr. myth)
Alda, Alan
Alda, Robert
Aldebaran (double star)
Alder, Kurt
Aldington, Richard
Aldous Huxley
Aldrich, Henry

Aldrich, Nelson Wilmarth
Aldrich, Thomas Bailey
Aldridge, Ira Frederick
Aldrin, Edwin E. 'Buzz', Astronaut
Alec Guinness, Sir
Aleichem, Sholom (pseud. Shalom
   Rabinowitz)
Aleksandr Blok
Aleksandr Borodin
Aleksandr Glazunov
Aleksandr Sergeyevich Pushkin
Aleksandr Scriabin
Aleksandr Solzhenitsyn
Aleksei N. Kosygin, Prem.
Aleksei Leonov, Cosmonaut
Aleksei Yeliseyev, Cosmonaut
Alemanni (Germanic tribes)
Alemannic (High German dialect)
Alessandria, Italy
Alessandro Scarlatti
Alessandro Volta, Conte
Aleut Indians, or the Aleuts
Aleutian Is.
Alex Karras
Alex Trebek
Alexander Archipenko
Alexander Calder
Alexander cocktail
Alexander Dubeck
Alexander Fleming, Sir
Alexander Godunov
Alexander Graham Bell
Alexander the Great, or Alexander III
Alexander M. Haig, Jr., Gen.
Alexander Hamilton
Alexander Mackenzie, P.M.
Alexander Mackenzie, Sir (explorer)
Alexander Pope
Alexander Selkirk (real Crusoe)
Alexander Woollcott
Alexander N. Yakovlev
Alexandra Danilova
Alexandre Dumas
Alexandre Logoya
Alexandre Millerand, Pres.
Alexandria, Eg.
Alexandria, VA
Alexio, Dennis

Alfa Romeo™ Spider
Alfie
Alfre Woodard
Alfred Bester
Alfred Dreyfus, Capt.
Alfred the Great
Alfred Hitchcock
Alfred Hitchcock's Mystery
  Magazine
Alfred C. Kinsey (*Kinsey Report*)
Alfred A. Knopf Inc.
Alfred Lunt and Lynn Fontanne
Alfred B. Nobel
Alfred Noyes
Alfred Sisley
Alfred Pritchard Sloan
Alfred Tennyson, Lord
Alfredo Cristiani, Pres.
Alfredo Stroessner, Pres.
Algeciras (seaport on Strait of Gibralter)
Alger Hiss
Alger, Horatio
Algeria
Algernon Swinburne
Algiers, Algeria
Algol
Algonquin Hotel, NY
Algonquin Indians, or Algonkin
Alhambra, CA
Alhambra, The
Ali Baba
Ali Khamenei, Pres.
Ali MacGraw
Ali Pasha
Ali, Haidar, or Ali, Hyder
Ali, Muhammad (Cassius Clay, Jr.)
Ali, Muhammad (pasha of Egypt)
Alice Cooper
Alice Dunbar-Nelson
Alice Faye
Alice Ghostley
Alice Munro
Alice B. Toklas
Alien and Sedition Acts
Alighieri Dante
Alistair Cooke
Alitalia™ Airlines
Alka Seltzer™

All-Bran™
All Fools' Day, or April Fools' Day
All Hallows Day
All Saints' Day
All Souls' Day
All's Well That Ends Well
All-Knowing (God)
All-Merciful (God)
All-Powerful (God)
All-Wise (God)
Allah (God)
Allan Carr
Allan Pinkerton
Allegany, NY
Allegheny Mts., PA
Allegheny Nat. Forest
Allegheny River (PA)
Allen Ginsberg
Allen Ludden
Allen wrench
Allen, Debbie
Allen, Ethan
Allen, Fred
Allen, Gracie
Allen, Mel
Allen, Woody
Allentown Morning Call
Allentown, PA
AllerAct™
Allergan Lens Plus™
Allessandra Ferri
Alley, Kirstie
Allez-Oop
Allhallows, or Allhallowmas
Allhallowtide
Allied Van Lines™
Allies (of WW II)
Alliluyeva, Svetlana
Allison, Fran (of *Kukla, Fran & Ollie*)
Allman Brothers, the
Allman, Gregg
Ally Sheedy
Allyce Beasley
Allyson, June
Almaden™ wine
Almagest (Ptolemy)
Almay™ cosmetics
Almighty, the

Almond Joy™
Alnu people
Alpenziger cheese
Alpert, Herb
Alpha Beta stores
Alpha-Bits™ cereal
Alpha Centauri
Alpo™ dog food
Alps, the
Alsace-Lorraine, Fr.
Alsatian (native of Alsace)
Altadena, CA
Altair (double star)
Altamira caves, or Caves of Altamira
Altamont racetrack
Altec™ speaker
Althea Gibson
Altman, Robert
Altoona, PA
Altovise Davis (Mrs. Sammy)
Altus Air Force Base, OK
Alundum™
Alvarez, Luis Walter
Alvin Ailey, Jr.
Alvin & the Chipmunks
Alysheba horse race
Alzheimer's disease
Amadeo Avogadro
Amadeus
Amadeus Quartet
Amadine Dupin (aka George Sand)
Amalekites people
Amalthea (Jupiter moon)
Amana™ appliances
Amana Church Society
Amanda Blake
Amarillo, TX
Amati violin
Amazing Stories
Amazon River
Amazon women
Amberlite™
Ambler, Eric
Amboise, France
Ambroise, Thomas
Ambrose Bierce
Ambrose E. Burnside, General
Ambrose, Saint

Ambrosian Library (Italy)
Amdek™ computer
Ameche, Don
Amedeo Modigliani
Amelia Bloomer (bloomers)
Amelia Earhart
Amelia-Bedelia
Amen Wardy boutique
Amenhotep I, or Amenophis I
Amenhotep III
Amerasian
America
America West Airlines
America's Cup
Americaine™
American Airlines™
American Ballet Theatre
American Bar Association
American Bar Association Journal
American Beauty rose
American Book Review
American cheese
American Civil Liberties Union
    (ACLU)
American Demographics
American Dream, or dream
American eagle
American English, or General
    American
American Express card
American Graffiti
American hotel plan
American Indian Movement
American Indians
American Institute of Architects
American Legion
American Legion Magazine
American Library Association (ALA)
American Medical Association
    (AMA)
American Opinion Bookstore
American Poetry Review
American Red Cross
American Revolution
American Saddle Horse
American Samoa
American Sign Language
Amer. Standard Version of the Bible

American water spaniel
American West
America West Airlines™
American wirehair cat
Americana
Americanism
Amerigo Vespucci
Ames Brothers, The
Ames Test
Ames, Leon
Amharic (language)
Amherst College
Amherst, Jeffrey, Gen./Baron
Amherst, MA
Amiens, France
Amiens, Treaty of
Amigaworld
Amilcare Ponchielli
Amin, Ida Dada Oumee, Pres.
Amish
Amityville Horror, The
Amityville, NY
Amman, Jordan (capital)
Ammens™
Ammon, or Amon
Ammonite people
Amnesty International
Amoco™ gas
Amorite people
Amory, Cleveland
Amos Alcott
Amos, Famous
Ampere, André
Amsterdam, Morey
Amsterdam, Netherlands
Amsterdam, NY
Amtico Vinyl Tile™
Amtrak Express
Amu Darya River
Amur River
Amy Alcott
Amy Lowell
Amy Madigan
Amy Tan
Amy Vanderbilt
Anabaptists
Anacin ™
Anacreon (poet)

Anadyr River, or Anadir
Anaheim, CA (Disneyland)
Anais Anais™ perfume
Analog
Anantapur, India
Anasazi Indians
Anastasia
Anastasio Somoza, Pres.
Anatolia
Anatoly Berezovoy, Cosmonaut
Anatoly Karpov
Anatoly, Dobrynin
Anaxagoras (Socrates' teacher)
Anaximander (Gr. philosopher)
Anchorage Daily News
Anchorage Times
Anchorage, AK
Ancient Chinese
Ancient of Days (God)
Ancren Riwle, or Ancrene Wisse
Andalusia region, Spain
Andaman Is.
Andaman Sea
Andamanese people
Anders Jonas Angström
Anders Celsius
Anders Zorn
Anders, William, Astronaut
Andersen, Hans Christian
Anderson, Dame Judith
Anderson, Marian
Anderson, Maxwell
Anderson, Richard Dean
Anderson, Sherwood
Andes Mountains
Andie MacDowell
Andorra (country)
Andorra, Andorra (city, country)
Andre Agassi
André Ampere
André Breton
Andre Cold Duck™
André Courréges
Andre the Giant
André Gide
Andre Kostelanetz
André Previn
Andre, Carl

18

Andre, John, Major
Andrea Doria
Andrea Doria, Admiral
Andrea Palladio
Andrea Pfister
Andrea Verrocchio
Andreas Papandreou, P.M.
Andrei Chesnokov
Andrei A. Gromyko, Pres., or Andrey
Andrei Dmitriyevich Sakharov
Andrés Segovia
Andress, Ursula
Andretti, Mario
Andrew Aguecheek, Sir
Andrew Carnegie
Andrew Dice Clay
Andrew Jackson, Pres.
Andrew Jergens Co., The
Andrew Johnson, Pres.
Andrew W. Mellon
Andrew Volstead, Rep.
Andrew Wyeth
Andrew Jackson Young, Mayor
Andrew, Saint
Andrews Air Force Base, MD
Andrews Sisters (Patti, Maxine, La
   Verne)
Andrews, Archie
Andrews, Julie
Andries Pretorius
Andriyan Nikolayev, Cosmonaut
Androcles & the lion
Andromache (Hector's wife)
Andromeda (Perseus' wife)
Andromeda Galaxy
Andromeda strain
Andronicus, Marcus
Andronicus, Titus
Andropov, Yuri, Gen. Secy.
Andy Capp
Andy Devine
Andy Gibb
Andy Griffith
Andy Rooney
Andy Warhol
Angel Falls in Venezuela
Angel Soft™ bath. tissue
Angela Davis

Angela Lansbury
Angeleno (native of L.A.)
Angelico, Fra
Angelou, Maya
Angelus prayer
Angie Dickinson
Angkor Wat, or Vat
Angkor, N.W. Cambodia
Angle (5th century people)
Anglican Church
Anglican Communion
Anglo-American
Anglo-Australian Observatory
Anglo-French
Anglo-Indian
Anglo-Saxon
Anglo-Saxon Chronicle
Anglophile
Anglophobia
Angola
Angora cat
Angora goat
Angora rabbit
Angora wool
Angostura bitters
Angst, often *angst*
Angström, Anders Jonas
Anguilla, W.I.
Anhalt, Prince Frederik von
Anheuser-Busch, Inc.
Animal's Voice magazine
Anita Ekberg
Anita Loos
Anjelica Huston
Anjou pear
Anjou region, France
Ankara, Turkey
Ann Arbor, MI
Ann Blyth
Ann Jillian
Ann Landers (Eppie Lederer)
Ann Rutledge
Anna Maria Alberghetti
Anna Held
Anna Karenina
Anna Magnani
Anna Pavlova
Anna Sewell

Annapolis Convention
Annapolis Naval Academy
Annapolis, MD.
Annapurna #1, Nep. (mtn. peak)
Anne of Austria
Anne Bancroft
Anne Boleyn
Anne Bradstreet
Anne of Brittany
Anne Brontë
Anne of Cleves
Anne of Denmark
Anne Frank
Anne Hathaway
Anne Jeffreys
Anne Klein™
Anne Spencer Lindbergh
Anne Sexton
Annette Funicello
Annie Besant
Annie Hall
Annie Oakley
Annie Potts
Annie, Little Orphan
Annunciation lily
Anointing of the Sick
Anon (abr. for anonymous)
Ansel Adams
Anselm, Saint
Anso Worryfree Carpet™
Anspach, Susan
Ant, Adam
Antabuse™
Antananarive, Madagascar
Antarctic Circle
Antarctic Peninsula
Antarctica (continent)
Antares (double star)
Anthony Eden, Sir, P.M.
Anthony Geary
Anthony Hopkins
Anthony Perkins
Anthony Pools ™
Anthony Quinn
Anthony Trollope
Anthony Van Dyck, Sir, or Vandyke
Anthony Wayne, Gen.
Anthony, Piers

Anthony, Susan B.
Anti-Corn-Law League
Anti-Masonic party
Anti-Saloon League
anti-Semite
anti-Semitism
Antibes, Fr.
Antichrist
Antietam campaign
Antigone
Antigua and Barbuda, N.A.
Antigua, Guatemala
Antilles, Greater
Antilles, Lesser
Antioch, CA
Antioch, Turkey, or Antakya
Antiquax™
Antoine Henri Becquerel
Antoine Emile Bourdelle
Antoine Cadillac, Governor
Antoine Laurent Lavoisier
Antoine Pevsner
Antoinette, Marie
Anton Bruckner
Anton Chekhov
Anton Dvorák, or Antonin
Anton Rubinstein (Russian pianist)
Anton, Susan
Antonio de Santa Anna, Gen.
Antonio Gaudí
Antonio Salieri
Antonio Sant'Elia
Antonio Stradivari, or Antonius
    Stradivarius
Antonio Vivaldi
Antony and Cleopatra
Antony van Leeuwenhoek
Antony, Mark, or Marc
Antron™
Antwerp, Belgium
Antwerpen prov., Belgium
Anubis
Anvers Island, Antarctica
Anwar Sadat, Pres., or Anwar al
Anza, Juan Bautista de
AP Broadcast Services
AP News Cable
AP Radio

Apache Indians
Apalachicola Nat. Forest
Apalachicola River
Apalachicola, FL
Apennines Mts.
Apgar score
Aphrodite (Gr. myth)
Apocalypse, the
Apocrypha
Apollo (god of the Sun)
Apollo Lunar Rover
Apollo-Soyuz Test Project
Apollo Space Program
Apollo space vehicle (*Apollo ll* first to
    Moon)
Apollo Theater (Harlem)
Apollodorus
Apollonius of Rhodes
Apollyon (the Devil)
Apostles' Creed
Apostolic Fathers
Appalachia
Appalachian Mts.
Appalachian Trail
Appaloosa horse
Appenzell, Switz.
Appian Way (Roman road)
Appian Way™ pizza
Apple Computer, Inc.
Apple Jacks™ cereal
Apple Newtons™ cookies
Apple Macintosh™
Appleby, John Francis
Applegate, Jesse
Appleseed, Johnny (John Chapman)
Appomattox Court House
Appomattox, VA
April Fools' Day, or All Fools' Day
Apure River
Apus (Bird of Paradise) constellation
Aqaba, Gulf of
Aqua Chem™
Aqua Net™
Aqua Velva™
Aqua-fresh™
Aqualung™
Aquarian
Aquarius (zodiac sign)

Aquarius constellation
Aquila (Eagle) constellation
Aquinas, Saint Thomas
Aquino, Corazon, Pres.
Aquitaine region, France
Aquitaine, Eleanor of
Ar (chem. sym. argon)
Arab League
Arab-Israeli Six-Day War
Arab-Israeli Wars
Arabia, or Arabian Peninsula
Arabian camel (one hump)
Arabian Desert
Arabian Nights, or *A Thousand and
    One Nights*
Arabian Sea
Arabic numerals
Arable, Fern
Arabs
Arachne (Gr. myth)
Arafat, Yasser, or Yasir
Aragon region, Spain
Aragon, Catherine of
Araguaia River
Arak, Iran
Araks River (Turkey)
Aral Sea, Sov. Un. (was Lake Aral)
Aram Ilich Khachaturian
Aramean, or Aramaean
Aramaic language
Aramis™
Arapaho Indians
Arapaho Nat. Forest
Ararat, Mt., Turkey
Araucanian Indians, or Araucan
Arawak Indians
Arbitron ratings
Arbor Day
Arbuckle, Fatty
Arby's™ fast food
Arc de Triomphe
Arcadia (reg. ancient Grc.)
Arcadia, CA
Arcaro, George 'Eddie'
Arch of Constantine
Arch Oboler
Arch of Titus
Archangel Gabriel

Archbishop of Canterbury
Arche Rivav™
Archeozoic era, or Archaeozoic
Archer, Corliss
Archerd, Army
Arches Nat. Park (UT)
Archfiend (the Devil)
Archibald MacLeish
Archie Andrews
Archie Bunker
Archie Goodwin
Archimedes
Archimedes' principle
Archimedes' screw
Archipenko, Alexander
Architectural Digest
Arcosanti community, AZ
Arctic (area)
Arctic Circle
Arctic Ocean
Arcturus (star)
Arden, Elizabeth
Arden, Eve
Aretha Franklin
Arezzo, Italy
Argentina
Argo (Jason's ship)
Argonauts
Argonne region, France
Argyll, Duke of
Ariadne (Gr. myth)
Ariel Durant (Will and)
Ariel Sharon
Aries (zodiac sign)
Aries (Ram) constellation
Arikha, Avigdor
Aris-Isotoner™ Gloves
Aristide Maillol
Aristophanes (poet)
Aristotelian logic, or Aristotelean
Aristotle
Aristotle Socrates Onassis
Aristotle, Christina
Arizona (AZ)
Arizona Daily Star
Arizona Highways
Arizona Republic
Ark of the Covenant

Ark, Joan Van
Arkansas (AR)
Arkansas River
Arkie™ computer game
Arkin, Alan
Arkwright, Sir Richard
Arledge, Roone
Arlen, Harold
Arlen, Richard
Arlene Dahl
Arlene Francis
Arles, Fr.
Arles, kingdom of
Arlington Hall Station
Arlington National Cemetery
Arlington, TX, VA
Arliss, George
Arlo Guthrie
Arm & Hammer™
Armada, Spanish
Armadeo Avogadro
Armageddon
Armagh county, N. Ire.
Armagnac brandy
Armand Assante
Armand Hammer
Armand Jean Richelieu, Cardinal, or
    Duc de Richelieu
Armani, Giorgio
Armbruster, Robert
Armed Forces Radio
Armenia Soviet republic
Armenian language
Armetale™ dinnerware
Armistice Day (now Veterans Day)
Armitage, Raymonde
Armond, Assante
Armor All™ cleaner
Armour™ meats
Armour Star™ meats
Armstrong, Louis 'Satchmo'
Armstrong, Neil A., Astronaut
Armstrong Floors™
Army Air Force
Army Archerd
Army Magazine
Army of the U.S.
Arnaz, Desi

Arnaz, Lucie
Arness, James
Arnie™ menswear
Arno, Peter
Arnold Palmer
Arnold Scaasi
Arnold Schoenberg
Arnold Schwarzenegger
Arnold Stang
Arnold Toynbee
Arnold, Benedict
Arnold, Eddy
Aroostock War
Arp, Jean, or Hans
Arquette, Cliff (aka Charlie Weaver)
Arquette, Rosanna
Arrau, Claudio
Arrid Extra Dry™
Arrigo Boito
Arrowhead™ water
Arsenio Hall
Arshile Gorky
Art Blakey
Art Buchwald
Art Carney
Art Deco
Art Forum
Art Garfunkel
Art News
Art Nouveau
Art Tatum
Arte Johnson
Artemis (goddess of hunt)
Artemis™ toiletries
Artemision at Ephesus
Artful Dodger
Arthur Ashe
Arthur Balfour, P.M.
Arthur C. Clarke
Arthur Compton
Arthur Dove
Arthur Conan Doyle, Sir
Arthur Fiedler
Arthur Fonzerelli, or 'the Fonz', or
   'Fonzie'
Arthur Godfrey
Arthur Hailey
Arthur Honegger

Arthur Kornberg
Arthur Miller
Arthur Murray
Arthur Quiller-Couch, Sir (aka 'Q')
Arthur Rubinstein (Pol.-Am. pianist)
Arthur M. Schlesinger
Arthur Schopenhauer
Arthur St. Clair, General
Arthur Sullivan, Sir
Arthur Treacher
Arthur, Bea
Arthur, Chester A., Pres.
Arthur, King
Arthurian Legend
Articles of War
Artie Shaw And His Orchestra
Artist's Magazine
Arts and Entertainment Network
Arturo Toscanini
Artweek
Aruba
Aryshire cattle
As (chem. sym. arsenic)
As You Like It
Asaf Masserer
Asbury Park Press
Ascension Day
Ascension Thursday
Ascot, races at
Ascriptin™
Asgard
Ash Wednesday
Ashburner, Charles
Ashcan Group, or School
Ashe, Arthur
Asher/Gould Advertising
Ashford, Evelyn
Ashkenazy, Vladimir
Ashkhabad, Turkmen (near the Iranian
   border)
Ashland, NH, OR
Ashley, Laura
Asia
Asia Minor
Asiaweek
Asimov, Isaac
Aslan (*Narnian Chronicles*)
Asmodeus (the Devil)

Asner, Ed
Aspartame™
Aspen Music Festival
Aspen, CO
Aspercreme™
Aspergum™
Assante, Armand
Assemblies of God Church
Assiniboin Indians
Assisi, Italy
Assisi, St. Francis of
Associated Broadcast News
Associated Dry Goods
Associated Press
Assyria
Assyrian art
Astaire, Adele
Astaire, Fred
Astin, Patty Duke, or Patty Duke
Aston Martin™
Astor, John Jacob
Astor, Mary
Astoria Coast Guard Air Station, OR
Astoria Coast Guard Base, OR
Astoria, OR
Astounding Science Fiction
Astrodome
Astroturf™
Asturias cheese
Asunción, Paraguay
Aswan High Dam
Aswan, Egypt
Atari™ computer
Athanasius, Saint
Athena Nike Temple (on Acropolis)
Athena, or Pallas Athena
Athenaeum, or Atheneum
Atheneum Publishers
Athens, GA
Athens, Greece
Atherton, Gertrude
Atkins, Chet
Atkinson, Brooks
Atlanta Braves
Atlanta Falcons
Atlanta Journal & Constitution
Atlanta, GA
Atlantic Beach, FL

Atlantic Charter
Atlantic City, NJ
Atlantic Monthly Press
Atlantic Ocean
Atlantic Richfield Co.
Atlantic Standard Time
Atlantic, The
Atlantis (legendary continent)
Atlantis space shuttle
Atlas (mythical hero)
Atlas Mts.
Atlas, Charles
Atomic Age
Atonement, Day of
Attenborough, Sir Richard
Attends™ undergarments
Attica, NY
Attila the Hun
Attlee, Clement R., P.M.
Atwater, Lee (Rep. Chair.)
Atwood, Margaret
Au (chem. sym. gold)
Auberjonois, René
Aubervilliers, Fr.
Aubrey Vincent Beardsley
Aubrey, John
Aubusson tapestry/rug
Auchincloss, Louis Stanton
Auckland, New Zealand
Audi™ car
Audrey Hepburn
Audrey Meadows
Audubon, John James
Auel, Jean M.
auf Wiedersehen
Augean stables
Auger effect
Auger shower
Augsburg, W. Ger.
August Macke
August Piccard
August Strindberg
August von Wassermann
Augusta Gregory, Lady
Augusta, GA, ME
Auguste Comte
Auguste Escoffier
Auguste Rodin

Augustin Eugène Scribe
Augustine, Saint
Augustus Caesar
Augustus Gloop
Augustus Saint-Gaudens
Auld Ane (the Devil)
Auld Clubfoot (the Devil)
Auld Lang Syne
Auld Nick (the Devil)
Aunt Jemima™
'Aunt Sally' (Br. slang for person set up
  as easy target)
Aureomycin™
Auriga (Charioteer) constellation
Aurora Australis (south), or aurora
  australis
Aurora Borealis (north), or aurora
  borealis
Aurora, CO
Auschwitz death camp
Auschwitz, Poland
Aussie (native, Australia)
Aussie™ shampoo
Austen, Jane
Austex™ chili
Austin American-Statesman
Austin, Stephen
Austin, Tracy
Austin, TX
Australia
Australian Alps
Australian Ballet
Australian crawl
Austria
Austro-Prussian War
Authorized Version of the Bible
Autodesk™
Autoharp™
Automat™
AutoSketch™
AutoWeek
Autry, Gene
Auvergne region, Fr.
Av (Jew. mo.)
Ava Gardner
Ava Maria (prayer)
Ava Maria (song)
Avalon , or Avallon (Arthurian)

Avedon, Richard
Averback, Hy
Avia™ shoes
Avianca Airlines
Aviation Week & Space Technology
Avigdor Arikha
Avignon, France
Avis™ rental car
Avogadro's law
Avogadro's number
Avogadro, Amadeo
Ax, Emanuel
Axel Stordahl
Axis (of WW II)
Axl Rose
Axminster™ carpet
Ayatollah Ruhollah Khomeini
Aykroyd, Dan
Ayres, Lew
Azazel (the Devil)
Azerbaijan, Soviet Socialist Republic
Azerbaijani (inhabitant)
Aziza™ cosmetics
Aznavour, Charles
Azoic Time
Azores Islands, or the Azores
Aztec Indians
Aztec Two-Step, or Montezuma's
  Revenge
Azuza, Ca

B (chem. sym. boron)
B Altman's, store
B Dalton Bookseller
B F Goodrich™ tire
B-2 Stealth bomber
B-52's

B-complex vitamin
B-horizon
B. B. King
B. F. Skinner
B. Kliban cats
Ba (chem. sym. barium)
Baalbek, Lebanon
Babar the Elephant
Babbage, Charles
Babbit, Bruce, Governor
Babbit, Milton Byron
Babbitt (Lewis)
Babbitt (narrow-minded middle class
    individual)
Babbitt™ metal
Babbitt, George F.
Babbitt, Harry
Babe Ruth (George)
'Babe' (Mildred) Didrikson Zaharias
Babe the Blue Ox (Paul Bunyan's)
Babel, Isaak
Babel, Tower of
Babism religion
Baby Boomer, or baby boomer
Baby Magic™
Baby Rose Marie
Baby Ruth™
Baby Snooks
Babylon, Hanging Gardens of
Babylonia
Babylonian captivity (historical Israel)
Bacall, Lauren
Bacardi™ rum
Baccarat™ crystal
Bacchanalia
Bacchus
Bach, Catherine
Bach, J. S. (Johann Sebastian)
Bach, Johann Ambrosia
Bach, Johann Christian (English Bach)
Bach, Johann Christoph
Bach, Johannes, or Hans
Bach, Karl Philipp Emanuel, or Carl
Bach, Richard (*Jonathan Livingston
    Seagull*)
Bach, Wilhelm Friedemann
Bacharach, Burt
Bachelor of Arts degree

Bachelor of Fine Arts degree
Bachelor of Science degree
Backus, Jim
Bacolod, Phil
Bacon, Francis (20th cent. artist)
Bacon, Sir Francis (17th cent.
    philosopher)
Bacon, Kevin
Bacon, Nathaniel
Bacon's Rebellion (Nathaniel)
BacOs™
Bactine™
Bactrian camel (2 humps)
Badajoz, Spain
Badalona, Spain
Baden-Baden, W. Ger.
Baden-Powell, Sir Robert (Boy Scouts)
Badenov, Boris
Badenov, Natasha, or Fataly
Badlands Nat. Pk. (SD)
Badlands plateau (SD)
Baedeker guidebooks, or 'Baedekers'
Baedeker, Karl
Baer, Jo
Baer, Max, Jr.
Baez, Joan
Baffin Bay, Can.
Baffin Island, Can.
Baffin, William
Bagehot, Walter
Baggies™
Baggins, Bilbo
Baggins, Frodo
Baghdad, Iraq
Bahái Faith
Bahaism religion
Bahamas, or Bahama Islands
Bahia, Brazil
Bahia Blanca, Argentina
Bahrain, or Bahrein
Baia-Mare, Romania
Baikal Lake
Bailey bridge (quickly assembled)
Bailey, DeFord
Bailey, F. Lee
Bailey, Nathan
Bailey, Pearl
Bailey's Irish Cream™

Bain de Soleil™
Bain, Conrad
Bainter, Fay
Baird, John Logie
Baizerman, Saul
Baja California Norte, state, Mexico
Baja California Sur, state, Mexico
Bajaia, Algeria
baked Alaska
Bakelite™
Baken-Ets™
Baker, James A., III, Secy. State.
Baker, Josephine
Bakersfield, CA
Bakhtaran, Iran
Bakker, Jim & Tammy Faye
Bakst, Leon
Baku, Azerbaijan
Bakula, Scott
Bakunin, Mikhail
Balakirev, Mili Alekseyevich
Balal Shem Tov
Balanchine, George
Balboa, CA
Balboa, Panama
Balboa, Vasco de
Baldassare Castiglione, Conte
Baldwin Park, CA
Baldwin, James
Baleares region, Spain
Balearic Is.
Balenciaga, Cristóbal
Balfe, Michael William
Balfour, Arthur, P.M.
Bali
Bali™ bra
Bali Ha'i
Balinese cat
Balkan Mts.
Balkan Peninsula
Balkan States, or the Balkans
Balkan Wars
Balkhash, Lake
Ball™ canning jars
Ball Park Franks™
Ball, Lucille
Balla, Giacomo
Ballantine™ Books

Ballantine's™ whisky
Ballarat, Australia
Ballard, J. G.
Ballard, Kaye
Ballatore™ champagne
Balleek ware
Ballet Folklórico de México
Ballet Russe de Monte Carlo
Ballington Booth
balm of Gilead
Balmer, Johann
Balmoral Castle, Scotland
balsam of Peru
Balsas river (Mexico)
Balthazar (1 of Wise Men)
Baltic Sea
Baltimore Colts
Baltimore oriole (bird)
Baltimore Orioles (team)
Baltimore Sun
Baltimore, Lord George
Baltimore, MD, OH
Baluchistan area, Iran/Pakistan
Balzac, Honoré de
Bambi
Ban Roll-On™ Anti-Perspirant
Ban-Lon™ (material)
Ban-Rol™ slacks
Banacek
Banana Republic stores
Banbury tarts
Bancroft, Anne
Bancroft, Judith
Band-Aid™
Banda Sea
Bandar Seri Begawan, Brunei
Bandaranaike, Sirimavo, P.M.
Bandini™
Bandung, Java
Bandyke brown
Banff Nat. Park
Banff, Alberta, Can.
Bang's disease
Bangalore, India
Bangkok, Thailand
Bangladesh
Bangor Daily News
Bangor Naval Submarine Base

Bangor, ME
Bangui, Central African Republic
Banjo Barons, The
Banjul, Gambia
Bank of America
Bankhead, Tallulah
Bannister, Roger
Banquet Cookin' Bag™
Banquet™ Dinners
Banquo (*Macbeth*)
Bantam Doubleday Dell Pub. Group
Bantu tribe
Banzai, Buckaroo
Baptists
Bar Harbor, ME
Bar-B-Que, also Bar-B-Q
Barabbas (Biblical thief)
Barbados
Barbara Bel Geddes
Barbara Bosson
Barbara Bush
Barbara Frietchie
Barbara Jordan, Rep.
Barbara Mandrell
Barbara Stanwyck
Barbara W. Tuchman
Barbara Walters
Barbara Woodhouse
Barbarosa (Turkish corsair)
Barbarosa, Frederick
Barbary ape
Barbary Coast (Africa)
Barbary Coast (San Francisco)
Barbary sheep
Barbary States (Africa)
Barbasol™
Barber of Seville, The
Barber, Red
Barber, Samuel
Barbers Point Coast Guard Air
   Station, HI
Barbers Point Naval Air Station, HI
Barbi Benton
Barbie™ doll
Barbirolli, Sir John
Barbizon School
Barbizon, France
Barbour, John

Barbra Streisand
Barcalounger™
Barcelona chair
Barcelona, Spain
Bard of Avon (Shakespeare)
Bardolino wine
Bardot, Brigitte
Barenboim, Daniel
Barents Sea
Baretta
Barker, Bob
Barkin, Ellen
Barkley, Alben W., V.P.
Barksdale Air Force Base, LA
Barlach, Ernst
Barleycorn, John
Barmecide (a false feast)
Barnabas, Saint
Barnard College
Barnard, Dr. Christiaan
Barnburners v. Hunkers
Barnes & Noble Bookstore
Barnes & Noble college outlines
Barney Google
Barney Kessel
Barney Oldfield
BarNone™ candy
Barnsley, Eng.
Barnum & Bailey's Circus
Barnum, P.T. (Phineas Taylor)
Barnum's Animals™ crackers
Barolo wine
Baron Lionel de Rothschild
Baron Carl Gustav Mannerheim
Baron Raglan, FitzRoy Somerset
   (raglan coat)
Barr body (after M. L. Barr)
Barr, Roseanne
Barranquilla, Columbia
Barres, Maurice
Barrett, Rona
Barrie Dunsmore
Barrie, Sir James M.
Barrie, Ont.
Barris, Chuck
Barron's
Barrow Point, Arctic
Barrow-in-Furness, Eng.

Barrows, Sydney Biddle
Barry Fitzgerald
Barry M. Goldwater, Sen
Barry M. Goldwater, Jr., Rep.
Barry Manilow
Barry Serafin
Barry, Philip
Barrymore, Diana
Barrymore, Drew
Barrymore, Ethel
Barrymore, John
Barrymore, John Jr.
Barrymore, Lionel
Barrymore, Maurice
Barstow Marine Corps Logistics
    Base, CA
Barstow, CA
Bart Giamatti
Barth, Karl
Barthes, Roland
Bartholdi, Frederic Auguste
Bartholomew, Saint
Bartles & Jaymes™ wine coolers
Bartlett pear
Bartlett's Quotations
Bartlett, John
Bartók, Béla
Bartolommeo, Fra
Barton Yarborough
Barton, Clara
Barty, Billy
Baruch Spinoza, or Benedict
Baruch, Bernard M.
Baryshnikov, Mikhail
Base Exchange™
Baseball Annies (groupies)
Baseball Hall of Fame
Basehart, Richard
Basel, Switzerland
Basenji dog, or basenji
Bashio (Jap. poet)
Basic English
Basie, Count (William)
Basil Rathbone
Basildon, Eng.
Basilica of the Savior, or Lateran
    basilica
Basinger, Kim

Baskerville type style
Baskerville, hounds of the
Baskerville, John
Basket Maker Indian culture
Baskin-Robbins™ 31 Flavors
Basque Country, Spain, or Basque
    Provinces, Sp.
Basque people
Basse-Normandie region, Fr.
Basse-Terre, Guadeloupe
Basset hound
Bastille Day
Bastille, the
Bastogne, Belgium
Bat Masterson
Bataan Death March
Bataan, Philippines
Batangas, Luzon, Phil.
Bath, Eng.
Bath, Order of the
Bathinette™
Bathsheba (David &), or Bath-Sheba
Batista y Zaldivar, Fulgencio (deposed
    Cuban leader)
Baton Rouge, LA
Battersea district (old Lon.)
Battle Creek, MI
battle of Brandywine
battle of Britain
battle of Bunker Hill (Breed's Hill)
battle of Chancellorsville
battle of Corregidor
battle of Hastings
battle of Lexington
battle of Monmouth
battle of Shiloh
battle of Trafalgar
Battlestar Galactica
Baudelaire, Charles
Baudouin, King (Belgium)
Baugh, Sammy
Bauhaus school of art
Baum, L. Frank
Baume & Mercier™ watch
Baumeister, Willi
Bausch & Lomb™ contacts
Bausch & Lomb Sensitive Eyes™
Bavaria, W. Ger.

Bavarian cream pie
Baxter-Birney, Meredith
Bay of Bengal
Bay of Biscay
Bay of Fundy
Bay of Pigs Invasion
Bay State (Massachusettes)
Bay Stater (MA native)
Bayard Taylor (James)
Bayer™ aspirin
Bayeux Tapestry
Baykal, Lake
Baylor University
Bayonne Military Ocean Terminal,
    NJ
Bayonne, France
Bayonne, NJ
Bayreuth Festival, Bavaria
Bayreuth, W. Ger.
Baziotes, William
Bazooka Joe™ bubble gum
Be (chem. sym. beryllium)
Bea Arthur
Beach Boys, The
Beale Air Force Base, CA
Bean, Judge Roy
Bean-Nighe
Beanee Weenee™
Bear Bryant
Beardsley, Aubrey Vincent
Beasley, Allyce
Beastie Boys, the
Beatitudes (Jesus' blessings)
Beatles, the
Beaton, Sir Cecil
Beatrice de' Bardi (married name
    Dante's love)
Beatrice Foods Co.
Beatrice Lillie
Beatrice Portinari (maiden name
    Dante's love)
Beatrix Potter
Beatrix, Queen of Netherlands
Beatty, Clyde
Beatty, Warren
Beau Brummell
Beau Nash
Beaufort Marine Corps Air Stn., SC

Beaufort scale
Beaufort Sea
Beaujolais wine
Beaumont, TX
Beauport, Québec, Can.
Beauregard, P.G.T., Gen.
Beauregarde, Violet
Beautyrest™ mattress
Beauvoir, Simone de
Beaver Cleaver (the Beaver)
Beaver Falls, PA
Beaverbrook, Baron William
Bechet, Sidney
Beck's™ beer
Becker, Boris
Becket, Thomas à, or St. Thomas
    Becket
Beckett, Samuel
Beckmann, Max
Becky Sharp
Becquerel rays (now gamma rays)
Becquerel, Antoine Henri
Bede, Saint, or the Venerable Bede
Bedford, MA, TX
Bedford-Stuyvesant (N.Y.
    neighborhood)
Bedfordshire, Eng.
Bedivere, Sir
Bedlem (Madhouse)
Bedlington terrier
Bedloe's Isl. (now Liberty Isl.)
Bedouin people
Bedrich Smetana
BedSack™
Bee Gees
Beebe, William
Beech-Nut Gum™
Beecham, Sir Thomas
Beecher, Henry Ward
beef Stroganoff
beef Wellington
Beefaroni™
Beefeater (Br. Yeoman of the Guard)
Beefeater™ gin
Beelzebub (the Devil)
Beene, Geoffrey
Beer-Nuts™
Beerbohm, Sir Max

Beersheba, Israel
Beery, Noah, Jr.
Beery, Wallace
Beethoven, Ludwig van
Beetle Bailey
Beetlejuice
Begin, Menachem, P.M.
Begley, Ed
Begley, Ed Jr.
Behrens, Peter
Behring, Emil von
Behrman, S. N.
Beiderbecke, Bix
Beijing, China (was Peking)
Beirut, Lebanon
Bekins™ Moving & Storage
Bel-Air, CA
Bel Geddes, Barbara
Bel Geddes, Norman
Bel Paese cheese
Béla Bartók
Bela Karolyi (gymnastics coach)
Bela Lugosi
Belafonte, Harry
Belasco, David
Belch, Sir Toby
Belfast, N. Ireland
Belgaum, India
Belgian Congo (now Zaire)
Belgian draft horse
Belgian endive
Belgian hare
Belgian sheepdog
Belgium
Belgrade, Yugoslavia, or Beograd
Belgrave Square, Lon.
Belial (the Devil)
Belinda Carlisle
Belize
Belize City, Belize
Belk Stores
Bell & Howell™
Bell, Alexander Graham
Bell's palsy
Bella Abzug
Bellamy, Ralph
Bellatrix
Belle Isle, Strait of

Belle Starr (b. Myra Belle Shirley)
Bellerophon (Gr. myth)
Belles Lettres
Bellevue Hospital (NYC)
Bellevue, WA
Bellflower, CA
Belli, Melvin, Atty.
Bellingham, WA
Bellini, Gentile
Bellini, Giovanni
Bellini, Jacopo
Bellini, Vincenzo
Bellisario, Donald P.
Bellow, Saul
Bellows, George Wesley
Belmont Race Track
Belmopan, Belize
Belo Horizonte, Brazil
Belorussia, or Belorussian Soviet
    Socialist Republic
Belshazzar (Biblical)
Beluga caviar, or beluga
Belushi, James
Belushi, John
Ben Blewitt
Ben Bogotá, Columbia
Ben Gazzara
Ben Grauer
Ben Hecht
Ben Hogan
Ben Hur
Ben Johnson (Can. athlete)
Ben Jonson (actor/author)
ben Joseph, Akiba
Ben Shahn (Benjamin)
Ben Vereen
Ben-Gay™ rub
Ben-Gurion, David, P.M.
Benadryl™
Benatar, Pat
Benay Venuta
Benazir Ali Bhutto, P.M.
Benchley, Robert
Bendix, William
Benedict Arnold
Benedict Spinoza, or Baruch
Benedict, Saint
Bénédictine liqueur

Benedictine Order of monks, or
    Benedictines
Benét, Stephen Vincent
Benetton™
Bengal light
Bengal region, India/Bangladesh
Bengal tiger
Bengasi, Libya, or Benghazi
Benglis, Lynda
Benguela Current
Benin (former Afr. kingdom)
Benitez, Jellybean
Benito Mussolini (aka *El Duce*)
Benjamin Disraeli, P.M.
Benjamin Britten, or Baron Britten of
    Aldeburgh
Benjamin Franklin
Benjamin Harrison, Pres.
Benjamin Henry Latrobe
Benjamin Rush
Benjamin 'Bugsie' Siegel
Benjamin Spock, Dr.
Benjamin Franklin Wade, Sen.
Benji
Benji's Moist 'n Chunky™
Bennett Cerf
Bennett, Tony
Bennie Maupin
Bennie Moten
Benny Goodman Orchestra
Benny, Jack (b. Benjamin Kubelsky)
Benoit, Joan
Benson, Ezra Taft
Bentham, Jeremy
Benton, Barbi
Benton, Thomas Hart (artist)
Benton, Thomas Hart, Sen.
Bentsen, Lloyd, Sen.
Benvenuto Cellini
Benzedrine™
Beothuk Indians
Beowulf
Berchtesgaden, W. Ger.
Berenger, Tom
Berenice's Hair constellation
Berenson, Bernard
Berenstain Bears, The
Berezovoy, Anatoly, Cosmonaut

Berg, Alban
Berg, Patty
Bergdorf Goodman store
Bergen, Candice
Bergen, Edgar
Bergen, Norway
Bergerac, Cyrano de
Bergman, Ingmar
Bergman, Ingrid
Bergonism
Bergson, Henri
Bergsonian philosophy
Bergstrom Air Force Base, TX
Bering Sea
Bering Strait
Berkeleian philosophy
Berkeleianism
Berkeley, Busby
Berkeley, CA
Berkeley, George
Berkley Publishing Group
Berkshire Music Festival
    (Tanglewood)
Berkshire Pigwig
Berkshire, Eng.
Berkshires, or Berkshire Hills
Berle, Milton ('Uncle Miltie')
Berlin Wall
Berlin, E. Germany
Berlin, Irving
Berlin, W. Germany
Berlioz, Hector, or Louis-Hector
Berlitz™ Language Center
Bermuda
Bermuda grass
Bermuda onion
Bermuda shorts
Bermuda Triangle
Bern, Switz., or Berne
Bernadette Peters
Bernadette, St. (Lourdes)
Bernard M. Baruch
Bernard Berenson
Bernard Lovell, Sir
Bernard Shaw
Bernard 'Toots' Shor
Bernardi, Herschel
Bernardo Bertolucci

Bernese Alps
Bernhard H. Goetz
Bernhard Riemann
Bernhardt, Sarah (actress)
Bernina™ sew. mach.
Bernini, Giovanni Lorenzo, or
    Gianlorenzo
Bernoulli, Daniel
Bernoulli, Jakob, or Jacques, or
    James
Bernoulli's principle
Bernsen, Corbin
Bernstein, Carl
Bernstein, Leonard
Bernstein's™ dressings
Berra, Yogi
Berry, Ken
Bert Convy
Bert Lahr
Bert Lytell
Berthe Morisot
Bertillon system
Bertinelli, Valerie
Bertolli Olive Oil™
Bertolucci, Bernardo
Bertrand Russell
Besançon, France
Besant, Annie
Beseler™ photo equip.
Bess Myerson
Bessemer process
Bessemer, Sir Henry
Bessie Smith
Best Foods™ mayonnaise
Bester, Alfred
Bestform™
Beta fiber
Betamax™, or 'Beta'
Betelgeuse, or Betelgeux
Bethe, Hans Albrecht
Bethesda Naval Hospital
Bethlehem, Jordan
Bethlehem, PA
Bethlehem, Star of
Bethune, Mary McCleod
Betsy Bloomingdale
Betsy Ross
Betsy-Wetsy™ doll

Bette Davis
Bette Midler
Better Business Bureau
Better Homes & Gardens
Betty Boop
Betty Crocker™
Betty Crocker™ Stir 'N Frost
Betty Crocker™ Snackin' Cake
Betty Ford (Mrs. Gerald)
Betty Ford Clinic
Betty Friedan
Betty Furness (Elizabeth)
Betty Garrett
Betty Grable
Beulah Bondi
Beulah, Land of
Beuys, Joseph
Beverly Crusher, Dr. (*Star Trek*)
Beverly Hillbillies
Beverly Hills, CA
Beverly Hills Hotel
Beverly Sills
Bewitched
Bexley (London borough)
Beyle, Marie Henri (aka Stendhal)
Beyond Good and Evil (Nietzsche's)
Bhagavad-Gita
Bhagwan Shree Rajneesh (now called
    Osho)
Bhavnagar, India, or Bhaunagar
Bhiwandi, India
Bhopal, India
Bhutan, Kingdom of
Bhutto, Benazir Ali, P.M.
Bi (chem. sym. bismuth)
Biafra, Republic of
Bialystok, Poland
Bianca Jagger
Biarritz, France
Bibb lettuce
Bible Belt
Bibliothèque nationale, Paris (library)
Bic™ pen/razor
Bichons Frise
Bickersons, The
Bicozene™
Biddle, John
Biddle, Nicholas

Biedermeier style
Biel, Switzerland
Bielefeld, W. Germany
Bierce, Ambrose
Big Apple (NYC)
Big Band Era
Big Bear City, CA
Big Ben (Lon.)
Big Bend Nat. Pk.
Big Bertha (WW I cannon)
"Big" Bill Tilden
Big Bird (Sesame Street)
Big Daddy
Big Dipper, also Ursa Major
'Big Foot', also Sasquatch
Big Mac 'attack'
Big Sid Catlett
Big Sur, CA
Bigelow™ carpet
Bigglesworth, James 'Biggles'
Biggs Restaurant, Chicago
Bighorn Mts.
Bijan™ perfume
Bikini atoll
Biko, Stephen
Bilbo Baggins
Bill Baird Puppets
Bill Bixby
Bill Blass
Bill Burrud
Bill Cosby
Bill Cullen
Bill (William) Mauldin
Bill Moyers
Bill Murray
Bill of Rights (Br.)
Bill of Rights (U.S.)
Bill 'Bojangles' Robinson
Bill 'Moose' Skowron
Bill Travilla
Bill, Pecos
Billboard Magazine
Billie Burke
Billie Holiday
Billie Jean King
Billings, Josh (pseud. Henry Wheeler Shaw)
Billings, MT

Billingsgate Market (Lon.)
Billionaire Boys Club
Billy Barty
Billy Budd
Billy Crystal
Billy (William) Graham, Rev.
Billy Idol
Billy Joel
Billy the Kid (Wm. H. Bonney)
Billy Ocean
Billy Rose
Billy Sol Estes
Billy Sunday (Wm. Ashley)
Billy Wilder
Biloxi, MS
Binaca™ Breath Drops
Binet test, or Binet-Simon test
Bing cherry
Bing Crosby (b. Harry Lillis)
Bing, Rudolph, Sir
Bingham, George Caleb
Biondi, Matt
Birch Society
Bird Watchers Digest
Bird, Larry Joe
Birdman of Alcatraz, the (Robert Stroud)
Birds Eye™ frozen foods
Birdseye, Clarence
Birkenhead, Eng.
Birkenstock™ shoes
Birki Dutch™ wooden clogs
Birman cat
Birmingham News
Birmingham, Eng.
Birnam Wood (in Scotland)
Birney, David
Birney, James Gillespie
Birobidzhan settlement, or Birobidjan
Birth of Venus, The (Botticelli)
Biscay, Bay of
Biscayne Blvd. (Miami)
Bishop, Elizabeth
Bishop, Joey
Bismarck Archipelago
Bismarck, ND
Bismarck, Prince Otto von ('Iron Chancellor')

Bismarck, the
Bisquick™
Bissau, Guinea-Bissau
Bissell™ sweeper
Bisset, Jacqueline
Bissinger's™ Chocolate
Bistro, The/Bistro Garden (Bev. Hills)
Bit-O-Honey™
Bitterroot Range
Bix Beiderbecke
Bixby, Bill
Biysk, Siberia
Biz™ bleach
Bizerte, Tunisia
Bizet, Georges
Bjorn Borg
Bk (chem. sym. berkelium)
Black & Decker™
Black and Tan troops
Black Angus cattle, or Aberdeen
    Angus
'Black Dahlia' (Elizabeth Short)
Black Death (plague)
Black Forest cake
Black Forest (W. Ger)
Black Friday
Black Hand
Black Hawk War
Black Hills of Dakota
Black Hole of Calcutta
Black Maria
Black Mass
Black Mts. (south U.S.)
Black Muslims
Black Panthers, or Black Panther
    party
Black Prince (Edward, Prince of Wales)
Black Sabbath (rock group)
Black Sea
Black Velvet™ Canadian whisky
Black Watch, or Royal Highland
    Regiment
Black, Justice Hugo
Black, Shirley Temple
Black Hawk, Chief
black-eyed Susan
Blackbeard, the Pirate (Edward Teach)
Blackburn Mt.

Blackett, Baron Patrick Maynard
Blackfoot Indians
Blackfriars Theatre
Blackie, Boston
Blackmun, Justice Harry A.
Blackpool, Eng.
Blackstone, Sir William
Blackwall hitch (a knot)
Blackwell, Elizabeth
Blackwood, Nina
Blaine, James G., Secy. State
Blaine, Vivian
Blair Underwood
Blair, Eric A. (aka George Orwell)
Blaize, Herbert, P.M.
Blake Edwards
Blake, Amanda
Blake, Eubie
Blake, Robert, Admiral
Blake, William
Blakeney, Sir Percival, (aka the Scarlet
    Pimpernel)
Blakey, Art
Blanc, Mel
Blanc, Mont, France
Blanca Peak, CO
Bland, Pigling
Blarney Castle/Blarney stone
Blass, Bill
Blaupunkt™ audio
Blavatsky, Madame Helena, or
    Helena Petrovna Hahn
Bleche-Wite™ car prod.
Blenheim spaniel (dog)
Blenheim, W. Ger.
Blessed Sacrament
Blessed Virgin
Blewitt, Ben
Bligh, William, Capt. (Bounty)
Blistex™ ointment
Blistik™ lip balm
Blitz, the, also *Blitzkrieg, or*
    blitzkrieg
Bloch, Ernest
Bloch, Felix
Bloch, Konrad Emil
Bloch, Ray
Blocker, Dan

Blois, France
Blok, Aleksandr
Blondell, Gloria
Blondell, Joan
Blondie & Dagwood Bumstead
Bloodhound
Bloods and Crips
Bloody Mary (alcoholic drink)
Bloody Mary (Mary I)
'Bloody____' (Br. curse)
Bloom Co.
Bloom, Claire
Bloomer, Amelia (bloomers)
Bloomfield, Leonard
Bloomfield, MI
Bloomingdale, Betsy
Bloomingdale's, or 'Bloomies'
Bloomington, IN
Bloomsbury group
Blossom Dearie
Blue Angels, The
Blue Bonnet™ Margarine
Blue Cross™ Insurance
Blue Ice™
Blue Mts. (west U.S.)
Blue Ridge Mts. (east U.S.)
Blue Shield™ Insurance
Blue Suede Shoes
Bluebeard (legendary murderer)
Bluegrass Country
Bluegrass music
Bluegum, Bunyip
Blues Brothers, The
Blume, Judy
Bly, Nellie
Blyth, Ann
Blytheville Air Force Base, AR
BMW Bayerische Motoren Werke
BMW™ car
B'nai B'rith
Bo Derek
Bo Jackson
Bo-Peep, Little
Boas, Franz
Bob Barker
Bob Clampett
Bob Costas
Bob Cousy

Bob Cratchit
Bob Dylan
Bob Eubanks
Bob Feller
Bob Fosse
Bob Geldof
Bob Hawke, P.M.
Bob Hope
Bob Hoskins
Bob Jamieson
Bob Keeshan (plays Capt. Kangaroo)
Bob Mackie
Bob Newhart
Bob Uecker (aka 'Mr. Baseball')
Bob Woodward
Bobbsey Twins
Bobby Breen
Bobby Darin
Bobby Fischer
Bobby Hull
Bobby Jones
Bobby McFerrin
Bobby Orr
Bobby Rahal
Bobby Seale
Bobby Shafto
Bobby Vinton
'Bobcat' Goldthwait
Bobo, Willie
Boca Raton, FL
Boccaccio, Giovanni
Boccherini, Luigi
Boccioni, Umberto
Bochco, Steven
Bochum, W. Ger.
Bodenheim, Maxwell
Bodleian Library (Oxford U.)
Bodoni type style
Bodoni, Giambattista
Body Glove™ casualwear
Bodyfuel™ drink
Boehm, Sydney
Boer people
Boer War, or South African War
Boesky, Ivan F.
Bogarde, Dirk
Bogart, Humphrey
Bogdanovich, Peter

Boggs, Dock
Bogor, Java
Bogotá, Columbia
Bohemia™ beer
Bohemia, Czech.
Bohemian
Bohr theory
Bohr, Niels
Boise Cascade Corp.
Boise, ID, or Boise City
Boitano, Brian
Boito, Arrigo
Bokhara rug
Bolero (dance)
Boléro (Ravel's)
Boleslaus, Polish rulers
Boleyn, Anne
Bolger, Ray
Bolingbroke, Henry of (King
  Henry IV)
Bolingbroke, Lord Henry (statesman)
Bolivar, Simon
Bolivia
Böll, Heinrich
Bolla Wine™
Bolling Air Force Base, DC
Bologna, Italy
Bolognese
Bolshevik
Bolshevik Revolution
Bolshevism
Bolshoi Ballet
Bolton, Eng.
Boltzmann constant
Boltzmann, Ludwig
Bolzano, Italy
Bombay™ gin
Bombay, India
Bombeck, Erma
Bomu river (Africa)
Bon Appetit
Bon Jovi, Jon
Bon Marche store
Bonanza TV show
Bonaparte, Joseph
Bonaparte, Louis
Bonaparte, Lucien
Bonaparte, Napoleon

Bonapartism
Bonaventura, or Saint Bonaventure
BonBons™ ice cream
Bond, James
Bondi, Beulah
Bonet, Lisa
Bongo
Boniface, Saint
Bonin Is.
Bonjour Tristesse
BonLait Fromage™
Bonn, W. Ger.
Bonnard, Pierre
Bonne Bell™ cosmetics
Bonneville Salt Flats (Utah)
Bonney, Wm. H. (aka Billy the Kid)
Bonnie Prince Charlie
Bonnie Raitt
Bono, Sonny
Bonwit Teller stores
Bonz™
Boogieboard™
Book Cache, The
Book of Changes (I Ching)
Book of Common Prayer
Book of the Dead
Book of Kells, The
Book-of-the-Month Club
Book of Mormon
Book of Numbers
Book of Proverbs
BookDealers World
Booker T. Washington
BookLover
BookNews
Bookstop Stores
Boolean algebra
Boomer State (Oklahoma)
Boone, Daniel
Boone, Pat
Boone, Richard
Boop, Betty
Boosler, Elayne
Booth Bay Harbor art colony
Booth Tarkington
Booth, Ballington
Booth, Edwin
Booth, Evangeline Cory

Booth, John Wilkes
Booth, Junius Brutus
Booth, Shirley
Booth, William
Boothia Peninsula
Boothia, Gulf of
Bootle, Eng.
Boötes constellation
Bophuthatswana
Borateem™
Boraxo™
Borazon™
Bordeaux mixture (poison)
Bordeaux wine
Bordeaux, Fr.
Borden™ dairy prod.
Borden, Lizzie
Border States (of Civ. War)
Borders region, Scotland
Borg, Bjorn
Borge, Victor
Borghese Gallery/Gardens
Borgia, Cesare
Borgia, Lucretia
Borglum, Gutzon
Borgnine, Ernest
Boris Badenov
Boris Becker
Boris Godunov, Czar
Boris Karloff
Boris Pasternak
Borman, Frank, Astronaut
Bormann, Martin
Born, Max
Borneo, Indonesia
Borodin, Aleksandr
Bors, Sir (Arthurian)
Borscht Belt
Borzoi
Bosc pear
Bosch™ power tools
Bosch, Hieronymous
Boskop skull (Boskop race)
Bosley, Tom
Bosporus strait
Bosson, Barbara
Bostic, Earl
Boston, MA

Boston baked beans
Boston Bay
Boston Blackie
Boston Braves
Boston brown bread
Boston bull terrier
Boston cream pie
Boston fern
Boston Globe
Boston Herald
Boston ivy
Boston lettuce
Boston Massacre
Boston Pops Orchestra
Boston Red Sox
Boston rocker
Boston Tea Party
Boston terrier
Bostonian
Boswell, James
Bosworth Field (England)
Bosworth, Brian 'The Boz'
Botany Bay, Australia
Botany wool
Botha, Louis, P.M. (Unionist party)
Botha, Pieter W., Pres. (National party)
Bothnia, Gulf of
Botswana
Botticelli, Sandro
Bottrop, W. Germany
Boucher, François
Boucheron™ perfume
Bougainville Is.
Bougainville, Louis de
Boulanger, Nadia
Boulder, CO
Boulder City, NV
Boulder Dam (now Hoover Dam)
Boulez, Pierre
Boulogne, Fr.
Boulogne-Billancourt, Fr.
Boult, Sir Adrian
Bountiful, UT
Bounty, H.M.S. (Capt. Bligh)
Bourbon, ruling family of France
Bourbon Street (New Orleans)
Bourdelle, Emile Antoine
Bourgeois, Louise

Bourgogne, Fr., or Burgundy
Bourke-White, Margaret
Bournemouth, Eng.
Bouviers de Flandres (dog), or
  bouviers
Bovary, Emma, Madame
Bow Bells (St. Mary-le-Bow church)
Bow, Clara (the 'It girl')
Bowdler, Thomas (bowdlerize)
Bowery, the (NYC)
Bowery Boys, The
Bowes, Major (*Amateur Hour*)
Bowie knife
Bowie, David
Bowie, James, Colonel
Bowling Green, KY
Boxer Rebellion, or Uprising
Boxing Day (Br. holiday)
Boxleitner, Bruce
Boy Scouts
Boycott, C. C., Capt. (boycott)
Boyer, Charles
Boyle, Peter
Boyle, Robert
Boyle's law
Boynton greeting cards
Boynton, Sandra
Boy's Life
Boys Ranch (in TX)
Boys Town (in NE)
Boz (pseud. Chs. Dickens)
Boz Scaggs
Bozcaada island (Turkish)
Bozeman Trail (John Bozeman)
Bozo the Clown
Br (chem. sym. bromine)
Brabant Copper™ cookware
Brach's™ candy
Bracken, Eddie
Bradbury, Ray
Braddock, Edward, Gen.
Bradford, Richard
Bradley, Ed
Bradley, Marion Zimmer
Bradley, Omar, General
Bradley, Tom, Mayor (L.A.)
Bradley, Truman
Bradstreet, Anne

Brady, Diamond Jim (James)
Brady, Mathew B.
Bragg, William Henry, Sir
Bragg, Wm. Lawrence
Brahma cattle
Brahma, or Brahman (supreme spirit)
Brahmanism (doctrine)
Brahmaputra River
Brahmin or Brahman (upper caste)
Brahms, Johannes
Braille Institute (L.A.)
Braille, Louis
Brain Trust (FDR's advisers)
Brakenbury, Sir Robert
Brampton, Ont., Can.
Bran Chex™
Brancacci Chapel (Italy)
Branch Rickey
Brancusi, Constantin
Brand, Vance, Astronaut
Brandauer, Klaus Maria
Brandeis, Justice Louis
Brandenburg Concerto
Brandenburg Gate
Brandenburg, E. Ger.
Brando, Marlon
Brandon De Wilde
Brandon Tartikoff
Brandt, Willy, Chancellor
Brandywine, battle of
Branestawm, Professor
Braniff™ airline
Branigan, Laura
Braque, Georges
Brasilia, Brazil
Brasselle, Keefe
Bratislava, Czech.
Bratwurst
Braun™ kitchen appliances
Braun, Eva (Mrs. A. Hitler)
Braunschweig, W. Ger.
Braunschweiger (sausage)
Brave New World
Braverman, Chuck
Brazil
Brazil nut
Brazzaville, Congo
Brazzi, Rossano

Breakstone™ dairy prod.
Breasted, James
Breathalyzer™
Breathless Mahoney (*Dick Tracy*)
Breckinridge, John C., V.P.
Breed's Hill (battle of Bunker Hill)
Breen, Bobby
Bremen, W. Ger.
Bremerton, WA
Brenda Vaccaro
Brennan, Walter
Brennan, Justice William J.
Brenner Pass (in Alps)
Brent Musburger
Brentano's Bookstore (chain)
Brentwood, CA
Br'er Fox
Br'er Rabbit
Brer Rabbit™ molasses
Breslin, Jimmy
Bret Harte, or Brett
Bret Maverick (James Garner role)
Bretagne, Fr., or Brittany
Breton, André
Breuer chair (Marcel)
Breuer, Marcel
Brewer, Teresa
Breyers™ ice cream
Brezhnev, Leonid I., Pres.
Brian Aherne
Brian Boitano
Brian 'The Boz' Bosworth
Brian De Palma
Brian Dennehy
Brian Donlevy
Brian Mulroney, P.M.
Brian Orser
Briarcliff College
Brice, Fannie 'Fanny'
Brick, NJ
Bride's Magazine
Bridgeport Post-Telegram
Bridgeport, CT
Bridger-Teton Nat. Forest
Bridges, Harry
Bridges, Lloyd
Bridgestone Tire Co. Ltd.
Bridgetown, Barbados

Bridgewater Courier-News
Brie cheese
Brigadoon
Briggs & Stratton™
Brigham Young (Mormon leader)
Brigham Young University
Bright's disease
Brighton, Eng.
Brighton, NY
Brigitte Bardot
Brigitte Nielsen
Brill's disease
Brillo™ pad
Brimley, Wilford
Brindisi, Italy
Brinell number/test/hardness
Brinkley, David
Brinkmann™ lights
Brisbane, Australia
Bristol, Eng.
Bristol Bay, AK
Bristol board
Bristol Channel
Bristol-Meyers Co.
Bristol-Myers Squibb Co.
Britain, or Great Britain
Britania™ Sportswear Ltd.
Britannia (poetic for Gr. Britain)
British Airways™
British Antarctic Territory
British Columbia, prov., Can.
British East India Co.
British Empire
British English (vs. Am. English)
British Grenadier Guards
British Guiana
British Honduras (now Belize)
British Hong Kong ('Honkers')
British Indian Ocean Territory
British Isles
British Knights™ shoes
British Museum, Lon.
British North America Act
British Somaliland
British thermal unit (Btu)
British West Indies
Britisher, or Brit, or Briton (native of Britain)

BritRail Pass
Brittany spaniel
Brittany, France
Britten, Benjamin, or Baron Britten of
  Aldeburgh
Brix scale
Broadway, or Great White Way
Broadway, The, department store
Brobdingnag (fictional land)
Brock, Lou
Brocklin, Norm Van
Brockton, MA
Broderick Crawford
Broderick, Matthew
Brodsky, Joseph
Brodsky, Vadim
Brokaw, Tom
Broken Arrow, OK
Bromo Seltzer™
Brompton cocktail (painkiller)
Bronica™ photo equip.
Bronson, Charles
Brontë sisters (Anne, Charlotte, Emily)
Bronx cheer
Bronx Co., NY
Bronx Zoo
Bronze Age
Bronze Star Medal
Brook Farm community (experimental)
Brooke Shields
Brooke, Edward William, Sen.
Brooke, Rupert
Brookhaven Nat'l Laboratory
Brookings Institution
Brookline, MA
Brooklyn, NY
Brooklyn Bridge
Brooklyn Coast Guard Air Station
Brooks Atkinson
Brooks Brothers
Brooks, Albert
Brooks, Mel
Brosco™ doors
Brosnan, Pierce
Brothers Grimm
Brothers Karamazov, The
Brothers, Dr. Joyce
Brown Derby restaurant (Hollywood)

Brown Jordan™ furniture
Brown 'N Serve™
Brown Swiss cattle
Brown, Edmund G. 'Pat', Gov.
Brown, Helen Gurley
Brown, Jerry, Gov. (Edmund G.
  Brown, Jr.)
Brown, John (abolitionist)
Brown, John M. (guns)
Browne, Jackson
Brownian movement, or motion
Brownie points
Browning machine gun/automatic
  rifle
Browning, Elizabeth Barrett
Browning, Robert
Brownsville, FL, TX
Broyhill™ furniture
Brubeck, David
Bruce Babbit, Governor
Bruce Boxleitner
Bruce Lee
Bruce Springsteen
Bruce Wayne (Batman)
Bruce Weitz
Bruce Willis
Bruce, Lenny
Bruce, Nigel
Brucker, Victoria
Bruckner, Anton
Brudenell, James, Earl of Cardigan
  (cardigan sweater)
Bruegel, Jan, also Brueghel, or
  Breughel (ak the 'Velvet Bruegel')
Bruegel, Pieter, the Elder, also
  Brueghel, or Breughel
Bruegel, Pieter, the Younger, also
  Brueghel, or Breughel
Brummell, Beau
Brunei, Sultan of
Brunelleschi, Filippo
Bruno Kirby
Brunswick Naval Air Station, ME
Brunswick stew
Brunswick, GA
Brussels Griffon (dog)
Brussels sprouts
Brussels, Belgium

Brussels, Ontario
Brut 33™ cologne
Bryan, William Jennings (politician)
Bryant Gumbel
Bryant, Bear
Bryant, William Cullen (poet)
Bryce Canyon Nat. Pk. (UT)
Brylcreem™
Bryn Mawr College
Bryn Mawr, PA
Brynner, Yul
Bryophyta
Bryson, Peabo
Bryston™ audio
Btu (British thermal unit)
Bubble Yum™
Bucaramanga, Columbia
Bucephalus (war horse Alexander the
  Great)
Buchanan, Pat
Buchanan, James, Pres.
Bucharest, Romania
Bucher, Lloyd 'Pete', Commander
Buchwald, Art
Buck Knives™
Buck Rogers
Buck, Pearl S.
Buckaroo Banzai
Bucket, Charlie
Buckingham Co., Eng.
Buckingham Palace
Buckley, William F. Jr.
Bucknell University
Bud Abbott
Bud Collyer
Bud Westmore
Bud Yorkin
Budapest, Hungary
Budd, Zola
Buddha (Siddhartha Gautama)
Buddhism
Buddig™ Meats
Buddy DeFranco
Buddy Ebsen
Buddy Hackett
Buddy Holly
Buddy Rich
Budge, Don

Budget™ car rental
Budget Gourmet™
Budweiser™
Buell Neidlinger
Buell Zazee
Buena Park, CA
Buena Vista Pictures™
Buenos Aires, Argentina
Buf-Puf™
Buffalo Bill (William F. Cody)
Buffalo Bills (team)
Buffalo Bob
Buffalo Evening News
Buffalo Spree
Buffalo, NY
Bufferin™
Buffett, Jimmy
Bugatti Royale™ car
Bugle Boy™ jeans
Bugs Bunny
'Bugs' Moran
Buick Starfire™
Building Design Journal
Bujumbura, Burundi
Bulfinch, Charles
Bulfinch's Mythology
Bulganin, Nikolai A., Premier
Bulgaria
Bull & Bear Financial Newspaper
Bull Moose party
Bull Run, battle of
Bull's-Eye™ sauce
Bulldog Drummond
Bullmastiff (dog), or bullmastiff
Bullock's dept. store
Bullock's Wilshire (now I. Magnin)
Bülow, Claus von
Bülow, Martha 'Sunny' von
Bumble Bee™ tuna
Bumstead, Blondie & Dagwood
Bunche, Ralph J.
Bundy, Ted
Bunker Hill, battle of
Bunker, Archie
Bunny, Bugs
Bunsen burner
Bunsen, Robert W. (burner)
Bunyan, John

Bunyan, Paul (& Babe the Blue Ox)
Bunyip Bluegum
Buonarroti, Michelangelo (artist)
Burbage, Richard
Burbank, CA
Burbank, Luther
Buren, Abigail Van ('Dear Abby')
Burger King™ restaurant
Burger, Ch. Justice Warren Earl
Burgess Meredith
Burghers of Calais (Rodin)
Burghoff, Gary
Burgos cheese
Burgoyne, John, Gen.
Burgundy region, France
Burgundy wine
Burke, Billie
Burke, Delta
Burke, Martha Jane (Calamity Jane)
Burkitt's lymphoma
Burl Ives
Burlington Free Press
Burlington, Ont., Can.
Burma
Burma Road (China)
Burma Shave signs
Burmese cat
Burmese language
Burn-Off™ sun screen
Burnaby, B.C., Can.
Burnett, Carol
Burns, George (b. Nathan Birnbaum)
Burns, Robert
Burnside, Ambrose E., General
Burpee, David
Burpee™ seeds
Burr, Aaron, V.P.
Burr, Raymond
Burroughs Corp.
Burroughs, Edgar Rice
Burrows Brothers
Burrows, Abe
Burrud, Bill
Burstyn, Ellyn
Burt Bacharach
Burt Lancaster
Burton, LeVar, also Levar
Burundi

Busby Berkeley
Buscaglia, Leo F.
Busey, Gary
Bush, Barbara
Bush, George Herbert Walker, Pres.
Bushman, Francis X.
Bushnell™ binocular
Business & Society Review
Business Advocate
Business Age
Business Book Review
Business Digest
Business Week
Busoni, Ferruccio
Buster Brown™ shoes
Buster Crabbe
Buster Keaton
Buster Poindexter
Butch Cassidy
Butchart Gardens (Can.)
Butcher's Blend™ dog food
Butler, Samuel
Butte, MT
Butter Buds Sprinkles™
Butterball™ turkey
Butterfield & Butterfield auctioneers
Butterfinger™
Butterick Patterns
Button, Richard 'Dick'
Buttram, Pat
Buzzards Bay, MA
Buzzi, Ruth
BWIA™ International Airline
Byington, Spring
Byrd, Richard E. (S. Pole explorer)
Byrd, Robert Carlyle, Sen.
Byrnes, Edd 'Kookie'
Byron R. White, Justice
Byron, Lord George
BYTE magazine
Byways Magazine
Byzantine architecture/art/music
Byzantine Empire
Byzantium (ancient city of Thrace)

C (chem. sym. carbon)
C & H™ sugar
C & R Clothiers
C-horizon
C-SPAN
C. C. Boycott, Capt. (boycott)
C. Everett Koop, Surgeon Gen.
C. S. Forester
C. S. Lewis
C3PO & R2D2
Ca (chem. sym. calcium)
Caan, James
Cab Calloway
Cabaret
Cabbage Patch Kids
Cabell, James
Cable Health Network
Cable Network
Cable News Network
Cabot, John
Cabot, Sebastian
Cabrini, St. Frances, or Mother
   Cabrini
Cacao tree
Cacharel™ perfume
Cadbury™ candy
Caddo Indian
Cadillac™ car
Cadillac, Antoine, Gov.
Cádiz, Spain
Caesar salad
Caesar, Augustus
Caesar, Julius
Caesar, Sid
Caesar's Tahoe hotel/casino
Caesarean section, also caesarean

Cage, John
Cage, Nicolas
Cagney & Lacey
Cagney, James
Cain (murdered Abel)
Cain, James M.
Caine, Michael
Cair Paravel (Narnia)
Cairo Museum
Cairo, Eg.
Cajun, or Cajan
Caladryl™ insect repellent
Calais, France
Calamity Jane (b. Martha Jane Burke)
Calaveras County Frog Jump Jubilee
Calcutta, India
Caldecott Medal
Caldecott, Dr. Helen
Caldecott, Randolph
Calder, Alexander
Caldor's Department Stores
Caldwell, Erskine
Caldwell, Sarah
Calgary Flames
Calgary Herald
Calgary Sun
Calgary, Alberta, Can.
Calgon™ water softener
Calhern, Louis
Calhoun, John C., V.P.
Cali, Columbia
Caliban (*Tempest*)
California (CA)
California Angels
California holly
California Horse Review
California, Gulf of
Caligula
Calistoga wagon
"Call me Ishmael..."
Callas, Charlie
Callas, Maria
Callaway™ carpet
Callejas, Rafael L., Pres.
Callimachus
Calliope, Muse of eloquence
Callisto (Jupiter moon)
Callot, Jacques

Calloway, Cab
Calphalon™ cookware
Calpurnia (Caesar's wife)
Calvary, also Golgotha
Calvin and Hobbes
Calvin Coolidge, Pres.
Calvin Klein™ clothes
Calvin, John
Calvinism
Calypso (Cousteau's ship)
Calypso (Gr. myth, sea nymph)
Calypso music
Camaro™
Cambodia, or Kampuchea
Cambrai, Treaty of
Cambrian period
Cambridge Platform
Cambridge University
Cambridge, Eng.
Cambridge, MA
Cambron™ lens
Camden Courier-Post
Camden, NJ
Camelot (Arthurian)
Camembert cheese
Cameroon, United Republic of
Camille
Camille Pissarro
Camille Saint-Saëns (Charles)
Camp Bullis, TX
Camp David accords
Camp David, MD
Camp Fire Girls
Camp Lejeune Marine Corps Base, NC
Camp Pendleton Marine Corps Base, CA
Campanella, Joseph
Campanella, Roy
Campari
Campbell Soup Co.
Campbell, Glen
Campbell, Mrs. Patrick
Campbell's™ Soups
Campeche, state, Mexico
Campho-Phenique™ cold sore gel
Campus USA
Camus, Albert

Canaan (ancient Palestine)
Canada
Canada Company
Canada Dry™ soft drinks
Canada First movement
Canada goose
Canada jay
Canada lily
Canada lynx
Canada mayflower
Canada thistle
Canadian Airlines International
Canadian Author & Bookman
Canadian bacon
Canadian Broadcasting Corporation
Canadian English
Canadian French
Canadian Mist™ whisky
Canadian Shield, also Laurentian Plateau
Canal Zone
Canaletto (b. Antonio Canal)
Canary Islands
Canaveral, Cape (FL)
Canberra, Australia
Cancun, Mex.
Candlemas
Candice Bergen
Candid Camera
Candida (genus)
Candide
Candie's™ shoes
Candy Candido
Candy, John
CandyTops™
Canes Venatici (Hunting Dogs) constellation
Caniff, Milton
Canis Major constellation
Canis Minor constellation
Cannery Row
Cannes Film Festival
Cannes, Fr.
Cannon Air Force Base, NM
Cannon Beach, OR
Cannon™ linens
Cannon, Dyan
Cannonball Adderly

Canon™ electronics
Canova, Judy
Canterbury bells
Canterbury Tales, The
Canterbury, Eng.
Canticle for Leibowitz, A
Canticles, also Song of Solomon, or
    Song of Songs
Cantinflas (Mex. superstar)
Canton crepe
Canton, Ch., also Guangzhou
Canton, OH
Cantonese food
Cantonese people
Cantor, Eddie
Cantor's deli, L.A.
Canuck (slang for French Canadian)
Canyon de Chelly Nat. Mo. (AZ)
Canyonlands Nat. Pk. (UT)
Capac, Manco
Cape Breton Is.
Cape Canaveral, FL
Cape Charles, VA
Cape Cod
Cape Cod cottage
Cape Fear, NC
Cape of Good Hope (Africa)
Cape Hatteras Lighthouse
Cape Horn (S. Am.)
Cape May Coast Guard Air Station,
    NJ
Cape Town, S. Africa, also Capetown
    or Kaapstad
Cape Verde republic
Capezio™
Capital Broadcast News
Capitol Hill (U.S. Congress)
Capitol Reef Nat. Park (UT)
Capitol, the (U.S. Capitol building)
Capitoline Hill (ancient Rome)
Capiz shell
Cap'n Crunch™ cereal
Cap'n Crunch's Crunch Berries™
Capone, Al 'Scarface' (Alphonse)
Capote, Truman
Capp, Al
Capra, Frank
Capri

Capricorn (zodiac sign)
Captain & Tennille (Daryl & Toni)
Captain Ahab
Captain America
Captain Kangaroo (Bob Keeshan)
Captain Kidd (William)
Capt. James T. Kirk (*Star Trek*)
Captain Midnight
Capt. Jean-Luc Picard (*Star Trek*)
Captain Pugwash
Captain Queeg
Capt. W. Rogers (*U.S.S. Vincennes*)
Captiva Isl., FL
Capucci™ shoes
Capulet family (*Romeo & Juliet*)
Car & Driver
Car-Temps™ car rental
Caracalla (Roman emperor)
Caracas, Venezuela
Caramello™ candy
Caravaggio, Michelangelo da
Caravelle™ candy
Caray, Harry
Carbondale, IL
Carboniferous period
Carborundum
Cárdenas, Lázaro, Pres.
Cardiff, Wales
Cardiff-by-the-Sea, CA
Cardinale, Claudia
Care Bears
Care*free™ gum
Carefree™ panty shields
Caress™ soap
Carew, Rod
Carew, Thomas
Carhartt™ work clothes
Caribbean Sea
Carillo, Leo
Carl Andre
Carl Philip Emanuel Bach, or Karl
Carl Bernstein
Carl Buddig™ meats
Carl Gustav Jung
Carl Gustaf Mannerheim, Baron
Carl Nielsen
Carl Reiner
Carl Sagan

Carl Sandburg
Carl Maria von Weber, also Karl
Carl's Jr.™
Carlin Glynn
Carlin, George
Carlisle Barracks, PA
Carlisle, Belinda
Carlisle, Kitty
Carlo Carra
Carlo Ponti
Carlo Rossi™ wine
Carlos Castaneda
Carlos Saul Menem, Pres.
Carlos Andres Perez, Pres.
Carlovingian style
Carlsbad Caverns Nat. Pk. (NM)
Carlsbad, CA, NM
Carlsberg™ beer
Carlton E. Morse
Carlton, Steve
Carlucci, Frank
Carly Simon
Carmel, CA
Carmelites, or Carmelite Order
Carmen Dragon
Carmen McRae
Carmen Miranda
Carmichael, 'Hoagy', or Hogie
Carnation Co.
Carnegie Corp. of NY
Carnegie Hall
Carnegie Steel Co.
Carnegie, Andrew
Carnegie, Dale
Carnegie-Mellon Univ.
Carnera, Primo
Carney, Art
Carol Burnett
Carol Channing
Carol Reed, Sir
Carole Landis
Carole Lombard
Caroline Affair
Caroline of Brunswick
Caroline Kennedy Schlossberg
Carolingian art/architecture
Carolyn Keene
Carolyne Roehm

Caron, Leslie
Carot, Jean Baptiste Camille
Carpathian Mts., or Carpathians
Carpenters, The
Carpeteria™ carpet store
Carr, Allan
Carra, Carlo
Carracci, Agostino
Carracci, Lodovico
Carradine, David
Carradine, Keith
Carre, John Le
Carrie Catt
Carrie Fisher
Carrie Nation, or Carry
Carrie Snodgress
Carroll & Co.™
Carroll O'Connor
Carroll, Diahann
Carroll, Leo G.
Carroll, Lewis (pseud. Chs. Dodgson)
Carruthers, Kitty & Peter
Carson City, NV
Carson McCullers
Carson, CA
Carson, Kit
Carson, Rachel
Carswell Air Force Base, TX
Carta Blanca™ beer
Carta Nevada™ wine
Cartagena, Columbia
Cartagena, Spain
Carter Hawley Hale (retail
   conglomerate)
Carter, Howard
Carter, James 'Jimmy' Earl, Pres.
Carter, Nick
Carter, Rosalynn
Cartesian coordinates
Carthage (ancient city)
Cartier™ jewelry
Caruso, Enrico
Carver, George Washington
Cary Grant
Caryatids, Porch of the
Caryl Chessman ('Red Light Bandit')
Caryn Kadavy
Casa Grande ruins

Casablanca
Casablanca Conference
Casablanca™ fan
Casablanca, Morocco
Casals, Pablo
Casals, Rosemary
Casanova
Casanova, Giovanni
Casbah, the
Cascade Range
Cascading Strings, the
Casey Jones (*Cannon Ball* express)
Casey Kasem
Casey Siemaszko
Casey (Charles) Stengel
Casey Tibbs
Cash, Johnny
Cash, Rosanne
Casio™ keyboard
Casio™ sport watch
Casite™ oil additive
Caslon type style
Caslon, William
Caspar (1 of the Magi)
Caspar Weinberger
Casper Milquetoast
Casper the Friendly Ghost
Casper, WY
Caspian Sea
Caspian, Prince (Narnia)
Cassandra (Gr. myth)
Cassatt, Mary
Cassavetes, John
Cassidy, Butch
Cassidy, Hopalong
Cassidy, Joanna
Cassini, Oleg
Cassiopeia (Gr. myth)
Cassius (a Roman family)
Cassius Clay, Jr. (Muhammad Ali)
Castaneda, Carlos
Castiglione, Baldassare, Conte
Castile region, Spain
Castilian
Castle Air Force Base, CA
Castle, Vernon and Irene
Castor and Pollux
Castro, Fidel, Pres.

Castrol GTX™ motor oil
CAT scan
Cat Chow PLUS™
Cat Stevens
Catacombs, the
Catalan language
Catalina Island, CA
Catalina™ sportswear
Catalonia region, Spain
Catawba
Catcher in the Rye, The
Caterpillar™ Tractor Co.
Cates, Phoebe
Catfish Hunter
Cathay Life Insurance
Cathedral of St. John the Divine
Cather, Willa
Catherine of Aragon
Catherine Bach
Catherine de Medici
Catherine Deneuve
Catherine the Great
Catherine of Siena, Saint
Cathleen Nesbitt
Catholic Apostolic
Catholic Emancipation
Catholic Epistles
Catholicism
Cathy Guisewite
Cathy Rigby
Catiline (Lucius Sergius Catilina)
Catlett, Big Sid
Catlin, George
Cato the Elder, also Cato the Censor
Cats (musical)
Cats Magazine
Catskill, NY
Catskills, or Catskill Mts.
Catt, Carrie
Catullus (Caius Catullus)
Caucasian race
Caulfield, Joan
Cavalier
Caves of Altamira, Spain
Cavett, Dick
Caxton, William
Cayenne, Fr. Guiana
Cayman Islands

Cayuga Indians
CB radio
CBS Radio
CBS Radio Stations News Service
CBS-TV
Cd (chem. sym. cadmium)
Ce (chem. sym. cerium)
Ceausescu, Nicolae (ex. Romanian dict.)
Cecchetti, Enrico
Cecil B. De Mille
Cecil Beaton, Sir
Cecrops
Cedar Rapids, IA
Cedars of Lebanon
Cedars-Sinai Medical Center
Cedric Hardwicke, Sir
Celebes Island, or Sulawesi
Celebes, Indonesia
Celeste Holm
Celeste™ pizza
Celestial Seasonings™
Celestine I, Saint
Celestine V, Saint
Cellini, Benvenuto
Celluloid™
Celsius temperature/scale
Celsius, Anders
Celtic Church
Celtic cross
Celtic languages
Celtic Sea
Celts
Cenozoic era
Centaurus (Centaur) constellation
Centers for Disease Control (CDC)
Central African Republic
Central America
Central Highlands, S. Viet.
Central Intelligence Agency (CIA)
Central Powers (of WW I)
Centrex™
Centrum™ vitamins
Centrum Jr.™ vitamins
Century 21™ Realtors
Cepacol™ mouthwash
Cepheid variables
Cerberus

Cerenkov radiation
Ceres asteroid
Cerf, Bennett
Cerro Tololo Inter-American Observatory, Chile
Certain Teed™ insulation
Certs™ breath mints
Cervantes Saavedra, Miguel de
Cerwin-Vega™ speakers
César Auguste Franck
Ccsar Chávez (Julio)
Cesar Romero
Cesare Borgia
Cessna™ plane
Cetus (Sea Monster) constellation
Ceylon (now Sri Lanka)
Ceylon tea
Cézanne, Paul
Cf (chem. sym. californium)
Chablis wine
Chablis, France
Chaco Canyon
Chad (country)
Chadwick, Florence
Chaffinch, Charley
Chagall, Marc
Chagas' disease
Chaim Soutine
Chairman Mao, or Mao Tse-tung, or Mao Zedong
Chaka Khan
Chakra, or chakra
Chaldea, or Chaldaea (part of Babylonia)
Chalcedon, Council of
Challenger space shuttle disaster
Chamaelon (Chameleon) constellation
Chamberlain, Neville, P.M.
Chamberlain, Richard
Chamberlain, Wilt (Norman)
Chambers, Sir William
Chamorro, Violeta de, Pres.
Champagne-Ardenne, Fr.
Champion™ battery
Champion, Gower
Champlain, Lake
Champlain, Samuel de
Champollion, Jean François

Champs-Elysees
Chan Chan ruins, Peru
Chan, Charlie
Chan, Dennis
Chancellor of the Exchequer
Chancellor, John
Chancellorsville, battle of
Chancellorsville, VA
Chandler wobble
Chandler, Raymond
Chanel, Gabrielle 'Coco'
Chaney, Lon, Jr.
Chang, Michael
Changchun, China
Changing Times
Changsha, China
Channel Islands, CA
Channel Islands, Eng.
Channing, Carol
Channing, Stockard
Chantilly lace
Chantilly, Fr.
Chanukah, or Hanukkah
Chaplin, Charlie (Sir Charles Spencer)
Chapman, John (aka Johnny Appleseed)
Chapman, Tracy
Chappaquiddick bridge (Kennedy/
    Mary Jo Kopechne)
Chappaquiddick, MA
ChapStick™
Chapultepec hill, Mex.
Char-Broil™ grill
Chardin, Jean-Baptiste-Siméon
Chardonnay wine
Charge of the Light Brigade
Charing Cross
Charisse, Cyd
Charlemagne, or Charles the Great,
    or Charles I
Charlene Tilton
Charles Greeley Abbot
Charles Ashburner
Charles Atlas
Charles Aznavour
Charles Babbage
Charles the Bald, or Charles II
Charles Baudelaire
Charles Boyer

Charles Bulfinch
Charles Bronson
Charles Coburn
Charles Cornwallis, Gen.
Charles Coulomb, or Chs.
    Augustin de
Charles A. Coulson
Charles Curtis, V.P.
Charles Robert Darwin
Charles G. Dawes, V.P.
Charles de Gaulle, Pres.
Charles de Talleyrand
Charles Dickens
Charles Dodgson (aka Lewis Carroll)
Charles Durning
Charles Eames
Charles W. Fairbanks, V.P.
Charles Farrell
Charles the Fat, or Charles III
Charles Lang Freer
Charles Frohman
Charles Gibson
Charles Goodyear
Charles Goren
Charles François Gounod
Charles the Great, or Charlemagne, or
    Charles I
Charles Grodin
Charles Haid
Charles Jeanneret (aka Le Corbusier)
Charles Jourdan™ shoes
Charles Kuralt
Charles Lamb
Charles Laughton
Charles' law
Charles A. Lindbergh
Charles Rennie Mackintosh
Charles Manson
Charles McGraw
Charles Osgood
Charles Pathé
Charles Perrault (wrote *Mother Goose*)
Charles Nelson Reilly
Charles M. Schulz
Charles Sheeler
Charles Sherrington, Sir
Charles 'Casey' Stengel
Charles Sumner, Sen.

Charles Hard Townes
Charles Townshend, Viscount
Charles Van Doren (TV scandal)
Charles Walgreen
Charles, Jacques
Charles, Ray
Charles-Augustin de Coulomb
Charlesbourg, Québec, Can.
Charleston Air Force Base, SC
Charleston Coast Guard Base, SC
Charleston dance
Charleston Gazette
Charleston Naval Shipyard, SC
Charleston Naval Station, SC
Charleston Naval Weapons Station,
   SC
Charleston News & Courier
Charleston, SC, WV
Charley Chaffinch
Charley Pride
Charley Wag
Charlie Bucket
Charlie Callas
Charlie Chan
Charlie Chaplin (Sir Charles Spencer)
Charlie Mingus
Charlie 'Bird' Parker
Charlie Ruggles
Charlie Sheen
Charlie Spivak
Charlie Weaver (pseud. Cliff Arquette)
Charlotte Amalie, V.I.
Charlotte Brontë
Charlotte Corday
Charlotte Observer
Charlotte, NC
Charlotte's Web
Charlottesville, VA
Charlottetown, Pr. Ed. Is., Can.
Charlton Heston
Charmin™ bath tissue
Charo
Charolais cattle
Charpentier, Gustav
Chartres Cathedral (Fr.)
Chartres, France
Chartreuse™
Charybdis

Chase Field Naval Air Station
Chase Manhattan Bank
Chase, Chevy
Chase, Ilka
Chasen's restaurant
Chateaubriand steak
Chateaubriand, François
Châteauguay, Québec, Can.
Chatelaine
Chatham Island
Chattahoochee Review
Chattahoochee, FL
Chattanooga campaign
Chattanooga Choo Choo
Chattanooga News-Free Press
Chattanooga, TN
Chatterley, Lady
Chatterton, Thomas
Chaucer, Geoffrey
Chausson, Ernest
Chautauqua movement
Chautauqua, NY
Chávez, Julio Cesar
Chayefsky, Paddy
Cheapside district, London
Checker™ cab
Checkpoint Charlie
Cheddar cheese
Cheech & Chong
Cheech, Marin
Cheektowaga, NY
Cheer™ detergent
Cheerios™
Cheese Dawgs™
Cheese Niblets™
Cheese Nips™
Chee-tos™
Cheever, John
Cheever, Susan
Cheez Doodles™
Cheez 'n Crackers™
Cheez Whiz™
Cheez-It™ crackers
Chef Boyardee™
Chekhov, Anton
Chellean man
Chelsea Antique Market
Chem-Dry™

Chengchow, China, or Zhengzhou
Chengdu, China, or Chengtu
Chennault, Claire Lee, Gen.
Cheops, Great Pyramid of
Cher (b. Cherilyn Sarkisian)
Cherbourg, Fr.
Chernenko, Konstantin, Gen. Secy.
Chernobyl, Russia
Cherokee™ casualwear
Cherokee Indians
Cherry Coke
Cherry Heering™
Cherry Orchard, The
Cherry Point Marine Corps Air
    Station, NC
Cheryl Ladd
Cheryl Tiegs
Chesapeake, VA
Chesapeake Bay
Chesapeake, U.S.S.
Chesapeake Bay retriever (dog)
Chesapeake Beach, MD
Chesebrough Ponds™
Cheshire cat
Cheshire Co., Eng.
Chesnokov, Andrei
Chessman, Caryl ('Red Light Bandit')
Chester A. Arthur, Pres.
Chester W. Nimitz, Adm.
Chesterfield, Lord Philip
Chet Atkins
Chet Huntley
Chevalier, Maurice
Cheviot hills, Eng./Scot.
Cheviot sheet
Chevrolet™ car
Chevrolet™ Corvette™
Chevrolet™ Lumina™
Chevron™ gas
Chevy Chase
Cheyenne Mountain Complex, CO
Cheyenne, WY
Chi, Tai, or Tai Chi Chuan
Chiang Kai-shek, Madame
Chiang Kai-shek, or Chiang
    Chung-cheng
Chianti wine
Chiba, Japan

Chic™ jeans
Chicago Art Institute
Chicago Bears
Chicago Cubs
Chicago Eight, the
Chicago Literary Review
Chicago Loop
Chicago Sun-Times
Chicago Tribune
Chicago, IL
Chicago White Sox
Chicano (slang for Mex. American)
Chichén Itzá
Chick Corea
Chickadee
Chickasaw (horse)
Chickasaw Indians
Chicken McNuggets™ (McDonald's)
Chicken of the Sea™ tuna
chicken Tetrazzini
Chiclets™
Chico Marx (Leonard)
Chico San™ rice cakes
Chief Black Hawk
Chief Cochise
Chief Mangas Coloradas
Chief Cornplanter
Chief Crazy Horse
Chief Executive (U.S. Pres. title)
Chief Justice of the U.S.
Chief Little Turtle
Chief Massasoit
Chief Pontiac
Chief Red Cloud
Chief Sitting Bull
Chief Tecumseh
Chihuahua (dog)
Chihuahua, state, Mexico
Child, Julia
Children's Crusade
Chile
Chillicothe, OH
Chillida, Eduardo
Chilliwack, B.C., Can.
Ch'in dynasty
Chin, Tiffany
China Lake Naval Weapons Center,
    CA

China rose
China, Great Wall of
China, Republic of
Chinatown
Chincoteague Isl., VA
Chincoteague Pony
Chinese cabbage
Chinese checkers
Chinese chestnut
Chinese Empire
Chinese lantern
Chinese puzzle
Chinese red
Chinese restaurant syndrome
Chinese Revolution
Chinese white
Ching dynasty, or Ch´ing, or Manchu
Chinon™ movie equip.
Chinook Indians
Chip-A-Roos™ cookies
Chipewyan Indian
Chippendale style
Chippendale, Thomas
Chippendales™ nightclub
Chippewa Falls, WI
Chippewa Indians, or Ojibwa
Chippewa Nat. Forest
Chips Ahoy!™ cookies
CHiPs TV show
Chirico, Giorgio de
Chisholm Trail (cattle drives)
Chisholm, Shirley
Chita Rivera
Chivas Regal™
Chloé ™ perfume
Chloromycetin™
Chlorophyta
Chocolatier
Choctaw Indians
Chong, Rae Dawn
Chong, Tommy (Cheech &)
Chopin, Frédéric
Chopsitcks
Chore Boy™ Dishscrub Sponge
Chorzow, Poland
Chou dynasty
Chou En-Lai, Prem.
Chouteau family (Am. fur traders)

Chow Chow (dog)
Chris Evert (Lloyd)
Chris Lemmon
Chris Schenkel
Chris-Craft™
Christ of the Andes
Christ, Jesus
Christa McAuliffe (*Challenger* teacher)
Christchurch, New Zealand
Christendom
Christhood
Christiaan Barnard, Dr.
Christian (believer in Christ)
Christian Broadcasting Network
Christian Brothers™ brandy
Christian Brothers religious order
Christian de Castelnau™
Christian Dior
Christian Doppler
Christian Endeavor meetings
  (Quakers)
Christian Era
Christian Huygens
Christian Science Monitor
Christian Science, or Church of
  Christ, Scientist
Christie, Dame Agatha
Christie's Auction House
Christina Onassis
Christina Pickles
Christina, Queen of Sweden
Christina's World (Wyeth)
Christine Ebersole
Christine Jorgensen
Christmas cactus
Christmas Carol (Dickens)
Christmas Day
Christmas Eve
Christmas Island, Australia
Christmas tree
Christmasberry
Christmastide
Christmastime
Christo (Christo Javacheff)
Christoph W. Gluck
Christopher Columbus
Christopher Fry
Christopher Isherwood

Christopher Lloyd
Christopher Marlowe
Christopher Plummer
Christopher Reeve
Christopher Robin
Christopher Wren, Sir
Christopher, Saint
Christy Mathewson (Christopher)
Christy, Edwin
Christy's Minstrels (Edwin Christy)
Chronicle of Higher Education
Chronicles
Chrysler Corp.
Chrysler™ Le Barron
Chrysler, Walter P.
Chrysophyta
Chubs™ Baby Wipes
Chuck Barris
Chuck Braverman
Chuck E. Cheese's restaurant
Chuck Jones
Chuck Mangione
Chuck Norris
Chuck Scarborough
Chuck Wagon™ dog food
Chuck Yaeger, Col.
Chun Doo Hwan, Pres.
Chun King™ foods
Chungking, China, or Chongqing
Chung, Connie
Chunky Soup™
Church of Scientology
Church of Scotland
Church of St. Basil (Moscow)
Churchill, Sarah
Churchill, Sir Winston
Ciao!™ shoes
Ciba Vision™ contacts
Cibola Nat. Forest
Cicero, Marcus Tullius
Cid Campeador, also 'The Cid'
Cicely Tyson
Cigna Companies
Cilea, Francesco
Cimarosa, Domenico
Cimarron, Territory of
Cimino, Michael
Cimmerians (myth. people)

Cincinnati Enquirer
Cincinnati Post
Cincinnati Reds
Cincinnati, OH
Cinco de Mayo
Cinderella
Cinefantastique
CinemaScope™
Cineplex Odeon Theaters
CineTelFilms
Cinzano wine
Circassia region, USSR
Circassian (inhabitant of Circassia)
Circe (myth.)
Circle K™ stores
Circuit City Stores
Circus Magazine
Circus Vargas
Cisco Kid
Citibank™
Citicorp™
Citizen Kane
Citrucel™ laxative
Citrus Hill™ juice
'City of David' (Zion)
City of Hope
City Lights
City of Seven Hills (Rome)
Ciudad Juárez, Mexico
Civil Aeronautics Board
Civil War, or War between the States,
    War of the Rebellion, War of
    Secession
Civil War Times
Civilian Conservation Corps
Civitan service club
CKO Network
Cl (chem. cym. chlorine)
Clabber Girl™ baking powder
Claiborne, Liz
Clair De Lune
Claire Bloom
Claire Lee Chennault, General
Clairol, Inc.
Clairol Nice 'N Easy™
Clairol Ultress™
Clamato™ juice
Clampett, Bob

Clampett, Elly May
Clampett, Jed
Clampett, Jethro
Clancy, Tom
Clapton, Eric
Clara Barton
Clara Bow, the 'It girl'
Clare Booth Luce
Clarence Birdseye
Clarence Darrow
Clarence Day
Clarion™ cosmetics
Clark Gable
Clark, George Rogers
Clark, Joe, P.M.
Clarke, Arthur C.
Claude Dauphin
Claude Debussy
Claude Garamond
Claude Levi-Strauss
Claude Monet
Claude Pepper, Rep.
Claude Rains
Claude Henri Saint-Simon
Claudette Colbert
Claudia Cardinale
Claudia 'Lady Bird' Johnson
Claudia O'Keefe
Claudine, Sidonie Gabrielle (aka
   Colette)
Claudio Abbado
Claudio Arrau
Claudio Monteverdi
Claus von Bülow
Claussen™ pickles
Clay, Andrew Dice
Clay, Cassius, Jr. (Muhammad Ali)
Clay, Henry, Sen. (Great Compromiser)
Claybrooke™ clothes
Clayton Antitrust Act
Clayton Moore (played Lone Ranger)
Clean & Clear™ cosmetics
Clearasil™ skincare
Clearwater, FL
Cleaver, Beaver ('the Beaver')
Cleese, John
Clemens, Wenzel Metternich
Clemens, Samuel (aka Mark Twain)

Clement R. Attlee, P.M.
Cleopatra (Shakespeare's)
Cleopatra, Queen of Egypt
Cleopatra's needles
Cleveland Amory
Cleveland Bay (draft horse)
Cleveland Browns
Cleveland Indians (team)
Cleveland Plain Dealer
Cleveland, Abbe
Cleveland, Grover, Pres.
Cleveland, OH
Clevon Little
Cliburn, Van
Cliff Arquette (aka Charlie Weaver)
Clifford Odets
Cliffs Notes
Clift, Montgomery
Clifton Fadiman
Clifton, NJ
Cline, Patsy
Cling Free™ fabric softener
Clingman's Dome
Clinique™ skincare
Clint Black
Clint Eastwood
Clinton, George, V.P..
Cloisters, the (NYC)
Clooney, Rosemary
Clootie (the Devil)
Clorox™ Bleach
Clorox Co.
Close Encounters of the Third Kind
Close, Glenn
Close-Up™ toothpaste
Club Med™
Clumber Spaniel (dog), or clumber
   spaniel
Clyde Beatty
Clydesdale (draft horse)
Clytemnestra (Gr. myth.)
CNN Newsroom
Cnossus, palace at, or Knossos
Co (chem. sym. cobalt)
Coahuiltec Indians
Coalinga, CA
Coast Magazine
Coats & Clark Wintuk™ yarn

Cobb, Lee J.
Cobb, Ty
COBOL, or Cobol
Coburn, Charles
Coca, Imogene
Coca-Cola™
Coca-Cola Co., The
Cochin China chicken
Cochin China, S. Viet.
Cochise, Chief
Cock Robbin
Cockaigne, or Land of Cockayne
Cocker Spaniel (dog)
Cocker, Joe
Cocky-Leeky, or Cock-a-Leekie
'Coco' Chanel (Gabrielle)
Coco, James
Cocoa Beach, FL
Cocoa Krispies™
Cocoa Pebbles™
Cocoa Puffs™
Cocoanut Grove (L.A.)
Coconino Nat. Forest
Cocos (Keeling) Islands
Cocteau, Jean
Cody, William 'Buffalo Bill'
Coeur d'Alene Nat. Forest (ID)
Coeur d'Alene, ID
Coffee-mate™
Cohan, George M.
Cohen, Mickey
Cointreau™
Coit Tower (in S.F.)
Coke™
Cokin™ photo. equip.
Colavita™ olive oil
Colbert, Claudette
Cold War
Coldstream Guards
Coldwell Banker™ Real Estate
Cole of California™
Cole Porter
Cole Younger
Cole, Cozy
Cole, Nat 'King'
Cole, Natalie
Coleman Hawkins
Coleman™ stove/lantern

Coleman, Dabney
Coleman, Gary
Coleman, Ornette
Coleridge, Mary Elizabeth
Coleridge, Samuel Taylor
Colette (pseud. Sidonie Gabrielle
    Claudine)
Colfax, Schuyler, V.P.
Colgate™ toothpaste
Colgate-Palmolive™
Colin Davis
Colleen Dewhurst
Colleen McCullough
College of Cardinals, or Sacred
    College
College of William and Mary, VA
Collins, Jackie
Collins, Joan
Collins, Pauline
Collis Potter Huntington
Collyer, Bud
Colman, Ronald
Cologne Cathedral
Cologne, W. Ger., or Köln
Coloma, CA
Colombia
Colombo (TV show)
Colombo, Sri Lanka
Colonel Blimp
Colonel Stoopnagle
Colonial Dames™
Colonial Penn Insurance
Coloradas, Mangas, Chief
Colorado (CO)
Colorado Springs, CO
Colosseum of Rome, or Coliseum
Colossi of Memon
Colossians
Colossus of Rhodes
Colt 45 gun
Colt, Samuel
Coltrane, John
Columbia Journalism Review
Columbia: Midwest Review of Books
Columbia Pictures
Columbia River
Columbia space shuttle
Columbia University

Columbia, MD, MO, SC
Columbus Day, or Discovery Day
Columbus Dispatch
Columbus, Christopher
Columbus, GA, OH
Comanche Indians
Comaneci, Nadia
Comédie Française
Comedy of Errors, The
Comet™ cleanser
Comet™ rice
Comics & Comix
Comics Journal
Comintern (Communist International)
Commedia dell' arte, or commedia
Commercialware™ cookware
Commodore Magazine
Commodore™ computer
Common Market
Common Prayer, Book of
Common Sense™ Oat Bran
Commonwealth Day
Commonwealth of Nations
Communism
Communist Manifesto
Communist Party
Como, Perry
Comoros, The, Federal Islamic
    Republic
Compaq Computer Corp.
Compazine™
Compound W™
Compromise of 1850
Compton, Arthur
Compute!
Computer Graphics World
Computerland™ store
Computerworld
Comstock Lode
Comstock, H. T.
Comstockery
Comte, Auguste
Conair™
Conakry, Guinea
Conan Doyle, Sir Arthur
Conan-the-Barbarian
Concepción, Chile
Concord grape

Concord Naval Weapons Station, CA
Concord, CA, MA
Concorde, place de la
Concorde, the (jet)
Conde' Nast
Conecuh Nat. Forest
Coneheads, the
Conestoga wagon
Coney Island (NY)
Confederate Memorial Day
Confederate States of America, or
    Confederacy
Confederation, Articles of
Confessions of Nat Turner, The
Confucianism
Confucius
Congo red
Congo River, or Zaïre River
Congo snake
Congoleum™ flooring
Congress of Racial Equality
Congress of the U.S.
Congressional Medal
Congressional Record
Congreve, William
Connecticut (CT)
Connecticut Wits, or Hartford Wits
Connections
Connemara Pony
Connery, Sean
Connie Chung
Connie Francis
Connie Sellecca
Conniff, Ray
Connoisseur
Connolly, Maureen "Little Mo"
Connors, Jimmy
Conoco Inc.
Conrad Aiken
Conrad Bain
Conrad Nagel
Conrad, Michael (*Hill Street Blues*)
Conrad, Robert (*Wild Wild West*)
Conrad, William (*Jake & the Fatman*)
Conried, Hans
Conservative Judaism
Conservative party
Constable, John

Constance Talmadge
Constantin Brancusi
Constantin Stanislavsky
Constantine, Emperor, or Constantine
  the Great
Constantinople (now Istanbul)
Constitution of the U.S.
Constitutional Convention
Construx™
Consumer Electronics
Consumer Price Index
Consumer Reports
Consumers Digest Magazine
Contac™
Contadina™ foods
Conté™ art crayon
Conte, Richard
Conti, Tom
Continental Airlines™
Continental breakfast
Continental Congress
Continental Divide (the Rockies)
Contras, the
Converse™ shoes
Convy, Bert
Conway Twitty
Coogan, Jackie
Cook Islands, N.Z.
Cook, James, Capt.
Cook, Robin
Cook, Thomas (Cook's Tours)
Cooke, Alistair
Cooked Goose Farm™
Cookies 'n Fudge™
Cool Whip™
Cooley, Spade
Coolidge, Calvin, Pres.
Coolmax™ shoes
Cooney, Gerry
Coonts, Stephen
Cooper, Alice
Cooper, Gary
Cooper, James Fenimore
Coors™ beer
Coos Bay, OR
Cootie Williams
Copas, Cowboy
Copenhagen, Den., or København

Copernican system
Copernicus, Nicholas
Copland, Aaron
Copley, John Singleton
Coppéliá
Copper Age
Copperfield, David
Copperheads
Coppertone™
Coppola, Francis Ford
Coptic Church
Coptic language
Coral Gables, FL
Coral Sea
Coral Sea Islands
Corazon Aquino, Pres.
Corbett, James "Gentleman Jim"
Corbin Bernsen
Corbin™ clothing
Corday, Charlotte
Cordell Hull, Adm./Secy. State
Cordilleras Mts.
Cordon Bleu
Córdoba, Spain
Cordova, Fred de
Corea, Chick
Coretta Scott King
Corey, Wendell
Corfu, Greece
Corian™
Corinth, Greece
Corinthian order
Corinthians
Coriolanus (Gnaeus Marcius)
Coriolanus (Shakespeare play)
Coriolis effect, or force
Cork, Ireland
Corliss Archer
Corn Chex™
Corn Laws
Corn Pops™
Cornel Wilde
Cornelia Guest
Cornelia Otis Skinner
Cornelius Vanderbilt
Cornell University
Cornell, Katharine
Corning Visions™ cookware

Cornish hen
Cornishman
Cornishwoman
Cornplanter, Chief
Cornwall & Isles of Scilly Co., Eng.
Cornwall County, Eng.
Cornwall, David (aka John Le Carre)
Cornwallis, Charles, Gen.
Corona™ beer
Corona Australis (Southern)
Corona Borealis (Northern)
Coronado Naval Amphibious Base,
    CA
Coronet™ paper prod.
Corot, Jean Baptiste Camille
Corps de Ballet
Corpus Christi Coast Guard Air
    Station/Naval Air Station, TX
Corpus Christi day
Corpus Christi, TX
Correctol™ laxative
Correggio (Antonio Allegri)
Corregidor
Corregidor, battle of
Corriedale sheep
Corry's™ slug bait
Corsica (island)
Cortaid™ cream
Cortés, Hernán, or Hernando
Corvette™ car
Corvus (crow) constellation
Corvus' Omninet network
Cosby, Bill
Cosco™ furniture
Cosell, Howard
Cosenza, Italy
Cosmoline™
Cosmopolitan
Cossacks
Costa Brava, Spain
Costa del Sol, Spain
Costa Mesa, CA
Costa Rica
Costas, Bob
Costello, Elvis
Costello, Lou
Costner, Kevin
Côte d'Azur

Cotillion (dance)
Cotler™ menswear
Cotlets™
Cotswold Hills, Eng.
Cotswold sheep
Cotten, Joseph
Cottian Alps
Cotton Mather, Rev.
Cotton, John (Puritan clergyman)
Coty™ cosmetics
Cougat, Xavier
Coulomb, Charles, or Charles-
    Augustin de (coulomb energy)
Coulson, Charles A.
Council of Chalcedon
Council of Pisa
Council of Trent
Count Basie (William)
Count Dracula (Vlad Tepes)
Count of Monte Cristo, Edmund
    Dantes
Country Home
Country Living
Country of the Gillikins
Country Washburn
County Armagh, N. Ire.
County Cork, Ire.
County Kerry, Ire.
County Mountie (slang-highway police)
County Tipperary, Ire.
Courbet, Gustave
Courréges, André
Court of St. James's (Br.)
Courvoisier™ cognac
Cousins, Norman
Cousteau, Jacques
Cousy, Bob
Covent Garden, London
Coventry, Eng.
Cover Girl™ cosmetics
Covington, KY
Coward, Sir Noël
Cowboy Copas
Cowper, William (jurist)
Cowper, William (poet)
Cowper's glands
Cox, Wally
Cozumel, Mex.

Cozy Cole
Cr (chem. sym. chromium)
Crab Nebula
Crabbe, Buster
Crabtree & Evelyn™
Crabtree, Lotta
Cracker Jacks™
Cracklin' Oat Bran™
Crafts Magazine
Craftsman™ tools
Crain, Jeanne
Crain's Chicago Business
Crain's New York Business
Crane, Stephen
Cratchit, Bob
Cratchit, Tiny Tim
Crate & Barrel™ furnishings
Crater Lake Nat. Pk. (OR)
Crater Mound (AZ)
Crave™ cat food
Craven, Wes
Crawford, Broderick
Crawford, Joan
Crayola™ crayons
Crazy Eights, also Wild Eights
Crazy Guggenheim (pseud. Frank
    Fontaine)
Crazy Horse, Chief
Cream of Wheat™
Creamette™ pasta
Creamsicle™ pops
Creative Loafing
Creator, the
Cree Plains Indians
Cree Woodland Indians
Creedence Clearwater Revival
Creek Indians
Cremona (commune in Lombardy, It.)
Cremora™
Crenna, Richard
Creole
crepes Suzette
Crest™ toothpaste
Cretaceous period
Crete (island)
Cribari™ wine
Crichton, Michael
Crick, Francis H. C.

Cricket magazine
Crimea peninsula
Crimean War
Crippen, Robert (first Space Shuttle)
Cripple Creek, CO
Cripps, Sir Stafford
Crips & Bloods
Cris & Pitt's™ BBQ sauce
Crisco™ vegetable shortening
Crispix™ cereal
Crist, Judith
Cristiani, Alfredo, Pres.
Cristina Ferrare
Cristobal Balenciaga
Crito (Plato's)
Cro-Magnon man
Croatia rep., Yugoslavia
Croatian
Crochet World
Crock
Crock-Pot™, or Crockpot™, or
    crock pot
Crockett, David 'Davy'
Crocodile Dundee
Crocodile Dundee II
Crohn's disease
Croix de Guerre
Cromwell current
Cromwell, Oliver
Cronin, A. (Archibald) J.
Cronkite, Walter
Cronyn, Hume
Crookes tube
Crookes, Sir William
Crosby, Bing (b. Harry Lillis)
Crosby, Stills & Nash
Crosby, Stills, Nash & Young
Crosman™ air gun
Cross & Blackwell™ preserves
cross of Lorraine
Crothers, Scatman
Crouse, Russel
Crow Indian
Crowley, John
Crown Books
Crown Royal™ whisky
Crucifixion, the
Cruella DeVille

Cruikshank, George
Cruise, Tom
Cruising World
Crunch 'n Munch™
Crunch Tators™
Crusade, Children's
Crusades, the
Crusher, Beverly, Dr. (*Star Trek*)
Crusher, Wesley, Ensign (*Star Trek*)
Crusoe, Robinson
Cryptophyta
Crystal Gayle
Crystal Light™
Crystal Palace (Lon.)
Crystal, Billy
CST Communications
CTV Television Network
Cub Scouts
Cuba
Cuba Libre (cocktail)
Cuban Missile Crisis
Cubism art
Cucamonga, CA
Cuenca, Ecuador
Cuernavaca, Mex.
Cuervo Gold™ tequila
Cugat, Xavier
Cuisinart™
Cukor, George
Cullen, Bill
Culligan man, the
Culligan™ Water Conditioning
Culp, Robert
Cultural Revolution
Cumberland Gap
Cumberland, MD
Cumbria Co., Eng.
cummings, e.e.
Cunard ships
Cuomo, Mario M., Gov.
Cup O' Noodles™
Cupid
Cuprinol™ stain
Curaçao Island, N.A.
Curad™ bandage
Curél™ skincare
Curie point, or temperature
Curie, Madam Marie

Curie, Pierre
Curie's law
Curity™ diapers
Curly Howard (1 of 3 Stooges)
Currier & Ives
Currier, Nathaniel
Curt Gowdy
Curt Jurgens
Curtin, Jane
Curtis Le May, Gen.
Curtis Strange
Curtis, Jamie Lee
Curtis, Charles, V.P.
Curtis, Tony
Curtiss, Glenn Hammond
Curtiss Aviation
Cushing's disease
Custer, George A. Lt. Col.
Custer, SD
Cut-Rite™ wax paper
Cutex™
Cuticura™ skincare
Cutty Sark™
Cuyahoga Falls, OH
Cuzco, Peru, or Cusco
Cy Young
Cybill Shepherd
Cyclades Islands
Cycle™ dog food
Cyclist Magazine
Cyclops (pl. Cyclopes)
Cyd Charisse
Cygnus (Swan) constellation
Cymbeline (play)
Cymbeline, King of Britain
Cymric (Celtic languages)
Cyndi Lauper
Cyndy Garvey
Cypress Gardens, FL
Cypress, CA
Cyprian, Saint
Cypriot
Cyprus
Cyrano de Bergerac
Cyril Ritchard
Cyrus McCormick
Cyrus R. Vance, Secy. State
Cyrus West Field

Czech (native of Czech.)
Czechoslovakia
Czerny, Karl
Czestochowa, Poland

D Day (WWII)
D region
D'Anjou pear
d'Arc, Jeanne, also Joan of Arc, or
    Maid of Orléans
D'Artagnan
d-Con™ pest control
D-horizon
d'Indy, Vincent
D'Oyly Carte Opera Co.
D'Oyly Carte, Richard
D. H. Lawrence (David Herbert)
D. W. Griffith (David Wark)
da Caravaggio, Michelangelo
da Gama, Vasco
Da Nang, Vietnam, or Da-nang
da Vinci, Leonardo
Dab Dab the duck
Dabney Coleman
Dacca, Bangladesh
Dachau concentration camp
Dachau, W. Ger.
Dachshund
Dacron™
Dada movement, or Dadaism, or
    Dadaist Art
Daedalus (Gr. myth)
Daffy Duck
Daffy-down-dilly
Dafoe, Willem
Dag Hammarskjöld, Secy. Gen. U.N.
Dagmar (pseud. Virginia Egnor)

Daguerre, Louis
Dagwood & Blondie Bumstead
Dagwood sandwich
Dahl, Arlene
Dahl, Roald
Dailey, Dan
Dailey, Janet
Daily Variety
Dairy Queen/Brazier
Daisy Miller
Daisy Plus™ razors
Dakar, Senegal
Dakota Indians, or Sioux
Daktari
Dalai Lama
Dale Carnegie
Dale Evans (& Roy Rogers)
Daley, Richard, Mayor
Dali, Salvador
Dallas Cowboys
Dallas Morning News
Dallas Times Herald
Dallas, George M., V.P.
Dallas, TX
Dalmatian (dog)
Dalton, John
Dalton's law
Daly, John Charles
Daly, Tyne
Damascus steel
Damascus, Syria
Damme, Jean-Claude Van
Damocles (Gr. myth)
Damocles, Sword of
Damon and Pythias
Damon Runyon
Damone, Vic
Dan Aykroyd
Dan Blocker
Dan Dailey
Dan Duryea
Dan Fogelberg
Dan O'Herlihy
Dan Rather
Dana Delany
Dance magazine
Dance Theater of Harlem
Dandie Dinmont terrier (dog)

Dandridge, Dorothy
Dandridge, Ruby
Danegeld (ancient tax)
Dangerfield, Rodney
Daniel arap Moi, Pres.
Daniel Barenboim
Daniel Bernoulli
Daniel Boone
Daniel Day-Lewis
Daniel Defoe, or De Foe
Daniel Frohman
Daniel Inouye, Sen.
Daniel Patrick Moynihan, Sen.
Daniel Ortega, Pres
Daniel Schorr
Daniel Shays (Shay's Rebellion)
Daniel D. Tompkins, V.P.
Daniel J. Travanti
Daniel Webster
Daniela Silivas
Danielle Steel
Danilova, Alexandra
Dannon™ yogurt
Danny Aiello
Danny De Vito
Danny Glover
Danny Kaye
Danson, Ted
Dante, Alighieri
Dante's inferno
Dantes, Edmund, (Count Monte Cristo)
Dantine, Helmut
Danube River
Danza, Tony
Danzig, or Gdansk
Daphne Du Maurier
Daphne Maxwell Reid
Daphne (nymph)
Daphnis and Chloë
Dar-es-Salaam, Tanzania
Dardanelles (ancient Hellespont)
Dare, Virginia
Darin, Bobby
Darius I,II,III (Perisan kings)
Darius Milhaud
Darjeeling tea
Darjeeling, India
Dark Ages

Dark Continent (old name of Africa)
Darley Arabian
Darling children (Wendy, John & Michael)
Darling River, Australia
Darnell, Linda
Darrin Stephens (of *Bewitched*)
Darrow, Clarence
Darryl F. Zanuck
Dart and Kraft Inc., or Kraft
Darth Vader
Dartmoor Prison (Eng.)
Darwin, Charles Robert
Darwin's theory, or Darwinism
Daryl Hall
Daryl Hannah
Dashiell Hammett
Data, Lt. Commander (*Star Trek*)
Dataproducts Corp.
Daumier, Honoré
Dauphin, Claude
Dauphin, the
Dave Garroway
Davenport, IA
David (Donatello's)
David (Michelangelo's)
David and Goliath
David Ackroyd
David Belasco
David Ben-Gurion, P.M.
David Birney
David Bowie
David Brinkley
David Brubeck
David Burpee
David Carradine
David Copperfield
David Cornwall (aka John Le Carre)
David 'Davy' Crockett
David Dinkins, Mayor
David Dubinsky
David Eddings
David Farragut, Adm.
David Friedkin
David Garrick
David Hartman
David Hasselhoff
David Hayes™

David Hayes Agnew
David Hockney
David Horowitz
David Hume
David Janssen
David Letterman
David Livingstone, Dr. (Stanley &)
David Lynch (Twin Peaks)
David McCallum
David Merrick
David Niven
David Ogilvy
David Rittenhouse
David Rockefeller
David Lee Roth
David Sarnoff, "General"
David Sarnoff Research Center
David Scott, Astronaut
David O. Selznick
David Malcolm Storey
David Susskind
David L. Wolper
David L. Wolper Productions
David, Jacques-Louis
Davidson, John
Davis vs. Davis
Davis, Altovise (Mrs. Sammy)
Davis, Angela
Davis, Bette
Davis, Colin
Davis, Eddie 'Lockjaw'
Davis, Jefferson, Pres. (Confederate)
Davis, Miles
Davis, Sammy, Jr.
Davis, Skeeter
Davis-Monthan Air Force Base, AZ
Davy (David) Crockett
Davy Jones's locker
DAW Books Inc.
Daw, Margery
Dawber, Pam
Dawes, Charles G., V.P.
Dawson, Richard
Dawson, Yukon, or Dawson City
Day, Clarence
Day, Dennis
Day-Glo™
Day-Lewis, Daniel

Dayan, Moshe, Foreign Def. Min.
Dayton Journal Herald
Dayton, OH
Daytona Beach, FL
Dayton-Hudson Department Stores
de Balboa, Vasco
de Balzac, Honoré
de' Bardi, Beatrice (married name
   Dante's love)
de Beauvoir, Simone
de Bergerac, Cyrano
de Bougainville, Louis
de Broglie waves
de Broglie, Louis
De Camp, Rosemary
de Chamorro, Violeta, Pres.
de Champlain, Samuel
de Chirico, Giorgio
de Cordova, Fred
de Coulomb, Charles-Augustin
de Cuellar, Javier Perez, U.N. Secy.
   Gen.
De Falla, Manuel
De Forest, Lee (radio)
de Gaulle, Charles, Pres.
de Givenchy, Hubert
de Greiff, Monica, Jus. Minister
De Haven, Gloria
De Havilland, Olivia
de Klerk, Frederik W., Pres.
de Kooning, Willem
de la Renta, Oscar
de Lafayette, Marie Joseph, Gen., or
   La Fayette
De Laurentiis, Dino
de León, Ponce, Juan
de Maupassant, Guy
dé Medici, Catherine
dé Medici, Lorenzo, the Magnificent
De Mille, Agnes
De Mille, Cecil B.
De Niro, Robert
De Palma, Brian
de Paul, St. Vincent
de Perón, Eva Duarte, Pres.
de Perón, María
de Rothschild, Lionel, Baron
de Sade, Marquis Donatien

de Santa Anna, Antonio, General
de Saussure, Ferdinand
De Sica, Vittorio
De Soto, Hernando
de Stijl art movement
de Talleyrand, Charles
de Toulouse-Lautrec, Henri
De Varona, Donna
De Vito, Danny
de Vlaminck, Maurice
De Vol, Frank
De Vries, Hugo, or de Vries
De Wilde, Brandon
De Wolf Hopper
de Young Museum, M. H.
Dead Sea Scrolls
Dead Sea, Israel-Jordan
Dead, Book of the
Dead-End Kids
Deadwood, SD
Dean Acheson, Secy. State
Dean Jagger
Dean R. Koontz
Dean Martin
Dean Rusk, Secy. State
Dean Wesley Smith
Dean Stockwell
Dean Witter Reynolds
Dean, Dizzy
Dean, Morton
Deanna Durbin
Deanna Troi, Counselor (of Star Trek)
Dear Abby (Abigail Van Buren)
Dear John letter
Dearborn, MI
Dearborn Heights, MI
Dearie, Blossom
Death Valley Nat. Mon. (CA/NV)
Deauville, France
Debbie Allen
Debbie Reynolds
DeBeers Consolidated Mines Ltd.
Debi Thomas
Deborah Kerr
Deborah Harry
Deborah Norville
Deborah Raffin
Debra Winger

Debussy, Claude
Decalogue, or Ten Commandments
Decameron tales
DeCarlo, Yvonne
Decatur, IL
Decatur, Stephen
Deccan region, India
Decker Slaney, Mary
Declaration of Independence
Decoration Day (now Memorial Day)
DeCorsia, Ted
Dede Slayton, Astronaut
Deep Sea Drilling Project
Deep South
Deep Woods Off!™
Defense Electronics
Defense, U.S. Dept. of
Def Leppard
Defoe, Daniel, or De Foe
DeFord Bailey
DeFore, Don
DeForest Kelley
DeFranco, Buddy
Dégas, Edgar
Deil (the Devil)
Deimos (Mars moon)
Deity (in ref. to God)
Dekker, Albert
Dekker, Thomas
DeKuyper™ Schnapps
Del Coronado Hotel (CA)
Del Mar, CA
Del Monte™
Del Rey Books™
Delacroix, Eugene
Delany, Dana
Delaroche, Paul
Delaware (DE)
Delaware Indians
Delaware River
Delco™ battery
Delft, Netherlands
Delftware™
Delhi, India
Delilah (and Samson)
Delius, Frederick
Dell Publishing Co., Inc.
della Robbia family

della Robbia wreath
DeLorean™ car
DeLorean, John
Delos Island (birthplace Artemis &
    Apollo)
Delphi, Greece
Delphic oracle, or Oracle of Delphi
Delphinus (dolphin) constellation
Delsarte system (calisthenics)
Delta™ Air Lines
Delta Burke
Delta Plan
Delta Sky
DeLuise, Dom
DeLuise, Peter
Delvaux, Paul
Delvecchio
Demarest, William
Demerol™
Demeter (myth)
Demetrius
Demi Moore
Democratic Party
Democritus (Gr. myth)
Demosthenes (Gr. orator)
Dempsey, Jack
Denali Nat. Park (AK)
Deneuve, Catherine
Deng Xiaoping
Denis Diderot
Denise Levertov
Denmark
Denmark Strait
Dennehy, Brian
Dennis Alexio
Dennis Chan
Dennis Day
Dennis Franz
Dennis Hopper
Dennis O'Keefe
Dennis Quaid
Dennis the Menace
Dennis Weaver
Dennison's™ Chili
Denon™ audio
Denorex™ dandruff shampoo
Dentyne™
Denver boot (police car clamp)

Denver Broncos
Denver Post
Denver, CO
Denzel Washington
Dep™ haircare
DePauw University
Depp, Johnny
Depression glass
der Führer
Der Spiegel
Derby County, Eng.
Derbyshire, Eng.
Derek, Bo
Derek, John
Deringer, Henry (derringer pistol)
Dermarest™
Dermocaine™
Des Moines Register
Des Moines, IA
Descartes, René
Deschutes Nat. Forest
Deschutes River
Desdemona (*Othello*)
Desenex™
Deseret Book Company
Desi Arnaz
Desiderata
Designer Imposter™ perfumes
Desilu Productions
DeskTop Graphics
Desktop Publishing
Desmond Tutu, Archbishop
Dessau, E. Ger.
Detroit Arsenal, MI
Detroit Coast Guard Air Station, MI
Detroit Coast Guard Base, MI
Detroit Free Press
Detroit Lions
Detroit News
Detroit Tigers
Detroit, MI
Deukmejian, George, Gov.
Deuteronomy
Deutschland
Devane, William
Devil, the
DeVille, Cruella
Devils Island

Devine Being (God)
Devine, Andy
Devon County, Eng.
Devon Rex cat
Devonian period
Dewar flask
Dewar, Sir James
Dewar's™ Scotch
Dewey Decimal System
Dewey, George, Adm.
Dewey, Thomas E.
Dewhurst, Colleen
DeWitt, Joyce
Dexatrim™
Dexedrine™ (slang- dexie, dexy)
Dey, Susan
Dhaka, Bangladesh
DiMaggio, Dom
Di Maggio, Joe
di Sant' Angelo, Giorgio
di Suvero, Mark
Di-Gel™
Diabetes Self-Management
Diaghilev, Sergei
Diahann Carroll
Dial Magazine
Diamond Head, Honolulu
Diamond International Corp.
Diamond Jim Brady (James)
Diamond, Neil
Diamond, Selma
Dian Fossey
Diana Barrymore
Diana Gregory
Diana Hyland
Diana Nyad
Diana Rigg
Diana Ross
Diana Vreeland
Diana, Princess of Wales (Lady Diana
    Spencer)
Diane Keaton
Diane Sawyer
Diane von Furstenberg
Dianetics
Dianne Feinstein, Mayor
Dianne Wiest
Diaparene™

Diar-Aid™
Diaspora (Jewish)
Diba, Farah
Dick Cavett
Dick Ebersol
Dick Enberg
Dick Francis
Dick Gregory
Dick Haymes
Dick Sargent
Dick Schaap
Dick Tracy
Dick Turpin (the highwayman)
Dick Van Dyke
Dick Vitale
Dick York
Dickens, Charles
Dickens, Little Jimmy
Dickies™ work clothes
Dickinson, Angie
Dickinson, Emily
Diconix™ printer
Dictaphone™
Dictograph™
Diderot, Denis
Didot, François
Die Fledermaus
Die Walküre
Diebenkorn, Richard
Diego Rivera
Diego Velázquez
Diem, Ngo Dinh, Pres.
Dien Bien Phu, Vietnam, or
    Dienbienphu
Diet Coke™
Diet Rite™ Cola
Dietrich, Marlene
Dieu et mon droit (motto British
    royalty)
Digital Equipment Corp.
Digger Indians
Digory Ketterley
Dijon mustard
Dijon, Fr.
Dilantin™
Dilaudid™
Diller, Phyllis
Dillinger, John

Dillon, Matt, Marshall
Dimetane™
Dimetapp™
Dimitri Shostakovich, or Dmitri
Dimitri Tiomkin
Dina Merrill
Dinah Shore
Diners Club International
Dinersaurs™ cereal
Dinkins, David, Mayor
Dino De Laurentiis
Dinty Moore™ stew
Diogenes (looking for "an honest man")
Diomedes (Gr. legend)
Dione (Saturn moon)
Dionne Quintuplets
Dionne Warwick
Dionysius, the Elder (tyrant of
    Syracuse)
Dionysus (god of fertility)
Dior, Christian
Dippity-do™
Dire Straits (rock group)
Directoire style
Dirk Bogarde
Dirty Dick's, London pub
Disarmament Conference
Disciples of Christ, or The Christian
    Church
Disciples, Twelve
Discovery Day, or Columbus Day
Discovery space shuttle
Dismal Swamp, VA/NC
Disney World™
Disney, Walt Elias
Disney-MGM Studio Theme Park
Disneyland™
Disraeli, Benjamin, P.M.
Distinguished Service Cross
District of Columbia (DC)
Distrito Federal, Mexico, or Federal
    District
Ditka, Mike
Ditmars, Ivan
Ditmars, Raymond
Diurex™
Divine Comedy
Divine Father (God)

Divine Liturgy
Divine, Major M.J., also Father
    Divine
Divorce Court
Dix, Otto
Dixie (song)
Dixie cup™
Dixiecrat
Dixieland, also Dixie Land
Dizzy Dean
Dizzy Gillespie
Djakarta, Java, or Jakarta
Djibouti (country)
Djibouti, Djibouti (city, country)
Djurgarden Park
DKNY™ sportswear
Dmitri Shostakovich, or Dimitri
Dmitry Sitkovetsky
Dnepr River, or Dnieper
Dnepropetrovsk, USSR
Dnestr River, or Dniester
Do, Tae Kwon
Doan's™ pills
Dobbins Air Force Base, GA
Doberman Pinscher (dog), or pinscher
Dobie Gillis
Dobrynin, Anatoly
Doc Holliday
Doc Severinsen
Dock Boggs
Doctor Doolittle
Doctor Zhivago
Dodd, Mead & Co.
Dodecanese Islands
Dodge™ Charger
Dodge City, KS
Dodger Stadium (L.A.)
Dodgson, Charles (aka Lewis Carroll)
Dodo bird
Dody Goodman
Doe, John
Doesburg, Theo van
Dog Fancy
Dog Star, also Sirus
Dog World
Dogpatch, U.S.A.
Dogrib Indians
Dohnányi, Ernst von

Dolby™ stereo
Dole™ fruit
Dole, Sanford B., Gov.
Dollar Rent A Car™
Dolley Madison (not Dolly)
Dolly Madison™ pastries
Dolly Parton
Dolph Lundgren
Dom DiMaggio
Dom Perignon™
Domenico Cimarosa
Domenico Scarlatti
Domingo, Placido
Dominic, Saint
Dominica,W.I.
Dominican Republic
Dominicans Catholic order
Dominick Dunne
Dominion Day (Can. holiday)
Domino, Fats
Domino's™ Pizza
Domsday Book, or Doomsday Book
Don Ameche
Don Budge
Don Carlos
Don DeFore
Don Diego (Zorro)
Don Drysdale
Don Giovanni
Don Ho
Don Juan
Don Knotts
Don Michael Paul
Don Quixote, or Don Quixote de la
  Mancha
Don Rickles
Donahue, Elinor
Donahue, Phil
Donahue, Troy
Donald P. Bellisario
Donald Duck
Donald E. Newhouse
Donald O'Connor
Donald Sutherland
Donald J. Trump
Donald E. Westlake
Donaldson, Sam
Donatello (It. sculptor)

Donegal tweed
Dong, Pham Van, Prem.
Donizetti, Gaetano
Donlevy, Brian
Donna De Varona
Donna Karen™ clothes
Donna Reed
Donna Rice
Donna Summer
Donnagel™
Donne, John
Donner Party
Donner Pass, CA
Donny Osmond
Doo Dads™ snack
Doobie Brothers, or The Doobies
Doodles Weaver
Doohan, James R. (Scotty on *Star Trek*)
Dooley, Dr. Thomas A.
Doolittle, Dr.
Doolittle, Eliza
Doom™ plant spray
Doomsday Book, or Domsday Book
Doonesbury
Doppelgänger
Doppler, Christian
Doppler effect/shift
Dorchester Hotel
Dore Schary
Doré, Gustave
Doren, Charles Van (scandal)
Doren, Mamie Van
Doria, Andrea, Admiral
Dorian Gray (picture of)
Dorians
Doric order
Doris Lessing
Dorking chicken
Dormouse, the
Dorothy (Gale) of Oz
Dorothy Chandler Pavilion (L.A.)
Dorothy Dandridge
Dorothy Gish
Dorothy Hamill
Dorothy Kilgallen
Dorothy Lamour
Dorothy McGuire
Dorothy Parker

Dorothy Sayers
Dorset County, Eng.
Dorset sheep
Dortmund, W. Ger.
Dos Equis™ beer
Dos Passos, John
Dostoyevsky, Feodor, or Dostoevsky
Dou, Dow, or Douw, Gerard or Gerrit
Douala, Cameroon
Douay Bible, or Version
Doubleday Book Shops
Doubleday Publishing Co.
Doubleday, Abner
doubting Thomas
Douglas Fairbanks
Douglas Fairbanks, Jr.
Douglas fir
Douglas MacArthur, Gen.
Douglas Wilder, Gov. (first U.S. black
   governor)
Douglas, Kirk
Douglas, Michael
Douglas, Stephen A.
Douglas, Justice William O.
Douglass, Frederick
Dove, Arthur
Dover Air Force Base, DE
Dover Strait, or Straits of Dover
Dovre™ wood stove
Dow Chemical Co., The
Dow Jones & Co.
Dow Jones Index
Down East Magazine
Down's syndrome
Downey, Morton
Downey, Morton, Jr.
Downs, Hugh
Downy™ fabric softener
Downyflake™ waffles
Doxsee™ clams
Doyle, Sir Arthur Conan
Doyle, Popeye
Dr. Doolittle
Dr. Faustus (Marlowe's)
Dr. Frankenstein
Dr. Jekyll & Mr. Hyde
Dr. Kildare
Dr. Joseph Mengele

Dr. Moreau (villian)
Dr. Pangloss
Dr Pepper™
Dr. Scholl's™
Dr. Seuss
Dr. Strangelove
Draco, or Dracon (Gr. politician)
Draco (Dragon) constellation
Draconian laws
Dracula, Count (Vlad Tepes)
Dragnet
Dragon, Carmen
Drake, Sir Francis
Dramamine™
Drambuie™ liqueur
Drano™
Draper, Ruth
Drechsler, Heike
Dred Scott Case
Dreiser, Theodore
Dresden china™
Dresden, E. Ger.
Dresser, Louise
Dressler, Marie
Drew Barrymore
Drew, John
Drew, Nancy
Drexel Burnham Lambert (junk bonds)
Dreyer's™ Frozen Yogurt
Dreyer's™ Ice Cream
Dreyfus Affair
Dreyfus Fund™
Dreyfus, Alfred, Capt.
Dreyfuss, Richard
Drinkwater, Terry
Dristan™ decongestant
Drixoral™
Drogheda, Ireland
Drood, Edwin
Drosselmeyer, Herr
Droste™ chocolate
Drottningholm Palace
Drug Emporium store
Druids, the
Drummond, Bulldog
Drummondville, Québec, Can.
Drumstick™ ice cream
Drury Lane theatre

Druses community, or Druze
Druten, John van
Dry Idea™ anti-perspirant
Dryden Flight Research Center, CA
Dryden, John
Drysdale, Don
Du Barry, Madame Jeanne Bécu
Du Bois, W.E. (William Edward of the NAACP)
Du Maurier, Daphne
Du Pont Co.
Du Pont family, or the Du Ponts
Dual Alliance
Duarte, Jose Napoleon, Pres.
Dubcek, Alexander
Dubinsky, David
Dublin, Ireland
Dubonnet™ wine
Dubrovnik, Yugoslavia
Dubuffet, Jean
Dubuque™ ham
Dubuque, IA
Duc de Richelieu, or Cardinal Armand Jean Richelieu
Ducal Palace
Duchamp, Marcel
Duchamp-Villon, Raymond
Dudley Do-Right, Mountie
Dudley Moore
Duel in the Sun
Duff, Howard
Duffy, Patrick
Dufy, Raoul
Dukakis, Katharine 'Kitty'
Dukakis, Michael, Gov.
Dukakis, Olympia
Dukas, Paul
Duke Ellington
Duke of Albuquerque
Duke of Paducah (pseud. Whitey Ford)
Duke Snider
Duke of Wellington (wellington boots)
Duke, Patty, or Patty Duke Astin
Duke, the (nick. John Wayne)
Dukhobors, or Doukhobors
Dulcolax ™ laxative
Dulles Airport (D.C.)
Dulles, John Foster, Secy. State

Duluth, MN
Dumas fils (A.Dumas' illegt. son)
Dumas, Alexandre
Dumbarton Oaks
Dumbo
Dumpster™
Dun & Bradstreet
Dun's Magazine
Dunaway, Faye
Dunbar-Nelson, Alice
Duncan Hines™
Duncan Phyfe (furniture)
Duncan, Isadora
Duncan, King of Scot.
Dundee, Scotland
Dungeness crab
Dungeons & Dragons
Dunkin' Donuts™
Dunkirk, France
Dunlop™ sports equip.
Dunlop™ tire
Dunne, Dominick
Dunne, Irene
Dunsinane (in Scotland)
Dunsmore, Barrie
Duny of Earthsea
Dupin, Amadine (aka George Sand)
DuPont Antron™
DuPont Stainmaster™
Durabeam™ flashlight
Duracell™ batteries
Duran Duran (rock group)
Durango, state, Mexico
Durant, Will and Ariel
Durante, Jimmy
DuraSoft™ contact lenses
Durbin, Deanna
Dürer, Albrecht
Durham County, Eng.
Durham, NC
Durkee™ foods
Durning, Charles
Durocher, Leo
Durrell, Lawrence
Durward Kirby
Duryea, Dan
Duse, Eleanora
Dushanbe, Tadzhik

Dussault, Nancy
Düsseldorf, W. Ger.
Dust Bowl (of '30s)
Dustin Hoffman
Dustin Nguyen
Dutch Belted cattle
Dutch bob
Dutch Borneo
Dutch door
Dutch East India Co.
Dutch elm disease
Dutch Guiana (now Suriname)
Dutch oven
Dutch Reformed Church
Dutch treat
Dutch uncle
Dutch West India Co.
Dutton, E. P.
Duvall, Robert
Duvall, Shelley
Dvořák, Anton, or Antonin
Dweezil Zappa
Dwight D. Eisenhower, Pres.
Dwight Hemion
Dwight Yoakam
Dy (chem. sym. dysprosium)
Dyan Cannon
Dyazide™
Dyck, Sir Anthony Van, or Vandyke
Dyke, Dick Van
Dylan Thomas
Dylan, Bob
Dynel™
Dynogen™ plant food
Dysart, Richard

E region
E-Z Load Trailer
E. & J. Gallo
E. B. White
E. M. Forster
E. P. Dutton, publisher
e. e. cummings
e.p.t.™
E.T.: Extra-Terrestrial
Eadweard Muybridge
Eagle™ potato chips
Eakins, Thomas
Eames chair/house
Eames, Charles
Earhart, Amelia
Earl of Albemarle
Earl Bostic
Earl of Cardigan , James Brudenell
    (cardigan sweater)
Earl Carrol's Vanities
Earl Grey tea
Earl 'Fatha' Hines
Earl of Northumberland
Earl of Sandwich, John Montagu
Earl Scheib™ auto painting
Earl Scruggs
Earl of Southhampton, Henry
    Wriothesley
Earl Burger Warren, Ch. Justice
Earle Naval Weapons Station, NJ
Earp, Wyatt
Earth Shoes™
Earth, Wind & Fire (rock group)
Eartha Kitt
East Berlin, E. Ger., or Ost-Berlin
East China Sea

East Germany, also German
    Democratic Republic
East Goths, or Ostrogoths
East India Co., British
East India Co., Dutch
East India Co., French
East Indies
East Lansing, MI
East Lynne
East of Eden
East Orange, NJ
East Sussex County, Eng.
East West Journal
Easter
Easter egg
Easter Island
Easter lily
Eastern Airlines
Eastern Church
Eastern Hemisphere
Eastern Orthodox Church
Eastern Review
Eastern Standard Time
Eastertide
Eastman Kodak Co.
Eastman, George
Eastwood, Clint
Easy Wash™ stain remover
Easy-Off™ Oven Cleaner
eau de Cologne
Ebbets Field
Ebenezer Scrooge
Eber, José
Ebersol, Dick
Ebersole, Christine
Ebert, Roger
Ebony magazine
Ebsen, Buddy
Ecclesiastes
Eckrich™ meats
Eckstine, Billy
Economic World
Ecotrin™
Ecuador
Ecumedia News Service
Ed Asner
Ed Begley
Ed Begley Jr.

Ed Bradley
Ed Harris
Ed Herlihy
Ed 'Too Tall' Jones
Ed Marinaro
Ed McMahon
Ed Sullivan
Ed Wynn
Edam cheese
Edberg, Stefan
Edd 'Kookie' Byrnes
Eddie Arcaro (George)
Eddie Bracken
Eddie Cantor
Eddie 'Lockjaw' Davis
Eddie Fisher
Eddie Foy
Eddie Foy, Jr.
Eddie Murphy
Eddie Rabbitt
Eddings, David
Eddy Arnold
Eddy, Mary Baker
Eden, Garden of
Eden, Sir Anthony, P.M.
Ederle, Gertrude
Edgar Bergen
Edgar Rice Burroughs
Edgar Dégas
Edgar Lee Masters
Edgar Allan Poe
Edinburg, TX
Edinburgh, duke of, Philip
    Mountbatten
Edinburgh, Scotland
Edison, Thomas Alva
Edith Evans, Dame
Edith Head
Edith Piaf
Edith Sitwell, Dame
Edith Wharton
Editorial Eye
Edmond Rostand
Edmonton Journal
Edmonton, Alberta, Can.
Edmund G. 'Pat' Brown, Gov.
Edmund Dantes, Count of Monte
    Cristo

Edmund Gwenn
Edmund Halley
Edmund P. Hillary, Sir
Edmund Kean
Edmund Muskie, Sen.
Edmund Randolph ("Randolph of
  Roanoke")
Edmund Spencer
Edna Ferber
Edna St. Vincent Millay
Édouard Victor Lalo
Edouard Manet
Edouard Vuillard
Edsel™ car
Edsel Ford (person)
Eduard A. Shevardnadze, For. Min.
Education Week
Educational Broadcasting Corp.
Edvard Grieg
Edvard Munch
Edward Albee
Edward the Black Prince
Edward Braddock, General
Edward Wm. Brooke, Sen.
Edward the Confessor
Edward Eggleston
Edward Elgar, Sir
Edward FitzGerald
Edward Gibbon
Edward Heath, P.M.
Edward Hopper
Edward Everett Horton
Edward Jenner
Edward Moore Kennedy, Sen.
Edward Koch, Mayor
Edward Mulhare
Edward R. Murrow
Edward 'Eddie' Rickenbacker, Capt.
Edward G. Robinson
Edward Steichen
Edward Lawrie Tatum
Edward Teach (aka Blackbeard)
Edward Teller, Dr.
Edward White, Astronaut
Edward Woodward
Edward, duke of Windsor
Edward, Prince of Wales (the Black
  Prince)

Edwards Air Force Base, CA
Edwards, Blake
Edwin E. 'Buzz' Aldrin, Astronaut
Edwin Booth
Edwin Christy
Edwin Drood
Edwin Powell Hubble
Edwin Meese, III, Atty. Gen.
Edwin Moses
Edwin Newman
Edwin Schrödinger
Edwin Stanton
Eero Saarinen
Eeyore (*Winnie-the-Poo*)
Efferdent™ Denture Cleanser
Efrem Zimbalist, Jr. (actor)
Efrem Zimbalist, Sr. (musician)
Egg Beaters™
Egg McMuffin (McDonald's)
Eggleston, Edward
Eggo™ waffles
eggs Benedict
Eglin Air Force Base, FL
Egnor, Virginia (aka Dagmar)
Egon Schiele
Egypt, or Arab Republic of Egypt
Egyptian Mau cat
Egyptology
Ehrlich, Paul
Ehrlichman, John
Eichmann, Adolf
Eielson Air Force Base, AK
Eiffel Tower
Eiffel, Gustave
Eigenwillig
Eight, the (group Am. artists)
Eikenberry, Jill
Eine Kleine Nachtmusik
Einstein, Albert
Eisaku Sato, P.M.
Eisenhower, Dwight D., Pres.
Eisner, Michael
Ekberg, Anita
Ekco™
El Al airline
El Cajon, CA
El Camino Real
El Dorado, CA

El Dorado, or Eldorado (legendary land)
El Duce (Benito Mussolini)
El Greco
El Niño current
El Paso, TX
El Salvador
El Toro Marine Corps Air Station, CA
Elaine Stritch
Elaine Zayak
Elam, Jack
Elat, Israel, or Eilat
Elayne Boosler
Elba Island
Elbe River
Elbis (the Devil)
Elbridge Gerry, V.P.
Elburz Mts.
Elder Beerman Department Stores
Eleanor of Aquitaine
Eleanora Duse
Electra (Gr. myth)
Electra complex
Electric Light Orchestra
Electrolux™
Elektra Records
'Elephant Man, the´ (John Merrick)
Eleusinian Mysteries
Elevators™ lift shoes
Elgar, Sir Edward
Elgin Marbles
Elgin™ watch
Elgin, IL
Eli Wallach
Eli Whitney
Elia Kazan
Elias Howe
Elias Sarkis, Pres.
Elijah, or Elias (prophet)
Elinor Donahue
Eliot, George (pseud. Mary Ann Evans)
Eliot, T. S.
Eliott Ness
Elisha Otis (elevator)
Eliza Doolittle
Elizabeth Arden™ cosmetics
Elizabeth Bishop
Elizabeth Blackwell

Elizabeth Barrett Browning
Elizabeth 'Betty' Furness
Elizabeth Kübler-Ross
Elizabeth Schwarzkopf
Elizabeth Cady Stanton
Elizabeth Taylor
Elizabethan sonnet
Elizabethan style
Elizabethtown, NY, PA
Elks Lodge (BPOE)
Elks Magazine
Ella Fitzgerald
Ella Raines
Elle magazine
Ellen Barkin
Ellen Terry, Dame
Ellen Tracy
Ellen Tree
Ellerbee, Linda
Ellery Queen
Ellery Queen's Mystery Magazine
Ellidyr, Prince
Ellington, Duke
Elliott Gould
Elliott, Sumner Locke
Ellis Island
Ellis, Perry
Ellison, Harlan
Ellroy, James
Ellsworth Air Force Base, SD
Elly May Clampett
Ellyn Burstyn
Elman, Mischa
Elman, Ziggy
Elmendorf Air Force Base, AK
Elmer Fudd
Elmer Gantry
Elmer Rice
Elmer Ambrose Sperry
Elmer's Glue-All™
Elmo Zumwalt III, Adm.
Elna™ sew. mach.
Elsa Lanchester
Elsa Schiaparelli
Elsinore, Denmark
Elton John
Elul (Jew. month)
Elvis Costello

Elvis Presley
Elysèe Palace
Elysian fields, or Elysium
Emancipation Proclamation
Emanuel Ax
Emanuel Swedenborg
Embargo Act of 1807
Emerald Isle
Emerson, Ralph Waldo
Emerson™ electronics
Emery™ Air Freight
Emil Nolde
Emil von Behring
Emile Zola
Emilio Estevez
Emilio Pucci
Emillo Aguinaldo
Emily Brontë
Emily Dickinson
Emily Lloyd
Emily Post
Emma Bovary, Madame
Emma Hamilton, Lady
Emma Lazarus
Emma Peel
Emma Samms
Emmeline Pankhurst
Emmy Awards
Emmylou Harris
Emperor Akihito
Emperor Caracalla (Roman)
Emperor Franz Joseph
Emperor Hadrian
Emperor Hirohito
Emperor Nero
Emperor Titus (Titus Flavius)
Empire State Building
Empire style
Emporium Capwell Store
Empress Eugènie
Empress Josephine
En-Lai, Chou, Premier
Enberg, Dick
Enceladus (Saturn moon)
Encore Books
Encyclopaedia Britannica
Enderby Land (region Antarctica)
Endust™

Energizer™ battery
Energizer™ bunny
Enerjee™ radiator
Enesco, Georges
Enfield rifle
Engelbert Humperdinck (Ger. composer)
Engelbert Humperdinck (pop. singer)
Engineering Digest
England
England Air Force Base, LA
England, Church of
English Channel
English cocker spaniel
English horn
English ivy
English muffin
English Restoration
English saddle
English setter
English sheepdog, or Old English sheepdog
English sonnet
English sparrow
English springer spaniel
English toy spaniel
English walnut
Englishman
Englishwoman
Eniwetok atoll, or Enewetak, or Enewetok
Enovid™
Enrico Caruso
Enrico Cecchetti
Enrico Fermi
Enriquez, Rene
Ensenada, Mex.
Ensign Chekov (*Star Trek*)
Ensor, James, Baron
Entebbe, Uganda
Enterprise, U.S.S.
Entertainment Tonight
Entrepreneur magazine
Entreprenurial Women
Environ-Sak™
Environmental Protection Agency (EPA)
Enzo Ferrari

Eocene epoch
Eolithic period
Eos (Gr. myth)
Epaminondas (Gr. statesman)
Ephesians (Biblical)
EPI™ Products
Epi™ smile
EPIC Productions
Epic Bookstores
Epictetus (philosopher - stoicism)
Epicurus (philosopher - pleasure)
Epilady™ hair removal system
Epiphany
Episcopal Church
Episcopalian (member of congregation)
Episcopalian magazine
Epsom Downs, Eng.
Epsom salts
Epson™ computer
Epstein-Barr virus
Equal™
Equal Rights Amendment
Equalactin™
Equatorial Guinea
Er (chem. sym. erbium)
ERA™ Real Estate
Erasistratus (Gr. physician)
Erasmus, or Desiderius Erasmus
Eratosthenes (Gr. scholar)
Erechtheum (on Acropolis)
Eric Ambler
Eric A. Blair (aka George Orwell)
Eric Clapton
Eric Fromm
Eric Leinsdorf
Eric Partridge
Eric the Red
Eric Sevareid
Eric Snowden
Erica Jong
Erich Segal
Erich von Stroheim
Ericsson, Leif
Erie Canal
Erie Times-News
Erie, Lake
Erie, PA
Erle Stanley Gardner

Erlenmeyer flask
Erma Bombeck
Ermanno Wolf-Ferrari
Ernest Bloch
Ernest Borgnine
Ernest Chausson
Ernest Glendinning
Ernest Hemingway
Ernest 'Ernie' Pyle
Ernest Rutherford, Baron
Ernest Shackleton, Sir
Ernest Truex
Ernest Tubb
Ernestine Schumann-Heink
Ernie Kovacs
Erno Laszlo™
Ernst Barlach
Ernst Lubitsch
Ernst Mach
Ernst von Dohnányi
Ernst, Max
Eros
Errol Flynn
Errol Garner
Erskine Caldwell
Erté
Erving, Julius 'Dr. J'
Erwin Rommel, Gen. (aka 'the desert
    fox')
Erwin Schrödinger
Es (chem. sym. einsteinium)
Esa-Pekka Salonen
Escoffier, Auguste
Escondido, CA
Esdraelon Plain, Israel
Eskimo dog
Eskimo Indians
Eskimo Pie™
Eskimo-Aleut Indians
Esperanto (language)
Esprit™
Esprit de Corp.
Esquimalt, B.C., Can.
Esquire
Essen, W. Ger.
Essence
Essex, MD
Essex County, Eng.

Essex House (NYC)
Essex, Robert, Earl of
Estée Lauder™ cosmetics
Estelle Getty
Estelle Parsons
Estes Kefauver, Sen
Estes, Billy Sol
Estevez, Emilio
Esther Rolle
Esther Williams
Estonia
Etch A Sketch™
Eteocles (7 against Thebes)
Ethan Allen
Ethan Frome
Ethel Barrymore
Ethel Kennedy (Mrs. Robert)
Ethel Merman
Ethel Smyth, Dame
Ethelred II, King (aka 'the Unready')
Ethiopia
Etna, Mt., or Aetna
Etobicoke, Ont., Can.
Eton collar
Eton College
Eton, Eng.
Etruria (now Tuscany/Umbria)
Etruscan civilization/art
Etticoat, Nancy
Etting, Ruth
Eu (chem. sym. europium)
Eubanks, Bob
Eubie Blake
Euclid (Gr. mathematician)
Euclidian geometry
Euell Gibbons
Eugene Delacroix
Eugene Fodor
Eugene Ionesco
Eugene Loring
Eugene McCarthy, Sen.
Eugene O'Neill
Eugene Ormandy
Eugénie, Empress
Eunice Kennedy Shriver
Euphrates River
Eurailpass
Eureka, CA

Eureka™ vacuum
Euripides (Gr. poet)
Euroclydon wind
Eurocurrency
Eurodollars
Europa (Jupiter moon)
Europe
European Community
European Economic Community
European hotel plan
European Monetary System
European Recovery Program, or
    Marshall Plan
European Southern Observatory,
    Chile
Eurydice (Gr. myth)
Eurythmics, the
Eustace Clarence Scrubb
Eva Braun (Mrs. A. Hitler)
Eva Duarte de Perón, Pres.
Eva Evdokimova
Eva Gabor
Eva Le Gallienne
Eva Marie Saint
Eva Tanguay
Evan Mecham, Gov. (impeached)
Evan Picone™
Evangelical Alliance
Evangeline Cory Booth
Evans, Dale
Evans, Dame Edith
Evans, Mary Ann (aka George Eliot)
Evans, Maurice
Evanston, IL
Evansville, IN
Evdokimova, Eva
Eve Arden
Evel Knievel
Evelyn Ashford
Evelyn Keyes
Evelyn Waugh
Evenflo™ baby bottle
Ever-Gard™ car alarm
Eveready™ battery
Everest, Mt.
Everglades Nat. Pk.
Everglades region, FL
Everly Brothers, The

Evers, Medgar
Evert (Lloyd), Chris
Everyman
Evian™ water
Evil One (the Devil)
Evinrude™ boat/engine
Evita
Evolutionism (Darwin's)
Evonne Goolagong
Ewell, Tom
Ewing, J. R.
Ewok (Star Wars creature)
Ex-Lax™
Excalibur (Arthurian)
Excedrin™
Executive Female magazine
Exercycle™
Exeter, England
Exodus, the
Explorer Magazine
Explorer space probe
Expressionism art, or expressionism
Extreme Unction
Exxon™
Exxon Valdez spill
Eyck, Hubert van
Eyck, Jan van
Eydie Gorme
Eyre, Jane
Eyre, Lake (Australia)
Ezekiel, or Ezechiel (Biblical)
Ezekiel's wheel
Ezio Pinza
Ezra Taft Benson
Ezra Loomis Pound

F (chem. sym. fluorine)
F. Lee Bailey
F. Scott Fitzgerald
F. W. Murnau
F.A.O. Schwarz
Fabergé Brut™
Fabergé egg
Fabergé, Peter Carl
Fabian Society
Fabray, Nanette
Fact Magazine
Fadiman, Clifton
Fahd, King, of Saudi Arabia
Fahlstrom, Oyvind
Fahrenheit 451
Fahrenheit scale/degree
Fahrenheit, G. D.
Fair Labor Standards Act
Fairbanks, AK
Fairbanks, Charles W., V.P.
Fairbanks, Douglas
Fairbanks, Douglas, Jr.
Fairchild Air Force Base, WA
Fairchild Space Co.
Fairfax, VA
Fairmont Hotel (S.F.)
Fairweather, Mount
Faisal I & II, kings of Iraq, or Feisal
Falabella Miniature Horse
Falkenburg, Jinx
Falkland Islands
Falla (FDR's dog)
Fallingwater (F.L.Wright)
Fallon Naval Air Station, NV
Falstaff, Sir John
Falwell, Jerry, Rev.

Family Circle
Family Computing
Family Magazine
Famous Amos Chocolate Chip
  Cookie Corp.
Fandango (dance)
Fannie 'Fanny' Brice
Fannie Farmer
Fannie Mae, or May, also Federal
  Nat'l Mortgage Assn.
Fantasia
Fantastik™ cleaner
Fantasy Island
Fantasy Review
Fantin-Latour, Ignace Henri
Far East
Faraday cage
Faraday, Michael
Farah Diba
Farah™ slacks
Fargo, ND
Farley Granger
Farm Family America
Farm Futures
Farm Journal
Farmer John™ meats
Farmer, Fannie
Farmer's Almanac, The
Farmington, NM
Farmstead
Farnese family of Italy
Farnese Palace, Rome
Farnsworth, Philo T.
Farouk, king of Egypt
Farr, Jamie
Farragut, David, Adm.
Farrah Fawcett
Farrar, Geraldine (opera star)
Farrar, Straus & Girous Inc.
Farrell, Charles
Farrell, Mike
Farrow, Mia
Fassbinder, Rainer Werner
Fasteeth™
Fatah (PLO organization)
Fataly, Natasha, or Badenov
Fates, three (Clotho, Lachesis, Atropos)
Father Time

Fatima, Miracle of
Fatima, Portugal
Fats Domino
Fats Navarro
Fats Waller
Fatty Arbuckle
Faulkner, William
Fauntleroy, Little Lord
Fauré, Gabriel
Faust (Goethe's)
Faust, Johann, or Faustus
Fauves
Fauvism art
Fawcett Books
Fawcett, Farrah
Fawkes, Guy
Fawn Hall
Fay Bainter
Faye Dunaway
Faye, Alice
Fayetteville, NC
FDR's New Deal
Fear, Cape, NC
February Revolution (Fr. 1848)
February Revolution (Rus. 1917)
Federal Constitutional Convention
Federal Express™
Federal Land Bank
Federal Republic of Germany
Federal Reserve Bank
Federal Reserve note
Federal Reserve Board
Federal Trade Commission
Federalist party
Federation of Malaysia
Federico Fellini
Feely, Paul
Feiffer, Jules
Feininger, Lyonel
Feinstein, Dianne, Mayor
Felipe Gonzales, P.M.
Felix Adler
Felix Bloch
Felix Mendelssohn
Fell, Norman
Feller, Bob
Fellini, Federico
Feltsman, Vladimir

80

Feminist Majority
Fendi
Fenian movement
Fennelman, George
Fens, or Fenland
Fenway Park
Feodor Dostoyevsky, or Dostoevsky
Ferber, Edna
Ferdinand de Saussure
Ferdinand E. Marcos, Pres.
Ferdinand Magellan
Ferdinand Graf von Zeppelin, Count
Ferguson, Maynard
Ferguson, Sarah 'Fergie', Duchess of
    York
Ferlin Husky
Fermi, Enrico
Fermilab (Fermi Nat'l Accelerator Lab.)
Fern Arable
Fernando Lamas
Fernando Valenzuela
Ferragamo, Salvatore
Ferrante & Teicher
Ferrare, Cristina
Ferrari™
Ferrari, Enzo
Ferraro, Geraldine
Ferrer, Mel
Ferri, Alessandra
Ferrigno, Lou
Ferris wheel
Ferruccio, Busoni
Fertile Crescent
Feynman, Richard
Fez, Morocco, or Fès
Fibber McGee and Molly
Fiber One™
Fiberall™
FiberCon™
Fibonaccí sequence
Fibonaccí, Leonardo
Fibranne™
Fibre Trim™
Fickett, Mary
Fiddler on the Roof
Fidel Castro, Pres.
Fidgi™ perfume
Fiedler, Arthur

Field & Stream
Field, Cyrus West
Field, Marshall
Field, Sally
Fielding, Henry
Fields, Gracie
Fields, W.C.
"Fifty-four forty or fight"
Fig Newtons™
Fiji, or Viti
Fiju Suva
Fila™ shoes
Fila Woman™ perfume
Filipino
Filippino Lippi
Filippo, Lippi, Fra
Filippo Brunelleschi
Fillmore, Millard, Pres./V.P.
Film World
Filofax™
Final Net™
Financial Analysts Journal
Financial News Network
Financial Post
Financial Times of Canada
Financial World
Findhorn community (Scotland)
Fine, Larry (1 of 3 Stooges)
Finesse™ haircare
Finger Lakes region, NY
Finland
Finlandia
Finn, Huckleberry
Finnair™ airline
Finney, Albert
Finnish language
Fiorello, La Guardia, Mayor
Firebird Suite (Stravinsky's)
Firestone™ tire
Firestone Tire and Rubber Co.
Firestone, Harvey
1st Interstate Bank
First Cause (God)
First Triumvirate
Firth of Forth, Scotland
Fischer, Bobby
Fischer™ skis
Fisher™ nuts

Fisher, Carrie
Fisher, Eddie
Fisher-Price™ toys
Fishri (Jew. mo.)
Fiske, Minnie Maddern, or Mrs. Fiske
Fittipaldi, Emerson
FitzGerald, Edward
Fitzgerald, Barry
Fitzgerald, Ella
Fitzgerald, F. Scott
FitzRoy Somerset, lst Baron Raglan
   (raglan coat)
Fitzsimmons Army Medical Center,
   CO
Fitzwater, Marlin
Five Alive™
Five Dynasties and Ten Kingdoms
   dynasty
Five-Year Plan (Stalin's)
Fixodent™
Fixx, Jim
Flack, Roberta
Flag Day (unofficial holiday)
Flanders field
Flash Gordon
Flathead Indians, or Salish
Flatt, Lester
Flaubert, Gustave
Flav-R-Pac™ foods
Fleet™ Enema
Fleet Street, London
Fleetwood Mac
Fleischmann's™ foods
Fleischmann's™ vodka
Fleming, Sir Alexander
Fleming, Ian
Fleming, Peggy
Fleming, Rhonda
Flemish language
Flex-Care™
Flinders, Jenny
Flintstone, Fred
Flintstones, The
Flintstones™ vitamins
Flippen, Jay C.
Florence Chadwick
Florence 'Flo Jo' Griffith Joyner
Florence Nightingale

Florence, Italy, or Firenze
Florenz 'Flo' Ziegfeld
Florida Keys
Florida (FL)
Florists' Transworld Delivery™, or
   FTD™
Florsheim™ shoes
Flotow, Friedrich von
Floyd Patterson
Fluorocarbon™
Flushing, NY
Flushing Meadows (NYC)
Flying Dutchman
Flying Karamazov Brothers
Flying Magazine
Flying Tigers Airline (merged with Fed.
   Express)
Flying Wallendas
Flynn, Errol
Foch, Nina
Fodor, Eugene
Fodor's Travel Guides
Fogelberg, Dan
Fogg Art Museum
Foghorn Leghorn
Foley, Red
Foley's Department Stores
Folger Shakespeare Library (D.C.)
Folgers™ coffee
Folies Berge're
Follett, Ken
Folsom Prison (CA)
Fonda, Jane
Fonda, Henry
Fonda, Peter
Fontaine, Frank (aka Crazy
   Guggenheim)
Fontaine, Joan
Fontainebleau, France
Fontainebleau, palace at
Fontainebleau, school of
Fontanne, Lynn
Fonteyn, Dame Margot
Fonzerelli, Arthur, or 'Fonzie', or
   'the Fonz'
Food & Beverage Marketing
Food & Wine
Food and Drug Administration (FDA)

Foot Locker store
Forbes
Forbes, Malcolm
Forbidden City, China
Ford Foundation
Ford Motor Co.
Ford Times
Ford, Betty (Mrs. Gerald)
Ford, Edsel (person)
Ford, Gerald Rudolph, Pres.
Ford, Henry
Ford, Mary (Les Paul &)
Ford, Tennessee Ernie
Ford, Whitey (aka Duke of Paducah)
Fordham University
Foreign Legion
Foreman, George
Foremost™
Forenza™ clothes
Forest E. Mars
Forest Hills, PA
Forest Lawn Memorial Parks (CA)
Forester, C. S.
Forman, Milos
Formby's™ refinishing prod.
Formfit Rogers™
Formica™
Formosa (now Taiwan)
Formosa Strait (now Taiwan Strait)
Formosan
Formula 409™
Fornax constellation
Forrestal, James, Secy. Navy/Def.
Forster, E. M.
Fort Belvoir, VA
Fort Benjamin Harrison, IN
Fort Benning, GA
Fort Bliss, TX
Fort Bragg, CA, NC
Fort Chaffee, AR
Fort Collins, CO
Fort Detrick, MD
Fort Devens, MA
Fort Dix , NJ
Fort Drum, NY
Fort Eustis, VA
Fort Gillem, GA
Fort Gordon, GA

Fort Greely, AK
Fort Hamilton, NY
Fort Hood, TX
Fort Huachuca, AZ
Fort Hunter Liggett, CA
Fort Irwin, CA
Fort Jonathan Wainwright, AK
Fort Knox, KY
Fort Laramie N.H.S., WY
Fort Lauderdale Sun-Sentinel
Fort Lauderdale, FL
Fort Leavenworth, KS
Fort Lee, VA
Fort Leonard Wood, MO
Fort Macon Coast Guard Base, NC
Fort McCoy, WI
Fort McHenry, MD
Fort McNair, DC
Fort McPherson, GA
Fort Meade, MD
Fort Monmouth, NJ
Fort Monroe, VA
Fort Myer, VA
Fort Myers, FL
Fort Ord, CA
Fort Polk, LA
Fort Richardson, AK
Fort Riley, KS
Fort Ritchie, MD
Fort Sam Houston, TX
Fort Shafter, HI
Fort Sheridan, IL
Fort Sill, OK
Fort Story, VA
Fort Sumter, SC
Fort Ticonderoga, NY
Fort Wayne Journal-Gazette
Fort Worth Star-Telegram
Fort Worth, TX
Fort-de-France, Martinique
Fortaleza, Brazil
Forth River in Scotland
Fortinbras, Prince of Norway
Fortnum and Mason
FORTRAN
Fortune
Fortune 500
Forty-Niner (Gold Rush participant)

Fosse, Bob
Fossey, Dian
Foster Farms™ chicken
Foster, Meg
Foster, Stephen
Fotomat™
Foul Fiend (the Devil)
Fountain of Youth
Four Aces, The
Four Freedoms of FDR
Four Horsemen of the Apocalypse
Four Lads, The
Fourth of July, or July Fourth, or
    Independence Day
Fowels, John
Fox Broadcasting Company
Fox Indians
Fox, Margaret (occult)
Fox, Michael J.
Foxx, Redd
Foy, Eddie
Foy, Eddie, Jr.
Foyt, A. J.
Fozzie Bear
Fr (chem. sym. francium)
Fra Angelico
Fra Bartolommeo
Fra Filippo Lippi
Fraggle Rock
Fragonard, Jean-Honoré
Framingham, MA
Frampton, Peter
Fran Allison (*Kukla, Fran & Ollie*)
Fran Tarkenton
France
Frances Langford
Francesco Cilea
Franchot Tone
Francine Pascal
Francis of Assisi, Saint
Francis Bacon (20th cent. artist)
Francis Bacon, Sir (17th cent.
    philosopher)
Francis X. Bushman
Francis Ford Coppola
Francis H. C. Crick
Francis Drake, Sir
Francis Scott Key

Francis 'Lightfoot' Lee
Francis Quarles
Francis 'Dick' Scobee (Challenger
    commander)
Francis E. Townsend
Francis T. Vincent Jr.
Francis E. Warren Air Force Base,
    WY
Francis, Arlene
Francis, Connie
Francis, Dick
Francis, Genie Ann
Francis, Marion (aka 'the Swamp Fox')
Franciscan monks, or Franciscans
Francisco Goya
Francistown, Botswana
Franck, César Auguste
Franco Zeffirelli
Franco-American™ foods
Franco-Prussian War, or Franco-
    German War
François Boucher
François Chateaubriand
François Didot
François Mansard, or Mansart
François Mitterrand, Pres.
François Rabelais
François Truffaut
François Villon
François Voltaire
Françoise Sagan
Frangelico™ liqueur
Frank Borman, Astronaut
Frank Capra
Frank Carlucci
Frank De Vol
Frank Fontaine (aka Crazy
    Guggenheim)
Frank Gifford
Frank Kupka
Frank Langella
Frank Lorenzo
Frank Reynolds
Frank Sinatra (Francis Albert)
Frank Slaughter
Frank R. Stockton
Frank Tuttle
Frank W. Woolworth

Frank Lloyd Wright
Frank Yankovic
Frank Yerby
Frank Zappa
Frank, Anne
Frankenstein, Dr.
Frankenstein
Frankenthaler, Helen
Frankfurt, E. Ger.
Frankfurt, W. Ger.
Franklin Pierce, Pres.
Franklin Delano Roosevelt, Pres.
   (FDR)
Franklin stove
Franklin, Aretha
Franklin, Benjamin
Frann, Mary
Frans Hals
Frans Snyders
Franz Boas
Franz Joseph Haydn
Franz Joseph, Emperor
Franz Kafka
Franz Lehar
Franz Liszt
Franz Marc
Franz Mesmer
Franz Schubert
Franz Joseph Strauss
Franz Waxman
Franz, Dennis
Franzia™ wines
Frasch process
Fraser River (B.C.)
Fratianne, Linda
Fraunhofer lines
Frawley, William
Freberg, Stan
Fred Allen
Fred Astaire
Fred de Cordova
Fred Flintstone
Fred MacMurray
Fred J. Muggs (TV chimp)
Fred Rogers (TV's Mr. Rogers)
Fred Savage
Fred Silverman
Fred Waring

Fred Zinnermann
Freddie Mac, or Federal Home Loan
   Mortgage Corp.
Freddie Prinze
Freddy Krueger
Frederic Auguste Bartholdi
Frédéric Chopin
Frederic Remington
Frederick & Nelson dept. stores
Frederick Barbarosa
Frederick Delius
Frederick Douglass
Frederick the Great
Frederick Loewe
Frederick Soddy
Frederick Winslow Taylor
Frederick the Winter King
Frederick, Pauline
Frederick's of Hollywood™
Fredericksburg, battle of
Fredericksburg, VA
Frederik W. de Klerk, Pres.
Frederik Pohl
Frederik von Anhalt, Prince
Fredric March
Free Enterprise
Free State
Free-Soil Party
Free-Soil territory
Freebies
Freedom of Information Act
Freeman, Morgan
Freemasonry (teachings)
Freemasons, or Free and Accepted
   Masons (order)
Freer Gallery of Art (D.C.)
Freer, Charles Lang
Freiburg, W. Ger.
Fremont, John Charles
French and Indian War
French bread
French bulldog
French Canadian
French cuff
French curve
French doors
French dressing
French East India Co.

French endive
French Equatorial Africa
French fries
French Guiana
French heel
French horn
French kiss
French knot
French leave
French letter (Br. slang-condom)
French Polynesia
French provincial style
French Revolution
French Revolutionary calendar
French Revolutionary Wars
French Riviera
French roll
French seam
French telephone
French toast
French twist
French West Africa
French windows
Frenchman
French's™ mustard
Frenchwoman
Freon™
Fresh Start™ detergent
Fresh Step™ cat litter
Fresnel™ lens
Fresno, CA
Freud, Sigmund
Friar John
Friar Lawrence
Friars Club
Frick Museum
Frick, Henry Clay
Frieburg, W. Ger.
Friedan, Betty
Friedkin, David
Friedkin, William
Friedrich Hund
Friedrich von Flotow
Friedrich Wilhelm Nietzsche
Friedrich Wilhelm von Schelling
Friedrich von Schiller
Friedrich von Steuben, Baron
Friends, Religious Society of

Friendly Exchange
Friendship 7
Frietchie, Barbara
Frigidaire™
Frigo cheese
Friml, Rudolf
Frisbee™
Friskies Buffet™
Friskies™ cat food
Frito Lay Inc.
Frito Lay's™ chips
Fritos™ chips
Fritz the Cat
Fritz Haber
Fritz Kreisler
Fritz Lang
Frizon, Maud
Frobisher, Sir Martin
Frodo Baggins
Frohman, Charles
Frohman, Daniel
Froman, Jane
Fromkess, Leon
Fromm, Eric
Fromme, Lynette 'Squeaky'
Frookie Cookie™
Froot Loops™ cereal
Frost, Robert
Frosted Mini-Wheats™
Frosted Wheat Squares™
Frostee-Freeze™
Frugal Gourmet
Fruit Of The Loom™
Fruit-Fresh™
FruitSlush™
Fruity Pebbles™ cereal
Fruity Yummy Mummy™
Frusen Glädjé™
Fry, Christopher
Fu Manchu
Fu, Tu (Chinese poet)
Fuchs, Klaus
Fudd, Elmer
Fudgsicle™
Fuji Electric Co. Ltd.
Fuji film™
Fuji, Japan
Fuji, Mount, or Mt. Fujiyama

Fujicolor™
Fukuoka, Japan
Fulbright Act (scholarship)
Fulbright, J. William, Sen.
Fulgencio Batista y Zaldivar (deposed
    Cuban leader)
Fuller Brush man
Fuller, R. Buckminster
Fuller, Margaret
Fullerton, CA
Fulton Fish Market
Fulton J. Sheen, Bishop
Fulton, Robert (steamship)
Funchal, Madeira
Fundy, Bay of
Funicello, Annette
Funk & Wagnalls
Funky Winkerbean
Funt, Alan
Furies, three (Alecto, Tisiphone,
    Megaera), or Erinyes
Furness, Elizabeth 'Betty'
Furstenberg, Diane von
Futurism art, or futurism
Futurist
Fuzzy Zoeller

G spot
G-man
G-string
G-suit
G. Gordon Liddy
Ga (chem. sym. gallium)
Gabel, Martin
Gable, Clark
Gabo, Naum
Gabon republic

Gabor, Eva
Gabor, Zsa Zsa
Gaborone, Botswana, or Gaberones
Gabriel Fauré
Gabriel Kaplan
Gabriel, Archangel
Gabriel, Jacques Ange
Gabriela Sabatini
Gabrielle 'Coco' Chanel
Gadhafi, Gaddafi, Qaddafi, or
    Khadafy, Moammar, Muammar, or
    Muammar-al
Gadsden Purchase
Gadsden, AL
Gaelic
Gaetano Donizetti
Gagarin Yuri A., Cosmonaut
Gage, Thomas, Gen./Gov.
Gaggenau™ stove
Gaillard, Slim
Gaines™ pet food
Gaines Gravy Train™
Gainesville, FL
Gainsborough, Thomas
Galanos™
Galanos, James
Galapagos Islands
Galatea (Pygmalion's statue)
Galatians
Galbraith, John Kenneth
Gale Storm
Gale, Zona
Galiceño (horse)
Galicia region, Spain
Galilee region, Israel
Galilee, Sea of
Galilei, Galileo, or 'Galileo'
Galileo space probe
Gallagher & Shean
Gallagher Report
Gallagher, Peter
Gallery magazine
Galliano liqueur
Gallic Wars
Gallico, Paul
Gallo™ wine
Gallo, Ernest & Julio
Galloping Gourmet, Graham Kerr

Galloway cattle
Gallup Poll
Gallup, George
Gallup, NM
Galoob™ toys
Galsworthy, John
Galveston, TX
Galway, Ireland
Galway, James
Gama, Vasco da
Gamal Abdal Nasser, Pres.
Gamay wine grape
Gambia, The
Gambia River
Gambling Times
Gandhi, Indira, P.M.
Gandhi, Mahatma Mohandas
Gandhi, Rajiv, P.M.
Ganges River, or Ganga
Gann, Paul (intro. CA Prop. l3)
Ganymede (Jupiter moon/Gr. myth)
Garagiola, Joe
Garamond type style
Garamond, Claude
Garand rifle
Garbo, Greta
Garden of Earthly Delights (Bosch)
Garden of Gethsemane
Garden Grove, CA
Gardena, CA
Gardenia, Vincent
Gardiner, Reginald
Gardner, Ava
Gardner, Erle Stanley
Garfield
Garfield, James A., Pres.
Garfunkel, Art
Garland, Judy
Garner, Errol
Garner, James
Garner, John N., V.P.
Garr, Teri
Garret A. Hobart, V.P.
Garrett, Betty
Garrett, Pat, Sheriff (shot 'Billy the
    Kid')
Garrick Utley
Garrick, David

Garrison Keillor
Garrison, Zina
Garroway, Dave
Garry Shandling
Garry Trudeau (Doonesbury)
Garson, Greer
Garter, Order of the
Garvey, Cyndy
Garvey, Steve
Gary Burghoff
Gary Busey
Gary Coleman
Gary Cooper
Gary Larson
Gary Morton
Gary Francis Powers (U-2 pilot)
Gary Puckett And The Union Gap
Gascony region, Fr.
Gasoline Alley
Gassman, Vittoro
Gaston Lachaise
Gates of Paradise (Ghiberti)
Gates, Horatio, Gen.
Gateway Books
Gatlin Brothers, The
Gatling gun
Gatling, Richard
Gatorade™
Gatsby, Jay
Gaudí, Antonio
Gauguin, Paul
Gaul (ancient European area)
Gaulle, Charles de, Pres.
Gaussian curve (bell curve)
Gavin MacLeod
Gaviscon™
Gaye, Marvin
Gayle, Crystal
Gaynor, Janet
Gaynor, Mitzi
Gaza Strip, or Ghazzah
Gazzara, Ben
Gd (chem. sym. gadolinium)
Gdansk, Poland, or Danzig
Ge (chem. sym. germanium)
GE™ appliances
GE Miser™ lightbulbs
GE Soft-White™ Light Bulbs

Geary, Anthony
Gebel-Williams, Gunther
Gebhardt™ Chili/Mex. foods
Geddes, Barbara Bel
Geddes, Norman Bel
Geech
Geer, Will
Geffron Records
Gehrig, Lou
Geiger counter
Geisel, Theodor (Dr. Seuss)
Geisha girl
Geisha™ Tuna
Geissler tube
Geldof, Bob
Geller, Uri
Gelsey Kirkland
Gelvan, Vladimir
Gemini (zodiac sign)
Gemini (Twins) constellation
Gemini Space Project
Gemini space vehicle
Gemini™ VHS tape
Geminides meteor shower (Dec.)
Gene Autry
Gene Hackman
Gene Kelly
Gene Krupa
Gene Roddenberry
Gene Shalit
Gene Siskel & Roger Ebert
Gene Tierney
Gene Tunney
Gene Wilder
Genealogy Today
General American English
General Assembly, UN
General Electric Co.
General Foods Corp.
General Foods™
General Mills™ foods
General Motors™
General Motors Corp.
General Secretary, USSR
General Tire™
Generra™ casualwear
Genesis (rock group)
Genesis Magazine

Genesis, Book of
Geneva Conference
Geneva Conventions
Geneva, Lake
Geneva, Switz.
Genghis Khan
Genie (legendary)
Genie Ann Francis
Genie™ remote-control
Genoa, Italy, or Genova
Gentile Bellini
"Gentleman Jim" (James) Corbett
Geoffrey Beene
Geoffrey Chaucer
Geordi La Forge, Lt. Cmdr. (of *Star Trek*)
Georg Jensen store
Georg Wilhelm Friedrich Hegel
Georg Ohm
Georg Solti, Sir
Georg Philipp Telemann
George Abbott
George Air Force Base, CA
George 'Eddie' Arcaro
George Arliss
George Balanchine
George Baltimore, Lord
George Wesley Bellows
George Berkeley
George Caleb Bingham
George Braque
George Burns (b. Nathan Birnbaum)
George Herbert Walker Bush, Pres.
George Byron, Lord
George Carlin (comedian)
George Washington Carver
George Catlett Marshall, Gen.
George Catlin (artist)
George Rogers Clark
George Clinton, V.P.
George M. Cohan
George Cruikshank
George Cukor
George A. Custer, Lt. Col.
George M. Dallas, V.P.
George Deukmejian, Gov.
George Dewey, Adm.
George Eastman

George Eliot (aka Mary Ann Evans)
George Enesco
George Fennelman
George Foreman
George Gallup
George Gershwin
George Gobel
George Washington Goethals
George Grenville, P.M.
George Frideric Handel
George Harrison
George Hepplewhite
George Jessel
George S. Kaufman
George Lucas
George Macready
George B. McClellan, Gen.
George S. McGovern, Sen.
George Meade, Gen.
George Meany
George Michael
George Jean Nathan
George Orwell (pseud. Eric A. Blair)
George Papadopoulos, Prem.
George Papandreou, P.M.
George S. Patton, Gen.
George Foster Peabody Award
George Peppard
George Plimpton
George Romney
George 'Babe' Ruth
George Sand (pseud. Amadine Dupin)
George Santayana
George Schaeffer
George Schlatter
George C. Scott
George Bernard Shaw
George P. Shultz, Secy. State
George Steinbrenner
George Stubbs
George Szell
George Takei (*Star Trek*)
George Wallace, Gov.
George Washington, Pres.
George Westinghouse
George Zuckerman
Georges Bizet
Georges Braque

Georges Enesco
Georges Pompidou, Pres.
Georges Rouault
Georges Seurat
Georgetown, Guyana
Georgetown, DC
Georgia (GA)
Georgia O'Keeffe
Georgia-Pacific Corp.
Georgian Soviet Socialist Republic
Georgian style
Gephardt, Richard A.
Geradus Mercator, or Gerhard
   Kremer
Gerald Rudolph Ford, Pres.
Gerald Grosvenor
Gerald McRaney
Geraldine Farrar (opera star)
Geraldine Ferraro (politician)
Geraldo Rivera
Gerber™ baby food
Gere, Richard
German measles
German shepherd
German shorthaired pointer
German wirehaired pointer
Germanic law
Germanic religion
Germany
Geronimo (Apache leader)
Geronimo, OK
Gerry Cooney
Gerry, Elbridge, V.P.
Gershwin, George
Gershwin, Ira
Gertrude Atherton
Gertrude Ederle
Gertrude Lawrence
Gertrude Stein
Gerulaitis, Vitas
Gestalt psychology/therapy
Gestapo
Gesundheit
Gethsemane, Garden of
Getty Oil Co.
Getty, Estelle
Getty, J. Paul
Gettysburg Address

Gettysburg military campaign
Gettysburg Nat'l Military Park
Gettysburg, PA
Getz, Stan
Gewürztraminer wine
Ghana, W. Africa
Ghent Altarpiece
Ghent, Belgium
Ghent, Treaty of
Ghiberti, Lorenzo
Ghirardelli™ chocolate
Ghirardelli Square
Ghostbusters
Ghostbusters II
Ghostley, Alice
GI Joe (Am. soldier)
GI Joe™ (toy)
Giacometti, Alberto
Giacomo Balla
Giacomo Meyerbeer
Giacomo Puccini
Giacomo, Laura San
Giamatti, Bart
Giambattista, Bodini
Gian Carlo Menotti, or Gian-Carlo
Giancana, Sam
Gibb, Andy
Gibbon, Edward
Gibbons, Euell
Gibbons, Leeza
Gibbs free energy
Gibbs, Josiah Willard
Gibbs, Marla
Gibraltar
Gibraltar, Rock of
Gibralter Savings & Loan
Gibran, Kahlil
Gibson cocktail
Gibson girl
Gibson, Althea
Gibson, Charles
Gibson, Hoot
Gibson, Kirk
Gibson, Mel
Gide, André
Gideon vs. Wainwright
Gideon Welles
Gideons Bible, or Gideon

Gideons International, The
Gidget
Gielgud, Sir John
Gifford, Frank
Gifford, Kathie Lee
Gigi
Gila monster
Gilbert & Sullivan
Gilbert Grosvenor (editor)
Gilbert Stuart
Gilbert, Melissa
Gilbert, Sir William (Gilbert & Sullivan)
Gilbey's™ gin
Gilda Marx™
Gilda Radner
Gillespie, Dizzy
Gillette™
Gillette Co., The
Gillette Daisy Plus™ razor
Gillette, King Camp (invented safety razor)
Gilligan's Island
Gillikins, Country of the
Gillis, Dobie
Gingold, Hermione
Ginnie Mae, or Govt. National Mortgage Assn.
Ginsberg, Allen
Ginza district, Tokyo
Gioacchino Rossini
Giordano, Umberto
Giorgio Armani™
Giorgio Beverly Hills™
Giorgio de Chirico
Giorgio di Sant´Angelo
Giorgione
Giotto (Giotto de Bondone)
Giotto space probe
Giovanni Bellini
Giovanni Lorenzo Bernini, or Gianlorenzo
Giovanni Boccaccio
Giovanni Casanova
Giovanni Schiaparelli
Giovanni Tiepolo
Giraudoux, Jean
Girl Before a Mirror (Picasso)

Girl Guides (Br.)
Girl Scouts (US)
Girolamo Savonarola
Gisele MacKenzie
Giselle
Gish, Dorothy
Gish, Lillian
Gitano™
Giuliani, Rudolph W.
Giuseppe Verdi
Givenchy, Hubert de
Givens, Robin
Giverny, France
Gîza, Egypt, or Gîzeh
Gîza, Great Pyramids of, or Gîzeh
Glacier Bay Nat. Pk. (AK)
Glad™ Cling Wrap
Glad™ Plastic Bags
Glad™ Trash Bags
Glad-Lock™ sandwich bags
Gladstone bag
Gladstone, William, P.M.
Gladys Knight & The Pips
Gladys Swarthout
Glakens, William
Glamour
Glasgow, Scotland
Glass Menagerie, The
Glass Plus™
Glass, Ron
Glastonbury Tor
Glazunov, Aleksandr
Gleason, Jackie
Gleason, Paul
Gleizes, Albert
Glen Campbell
Glen Canyon Dam
Glenda Jackson
Glendale, CA
Glendinning, Ernest
Glenlivet™ scotch
Glenn Close
Glenn Hammond Curtiss
Glenn Gould
Glenn Miller Orchestra
Glenn T. Seaborg, Dr.
Glenn, John H., Astronaut/Sen.
Glenn, Scott

Glenview Naval Air Station, IL
Gless, Sharon
Glidden™ paint
Glidden™ Spread Satin
Glinka, Mikhail Ivanovitch
Globe Theatre
Gloccamorra, Ireland
Gloop, Augustus
Gloria Blondell
Gloria De Haven
Gloria Grahame
Gloria Loring
Gloria Steinem
Gloria Swanson
Gloria Vanderbilt™ perfume/clothes
Glorious Revolution
Gloucester Co., Eng.
Gloucester, MA
Gloucestershire Co., Eng.
Glover, Danny
Gluck, Christoph W.
Glue Stic™
Glyndebourne Festival, Eng.
Glynis Johns
Glynn, Carlin
Gnaeus Agricola
Gnosticism
Go-Jo™ hand cleaner
Gobel, George
Gobi Desert
God Almighty
God the Father
Godchaux's department stores
Goddard, Paulette
Godey's Lady's Book
Godfrey, Arthur
Godhead
Godiva™ chocolates
Godiva, Lady
'Gods little acre´
Godspell
Godthåb, Greenland
Godunov, Alexander
Godunov, Boris, Czar
Goebbels, Paul J. (Nazi)
Goering, Hermann Wilhelm, ot
  Göring
Goethals, George Washington

Goethe, Johann Wolfgang von
Goetz, Bernhard H.
Gog and Magog
Gogh, Vincent Van
Golan Heights
Gold Rush, The
Gold Star Medal
Golda Meir, P.M.
Goldberg, Rube
Goldberg, Whoopi
Goldblum, Jeff
Golden Age of Spain
Golden Ass, The (early Latin novel)
Golden Delicious apple
Golden Dipt™ marinade
Golden Fleece (Jason's)
Golden Gate Bridge
Golden Gate Park (S.F.)
Golden Griddle™ Syrup
Golden Horde, Empire of the
Golden Horn
Golden Rule
Golden Years
Goldie Hawn
Goldilocks
Golding, William
Goldmark, Karl
Goldsmith, Oliver
GoldStar™ microwave
Goldthwait, Bobcat
Goldwater, Barry M., Sen.
Goldwater, Barry M., Jr., Rep.
Goldwyn Girls, the
Goldwyn, Samuel
Golf Digest
Golf Illustrated
Golf Magazine
Golfinopoulos, Peter
Golgi apparatus
Golgotha
Goliardic songs
Goliards (wandering scholars)
Goliath, David and
Golliwogg, or Golliwog (character)
Gollum
Gomer Pyle
Gomorrah (Sodom &)
Gompers, Samuel

Gone With The Wind
Goneril (*King Lear*)
Gonzales, Felipe, P.M.
Gonzalez, Pancho
Good & Fruity™ candy
Good & Plenty™ candy
Good Book, the (Bible)
Good Friday
Good Hope, Cape of
Good Housekeeping
Good Humor™
Good Humor man
'good' King Wenceslaus, or St.
    Wenceslaus
Good Samaritan
Good Seasons™ salad dressing
Good-bye Columbus
'good-time Charlie'
Goodall, Jane
Goodfellow, Robin (Puck)
Goodman, Benny
Goodman, Dody
Goodman, Mark
GoodNews™ razor
Goodson-Todman Productions
Goodwill Industries
Goodwin, Archie
Goody™ hair prod.
Goodyear™ Tire & Rubber Co.
Goodyear, Charles
Goolagong, Evonne
Goop™ glue
Goop™ hand cleaner
Goose Tatum
Gorbachev, Mikhail S., Pres.
Gorbachev, Raisa
Gorcey, Leo
Gordian knot
Gordie Howe
Gordon Lightfoot
Gordon MacRae
Gordon setter
Gordon, Flash
Gordon, Ruth
Gordon's™ vodka/gin
Gore Vidal
Gore, Albert, Jr. Sen.
Gore-Tex™

Goren, Charles
Gorgonzola cheese
Gorham™ silverware
Gorky, Arshile
Gorky, USSR
Gorman, R. C.
Gorme, Eydie
Gorton's™ fish products
Goshen (Biblical fertile land)
Gospels, Synoptic
Gospels, the
Gossett, Louis, Jr.
Goth
Gotham (nick. NYC)
Gotham City (Batman's)
Gothic architecture/art
Gothic revival
Gothic romance
Gotland Pony
Götterdämmerung
Gottfried Lebniz, or Leibnitz
Gottschalk, Louis Moreau
Gouda cheese
Gouda, Netherlands
Gould, Elliott
Gould, Glenn
Gould, Jay
Goulet, Robert
Gounod, Charles François
Gourmet
Government Product News
Gowdy, Curt
Gower Champion
Goya, Francisco
GQ Magazine
Grable, Betty
Grace Metalious (Peyton Place)
Grace, Princess, Consort of Monaco
   (Grace Kelly)
Graces, or Charities (Gr. myth)
Gracie Fields
Graco™ baby stroller
Graf Zeppelin
Graf, Steffi
Graham Kerr, Galloping Gourmet
Graham Sutherland
Graham, Katherine
Graham, Martha

Graham, Rev. (William) 'Billy'
Grahame, Gloria
Grahame, Kenneth
Grail, or Holy Grail
Gram Parsons
Gram's method
Gram's stain
Gramercy Park hotel (NYC)
Gramercy Park (NYC)
Granada, Spain
Granby, Québec, Can.
Grand Army of the Republic
Grand Canal (China)
Grand Canyon (AZ)
Grand Coulee Dam (WA)
Grand Duchy
Grand Forks Air Force Base, ND
Grand Forks, ND
Grand Gourmet™ dog food
Grand Marnier™ liqueur
Grand Ole Opry
Grand Prix race
Grand Rapids Press
Grand Rapids, MI
Grand Teton Nat. Pk. (WY)
Grandma Moses (Anna Mary Moses)
Grandparents
Grange, Red (Harold)
Granger, Farley
Granger, Stewart
Granny Smith apple
Granolith™ concrete
Grant Tinker
Grant Wood
Grant, Cary
Grant, Ulysses Simpson, Pres.
Granville, Fr.
Grape-Nuts™ cereal
Grapes of Wrath, The
Graphic Arts Monthly
Grateful Dead (rock group)
Grauer, Ben
Gravella Roller
Gravenstein apple
Graves, Peter
Graves' disease
Gravy Train™ dog food
Gray, Dorian (picture of)

Gray, Linda
Grayson, Kathryn
Graz, Austria
Graziano, Rocky
Great Awakening, the
Great Barrier Reef
Great Basin desert
Great Britain, or United Kindgom of
   Great Britain & Northern Ireland
Great Compromiser (Sen. Henry Clay)
Great Dane (dog)
Great Depression, the
Great Dictator
Great Divide
Great Falls, MT
Great Gatsby, The
Great Gildersleeve, The
Great Lakes Naval Training
   Center, IL
Great Lakes, the
Great Mosque of Samarra
Great Plains region
Great Pyramid of Cheops
Great Pyramid of Khufu
Great Pyramids of Gîza, or Gîzeh
Great Pyrenees, dog
Great Salt Lake
Great Schism or Schism of the West
Great Slave Lake
Great Smoky Mts.
Great Sphinx
Great Starts™ breakfasts
Great Wall of China
Great Western Savings & Loan
Great White Way, or Broadway
Greater Antilles, W.I.
Greatest Show on Earth, The
Grecian Formula™ haircare
Grecian profile
Greco, El
Greco-Roman wrestling
Greece
Greek chorus
Greek Church, or Greek Orthodox
   Church
Greek fire
Greeley, Horace
Green Bay Packers

Green Bay, WI
Green Giant™ ('Jolly Green Giant')
Green Giant™ Niblets corn
Green Mountain Boys
Green River Ordinance
Greenaway, Kate
Greenback party
Greene, Joe
Greene, Lorne
Greene, Michele
Greene, Shecky
Greenland
Greenpeace organization
Greensboro News & Record
Greensboro, NC
Greenstreet, Sydney
Greenville News-Piedmont
Greenville, SC
Greenwich Mean Time
Greenwich meridian
Greenwich Observatory (Eng.)
Greenwich Village Theatre
Greenwich Village (NYC)
Greenwich, CT
Greenwich, London
Greer Garson
Greg Gumbel
Greg Le Mond
Greg Louganis
Gregg Allman
Gregor Johann Mendel
Gregorian calendar
Gregorian chant
Gregory Griggs
Gregory Peck
Gregory, Diana
Gregory, Dick
Gregory, Lady Augusta
Gregory, Lisa Lynn
Greiff, Monica de, Jus. Minister
Grenada, W.I.
Grenadines, W.I.
Grenoble, France
Grenville, George, P.M.
Grenville, Sir Richard
Gresham's law of economics
Gresham, Sir Thomas
Greta Garbo

Gretna Green ('any' town for eloping couples)
Gretna Green, Scot.
Gretzky, Wayne
Grey Poupon™ mustard
Grey, Lady Jane
Grey, Zane
Greyhound™ Bus
Greyhound Corp.
Greystoke, Lord
Grieg, Edvard
Grier, Rosey
Griffin, Merv
Griffiss Air Force Base, NY
Griffith Park (Hollywood)
Griffith, Andy
Griffith, D.W. (David Wark)
Griffith, Melanie
Griggs, Gregory
Grigori Aleksandrovich Potemkin, Prince
Grigori, Rasputin ('Rasputin')
Grim Reaper
Grimes, Tammy
Grimes, Tiny
Grimm, Brothers
Grimm's Fairy Tales
Grimm's law of language
Grimsby, Eng.
Gris, Juan
Grissom Air Force Base, IN
Griswold vs. Connecticut
Grodin, Charles
Gromyko, Andrei A., Pres.
Grooms, Red
Gross, Mary
Grosse Point, MI
Grossinger's resort (NY)
Grosvenor, Gerald
Grosvenor, Gilbert
Groucho Marx (Julius)
Groundhog Day
Group W Productions
Grove, Lefty
Grover Cleveland, Pres.
Grünewald, Mathias
Gruyère cheese
Gstaad, Switzerland

GTE™ phone
Guadalajara, Mex.
Guadalajara, Spain
Guadalcanal island
Guadalcanal Diary
Guadalupe Hidalgo, Treaty of
Guadalupe Victoria, Pres.
Guadeloupe (Fr. overseas dept.)
Guam
Guangdong, prov., Ch.
Guantánamo Bay
Guantánamo, Cuba
Guardian Angels
Guatemala (country)
Guatemala, Guatemala (city, country)
Guayaquil, Ecuador
Guaymas, Mexico
Gub Gub the pig
Gucci™
Guelph, Ont., Can.
Guerlain™
Guernica (Picasso)
Guernica, Spain
Guernsey cattle
Guernsey, Isle of
Guerrero, state, Mexico
Guess™ jeans
Guest, Cornelia
Guggenheim Art Museum
Guggenheim, Crazy (pseud. Frank Fontaine)
Guggenheim, Solomon R.
Guglielmo Marconi (telegraph)
Guiana, Dutch (now Suriname)
Guideposts
Guilaroff, Sidney
Guildenstern (Hamlet)
Guillain-Barré syndrome
Guillaume, Robert
Guinea (Africa)
Guinea-Bissau (Africa)
Guinevere, Queen (Arthurian)
Guinness Book of World Records
Guinness Extra Stout
Guinness, Sir Alec
Guisewite, Cathy
GULAG (USSR prison system)
Gulden's™ mustard

Gulf + Western Industries Inc.
Gulf of Aqaba
Gulf of Boothia
Gulf of Bothnia
Gulf of Thailand, or Siam
Gulf of Tonkin, or Tonkin Gulf
Gulf Oil Corp.
Gulf States, U.S.
Gulf Stream
Gulfport, MS
Gulliver's Travels
Gumbel Greg
Gumbel, Bryant
Gummi Bears, The
Gummi Bears™
Gummidge, Worzel
Gummo Marx (Milton)
Gumout™
Gump's store
Gunga Din
Gunk™ Puncture Seal
Gunn, Peter
Guofeng, Hua, Premier
Gunpowder Plot (Br.)
Guns N' Roses
Guns of August, The
Gunsmoke
Gunter's chain (surveyor's measure)
Gunther Gebel-Williams
Gurkha soldier
Gustav Charpentier
Gustav Holst
Gustav Klimit
Gustav Mahler
Gustave Courbet
Gustave Doré
Gustave Eiffel
Gustave Flaubert
Gutenberg Bible, or Mazarin Bible
Gutenberg Johann
Guthrie Theater (MN)
Guthrie, Arlo
Guthrie, Sir Tyrone
Guthrie, Woody
Guttenberg, Steve
Gutzon Borglum
Guy de Maupassant
Guy Fawkes Day

Guy Kibbee
Guy Lombardo
Guy, Jasmine
Guyana (was Br. Guiana)
Guzzini™ dinnerware
Gwen Verdon
Gwenn, Edmund
Gwyn, Nell, or Gwynn
Gynt, Peer
Gypsies, or gypsies, gipsies
Gypsy language
Gypsy Rose Lee

H (chem. sym. hydrogen)
H & R Block
H-Bomb
H. G. Wells
H. H. (pseud. Helen Hunt Jackson)
H. J. Heinz Co.
H. L. Mencken
H. R. Haldeman
H. T. Comstock (Henry Tomkins)
H.M.S. Bounty
H.M.S. Pinafore
Haacke, Hans
Häagen-Dazs™ ice cream
Haarlem, Netherlands
Haber process
Haber, Fritz
Hackensack, NJ
Hackett, Buddy
Hackman, Gene
Hackney Pony
Hadassah
Hades (Hell)
Hadrian, Emperor, or Adrian
Hadrian's Wall

Hafenites
Hagar the Horrible
Hagerstown, MD
Haggar™ slacks
Haggard, Merle
Hagia Sophia, or Santa Sophia
Hagler, Marvin
Hagman, Larry
Hague Conferences
Hague Tribunal
Hague, The, Holland
Hahn, Helena Petrovna, or Madame
   Helena Blavatsky
Hahn, Jessica
Hai Duong, Vietnam
Haid, Charles
Haida Indians
Haidar Ali, or Hyder Ali
Haifa, Israel, or Hefa
Haig, Alexander M., Jr., Gen.
Hail Mary (prayer)
Hail Mary (song)
Haile Selassie, Emperor
Hailey, Arthur
Haiphong, N. Vietnam
Haiti
Hal Holbrook
Hal Linden
Hal Roach
Hal Roach Studio (old Hollywood)
Hal B. Wallis
Haldeman, H.R.
Hale, Nathan
Haleakala Nat. Pk. (HI)
Halen, Van
Haley, Jack
Haley's M-O™
Half Moon Bay, CA
Half Price Books
Haliburton, Thomas (aka Sam Slick)
Halifax, Nova Scotia, Can.
Hall & Oates
Hall of Fame (NY)
Hall, Arsenio
Hall, Daryl
Hall, Fawn
Hall, Monty
Hall, Tom T.

Halley, Edmund
Halley's Comet
Halloween
Halls Mentho-Lyptus™
Halpern, Steven
Hals, Frans
Hälsa Hair™
Halston™
Hambletonian race
Hamburg, W. Ger.
Hamburger Helper™
Hamden, CT
Hamel, Veronica
Hamill, Dorothy
Hamilton, Alexander
Hamilton, Lady Emma
Hamilton, Ont., Can.
Hamilton, Scott
Hamites
Hamlet, Prince of Denmark
Hamlin, Hannibal, V.P.
Hamlin, Harry
Hamm's™ beer
Hammacher Schlemmer
Hammarskjöld, Dag, Secy. Gen. UN
Hammer and Sickle Gold Medal
Hammer, Armand
Hammer, Mike
Hammerstein, Oscar
Hammett, Dashiell
Hammond, IN
Hammurabi, king of Babylon
Hampshire County, Eng.
Hampton Court Conference
Hampton Court Palace
Hampton Institute (VA)
Hampton Roads Channel (VA)
Han dynasty
Han Soio
Hancock, Herbie
Hancock, John, Gov.
Hand, Learned, Judge
Handel, George Frideric
Handy, W.C.
Hanes Her Way™
Hanes™ pantyhose/underwear
Hanging Gardens of Babylon
Hangouts™ hammocks

Hangzhou, China (was Hangchow)
Hanimex™ movie equip.
Hank Snow
Hank Williams, Jr.
Hanks, Tom
Hanna-Barbera Productions
Hannah, Daryl
Hanni Wenzel
Hannibal (crossed Alps)
Hannibal Hamlin, V.P.
Hannover, W. Ger.
Hanoi, N. Vietnam
Hanover, House of (ruling family)
Hans Christian Andersen
Hans Albrecht Bethe
Hans Conried
Hans Haacke
Hans Holbein, the Elder
Hans Holbein, the Younger
Hans Krebs, Sir
Hans Oersted
Hans Sachs
Hans Zinsser
Hanscom Air Force Base, MA
Hansel and Gretel
Hansen's disease (leprosy)
Hansom, J.A. (hansom cab)
Hanukkah, or Chanukah
Happy Face
Hapsburg family, or Habsburg
Harcourt Brace Jovanovich Inc.
Hardee's™
Harding, Warren G., Pres.
Hardishake™ shingles
Hardwicke, Sir Cedric
Hardy Boys (Joe & Frank)
Hardy, Oliver
Hardy, Thomas
Hare Krishna
Hari, Mata
Harlan Ellison
Harlan Fiske Stone, Justice
Harlem Globetrotters
Harlem Renaissance
Harlem River
Harlem (NYC)
Harlequin (traditional buffoon)
Harley-Davidson™ motorcycle

Harlow Shapley
Harlow, Jean
Harman/Kardon™ stereo
Harmonicats, The
Harold Arlen
Harold 'Red' Grange
Harold Lloyd
Harold Macmillan, P.M.
Harold Pinter
Harold Ramis
Harold 'Pee Wee' Reese
Harold Robbins
Harold Wilson, Sir (P.M.)
Harper & Row, Pub. Inc.
Harper's
Harper's Bazaar
Harpers Ferry (VA)
Harpo Marx (Arthur)
Harriet Beecher Stowe
Harriet Tubman
Harriman, W. Averell
Harrington, Pat
Harris Poll
Harris tweed
Harris, Ed
Harris, Emmylou
Harris, Julie
Harris, Phil
Harrisburg Patriot-News
Harrisburg, PA
Harrison, Benjamin, Pres.
Harrison, George
Harrison, Rex
Harrison, Wm. Henry, Pres.
Harrods store (Lon.)
Harrowborough, Lon.
Harrowsmith
Harry Babbitt
Harry Belafonte
Harry A. Blackmun, Justice
Harry Bridges
Harry Caray
Harry Diamond Laboratories, MD
Harry Hamlin
Harry Hershfield
Harry Houdini
Harry M. Popkin
Harry Reasoner

Harry Stack Sullivan
Harry S. Truman, Pres.
Harry VonZell
Harry Winston (diamonds)
Harry, Deborah
Hart, Moss
Hart, William S.
Harte, Bret, or Brett
Hartford Courant
Hartford Wits
Hartford, CT
Hartman, David
Harunobu (Suzuki Harunobu)
Harvard Business Review
Harvard Magazine
Harvard University
Harvard University Library
Harvey Firestone
Harvey Korman
Harvey Milk
Harvey, Laurence
Harvey, Paul
Harveys Bristol Cream
Harwood, Vanessa
Hasbro™ toys
Hashemi Rafsanjani, Pres.
Hashemite Kingdom of Jordan
Hasidim (Jewish sect)
Haskapi Indian
Hassan II, King
Hasselblad™ camera
Hasselhoff, David
Hasso, Signe
Hastings, battle of
Hastings, Eng.
Hatfields & McCoys
Hatha yoga
Hathaway, Anne
Hatshepsut, Queen
Hatteras, Cape (NC)
Hauer, Rutger
Hava Nagilah (Israeli dance)
Havana brown cat
Havana, Cuba
Havilland, Olivia De
Havoc, June
Hawaii (HI)
Hawaii Blend™ tan lotion

Hawaiian Airlines™
Hawaiian Punch™
Hawaiian guitar
Hawke, Bob, P.M.
Hawkeye State (Iowa)
Hawking, Stephen
Hawkins, Coleman
Hawkshaw Hawkins
Hawley-Smoot Tariff Act
Hawn, Goldie
Hawthorne, Nathaniel
Hayakawa, S. I. (Samuel Ichiye)
Hayden Planetarium
Hayden, Sterling
Haydn, Franz Joseph
Hayes, Helen
Hayes, Peter Lind
Hayes, Rutherford B., Pres.
Hayley Mills
Haymarket Square riot (1886)
Haymes, Dick
Hayward, CA
Hayward, Susan
Hayworth, Rita
He (chem. sym. helium)
Head & Shoulders™ shampoo
Head™ sports equip.
Head Start program
Head, Edith
Headroom, Max
HeadStart™ computer
Health-tex™ clothes
Heard, John
Hearns, Thomas
Hearst, Patricia 'Patty'
Hearst, William Randolph
Hearst castle (San Simeon)
Hearty Chews™ dog treat
Heath, Edward, P.M.
Heathcliff
Heather Locklear
Heatherton, Joey
Heathrow Airport, Lon.
Heatilator™ wood stove
Heaven
Hebrew
Hebrew calendar
Hebrew language

Hebrew National™ meats
Hebrew-Aramaic
Hebrides, Inner
Hebrides, Outer
Hecate
Hecht, Ben
Hector Berlioz, or Louis-Hector
Hecuba, Queen of Troy
Hedda Gabler
Hedda Hopper
Hedren, Tippi
Hedy Lamarr
Hee, Park Chung, Pres.
Heep, Uriah
Heet™
Heffner, Hugh
Heffner, Kimberley (Mrs. Hugh)
Heflin, Van
Hefty™ Cinch Sak
Hegel, Georg Wilhelm Friedrich
Heian period
Heidelberg man
Heidelberg, W. Ger.
Heidi
Heidt, Horace
Heifetz, Jascha
Heigh-Ho
Heike Drechsler
Heimlich maneuver
Heineken™ beer
Heineken Group, The
Heinlein, Robert
Heinrich Böll
Heinrich Hertz
Heinrich Himmler
Heinrich Lenz
Heinrich Schliemann
Heinz™ catsup
Heinz™ Pork 'N' Beans
Heisenberg uncertainty principle
Heisenberg, Werner
Heisman trophy
Held, Anna
Helen Gurley Brown
Helen Caldecott, Dr.
Helen Frankenthaler
Helen Hayes
Helen Hunt Jackson (aka H.H.)

Helen Keller
Helen MacInnes
Helen Wills Moody
Helen Reddy
Helen Traubel
Helen of Troy
Helena Blavatsky, Madame, or Elena
    Petrovna Hahn Blavatsky
Helena Modjeska
Helena Rubinstein™ cosmetics
Helena, MT
Helene Curtis™ cosmetics
Heliopolis (ancient Eg. city)
Helios (Gr. myth)
Helios space probe
Hellenism
Hellenist
Hellenistic civilization
Heller, Joseph
Hellespont, the (ancient)
Hellinger, Mark
Hellman, Lillian
Hellmann's mayonnaise
Helms, Jesse, Sen.
Helms, Richard (CIA)
Helmsley, Leona
Helmut Dantine
Helmut Kohl, Chanc.
Helmut Schmidt, Chanc.
Helsinki, Finland
Hemingway, Ernest
Hemingway, Margaux
Hemingway, Muriel
Hemion, Dwight
Hemsley, Sherman
Hendrick Terbrugghen
Hendricks, Thomas A., V.P.
Hendrix, Jimi
Henie, Sonja
Henner, Marilu
Hennessy™ cognac
Henredon™ furniture
Henri Bendel store
Henri Bergson
Henri de Toulouse-Lautrec
Henri Fantin-Latour
Henri Matisse
Henri Rousseau

Henrik Ibsen
Henry 'Hank' Aaron
Henry Aldrich
Henry Bessemer, Sir
Henry Bolingbroke (K. Henry IV)
Henry Bolingbroke, Lord (statesman)
Henry Clay, Sen. ('Great
    Compromiser')
Henry Deringer (derringer pistol)
Henry Fielding
Henry Fonda
Henry Ford
Henry the Fowler
Henry Hudson
Henry Huntington Library, CA
Henry J. Kaiser
Henry A. Kissinger, Dr./Secy. State
Henry Kravis
Henry the Lion
Henry Cabot Lodge, Sen.
Henry Cabot Lodge, Jr., Sen.
Henry Wadsworth Longfellow
Henry Robinson Luce
Henry Mancini
Henry Miller
Henry Moore
Henry Morgan, Sir
Henry Morgenthau, Jr., Secy. Treas.
Henry the Navigator
Henry Purcell
Henry Wheeler Shaw (aka Josh
    Billings)
Henry M. Stanley, Sir
Henry Steinway
Henry Lewis Stimson, Secy. War
Henry David Thoreau
Henry Vauxhall, Prince
Henry A. Wallace, V.P.
Henry Ward Beecher
Henry Wilson, V.P.
Henry Winkler
Henry Wriothesley, Earl of
    Southhampton
Henry, Joseph
Henry, O. (pseud. Wm. Sydney Porter)
Henry, Patrick
Henson, Jim (Muppets creator)
Hepburn, Audrey

Hepburn, Katharine
Hephaestus (Gr. myth)
Heppenheimer, Thomas A
Hepplewhite style
Hepplewhite, George
Hera
Heraclitus (Gr. philosopher)
Heralds' College (heraldry)
Herb Alpert & The Tijuana Brass
Herb Shriner
Herb-Ox™ bullion cubes
Herbalife™
Herbert Blaize, P.M.
Herbert C. Hoover, Pres.
Herbert Tree, Sir
Herbert von Karajan
Herbert, Victor
Herbie Hancock
Herbie Mann
Hercule Poirot
Hercules, also Heracles, or Herakles
Hereford cattle
Hereford Co., Eng.
Heritage USA theme park (PTL)
Herlihy, Ed
Herman Melville
Herman Tarnower, Dr.
Herman Wouk
Herman, Pee-Wee
Hermann Hesse
Hermann Wilhelm Goering, or
    Göring
Hermes (messenger of the Gods)
Hermès™ designer wear
Hermione Gingold
Hermitage museum (USSR)
Hermitage wine
Hernando De Soto
Hernán Cortés, or Hernando
Herod Agrippa
Herod the Great
Herodotus (Gr. historian)
Herr Drosselmeyer
Herriot, James
Herschel Bernardi
Hershey Bar™
Hershey, Milton
Hershey, PA

Hershfield, Harry
Hershiser, Orel
Hertz™ Rent A Car
Hertz, Heinrich
Herve Villechaize
Herzog
Herzog, Werner
Heshvan (Jewish mo.)
Hesiod (Gr. poet)
Hess, Rudolf
Hess's Department Stores
Hesse, Hermann
Hesseman, Howard
Hessian boots
Hessian troups
Hestia (Gr. myth)
Heston, Charlton
Heusen, James 'Jimmy', Van
Hewlett-Packard™
Heyerdahl, Thor (Kon Tiki)
Hezbollah militia (Party of God)
Hf (chem. sym. hafnium)
Hg (chem. sym. mercury)
Hi & Lois
Hi Ho™ Crackers
Hi-C™ drink
Hi-Dri™ Paper Towels
Hialeah Park Race Track
Hiawatha
Hiawatha Nat. Forest
Hickam Air Force Base, HI
Hickok, Wild Bill (James)
Hickory Farms™
Hidatsa Indians
Hidalgo, state, Mexico
Hide-A-Bed™
Hideki, Tojo, Prem.
Hieronymous Bosch
Higbee Company
Higgins, William R., Lt. Col.
Higgledy-Piggledy
High Church
High German
High Renaissance
High Technology
High Times
Highlands region, Scot.
Highlights for Children

Hildegarde (entertainer)
Hildegarde Neff
Hill House chair
Hill Street Blues
Hillary™ tents
Hillary, Sir Edmund P.
Hillel (Jewish scholar)
Hills Bros™
Hillshire Farm™
Hilo, HI
Hilton Hotels
Himalayas, or Himalaya Mts.
Himmler, Heinrich
Hinckley, John, Jr.
Hindemith, Paul
*Hindenburg disas*ter
Hindenburg, Poland, or Zabrze
Hindu (native)
Hindu Kush Mts.
Hinduism (philosophy)
Hindustan region, India
Hindustani (native/language)
Hines, Earl 'Fatha'
Hinton, S. E.
Hippocrates
Hippocratic oath
Hippolyta (Queen of Amazons)
Hippolyte Taine
Hippolytus (Gr. myth)
Hirohito, Emperor
Hiroshima, Jap.
Hirsch, Judd
Hirshhorn Museum & Sculpture
    Garden (DC)
Hirshhorn, Joseph
Hispanic Americans
Hispanic USA
Hispaniola, W.I.
Hiss, Alger
Histoire d'Amour™ perfume
Hitachi Ltd.
Hitachi™ TV/stereo
Hitchcock, Alfred
Hitler, Adolf
Hittite (language)
Hittites (people)
Ho (chem. sym. holmium)
Ho, Don

Ho Chi Minh City, Vietnam (formerly Saigon)
Ho Chi Minh Trail
Ho Chi Minh, Pres.
Hoagy Carmichael, or Hogie
Hobart, Garret A., V.P.
Hobbes, Thomas
Hobbit, The
Hockney, David
Hodgkin's disease
Hodiak, John
Hoffa, James R.
Hoffa, Portland
Hoffman, Abbie
Hoffman, Dustin
Hogan, Ben
Hogan, Hulk
Hogan's Heroes
Hogarth, William
Hogg, James
Hoity Toity
Hokey-Pokey
Hokkaido, Jap.
Hokusai (b. Katsushika Hokusai)
Holbein, Hans, the Elder
Holbein, Hans, the Younger
Holbrook, Hal
Holiday, Billie
Holland
Holle, Mother
Holliday, Doc
Holliday, Judy
Holloman Air Force Base, NM
Holly Harp™
Holly Hunter
Holly, Buddy
Hollywood bed
Hollywood Park racetrack
Hollywood Reporter, The
Hollywood Squares
Hollywood Wives (novel)
Hollywood wives (movie biz wives)
Hollywood, CA, FL
Holm, Celeste
Holmby Hills, CA
Holmes, Larry
Holmes, Oliver Wendell (author/ physician)

Holmes, Oliver Wendell, Jr., Justice
Holmes, Sherlock
Holocaust, the
Holocene epoch
Holst, Gustav
Holstein area, W. Ger.
Holstein cattle
Holy Alliance
Holy Bible
Holy Communion
Holy Cross, Mount of the
Holy Father (Pope's title)
Holy Ghost
Holy Grail
Holy One
Holy Roller
Holy Roman Empire
Holy Saturday
Holy Scripture
Holy Sepulcher
Holy Spirit, or *Spiritus sanctus*
Holy Week
Holy Writ
Holyoke, MA
Home Box Office, or HBO
Home Business
Home Magazine
Home Mechanix
Home Rule (Br.)
Home Savings & Loan
Homeir, Skippy
Homelite™ saw
Homemakers Magazine
Homer (*Illiad & Odyssey*)
Homer & Jethro (Henry Haynes & Kenneth Burns)
Homer, Winslow
Homeric Hymns
Homestead Act
Homestead Air Force Base, FL
Homestead, FL
Homo erectus
Homo sapiens
Honda™ cars/motorcyles
Honda™ Accord
Honda™ Acura
Honduras
Honegger, Arthur

Honey Hill Farms™ frozen yogurt
Honey Maid™ crackers
Honeycomb™ cereal
Honeywell Inc.
Hong Kong, British
Honolulu Star-Bulletin
Honolulu, HI
Honoré Daumier
Honoré de Balzac
Honoré Gabriel Mirabeau
Honshu Is., Jap.
Hooke, Robert
Hooke's law of elasticity
Hooker, Joseph, Gen.
Hooker, T. J.
Hoosier (Indiana resident)
Hoot Gibson
Hoover Dam (now Boulder Dam)
Hoover, Herbert C., Pres.
Hoover, J. Edgar (of FBI)
Hopalong Cassidy
Hope Lange
Hope, Bob
Hopi Indians
Hopkins, Anthony
Hopper, De Wolf
Hopper, Dennis
Hopper, Edward
Hopper, Hedda
Horace Greeley
Horace Heidt
Horace Mann
Horace Walpole
Horatio Alger
Horatio Heavyside Dragon
Horatio Gates, Gen.
Horatio Nelson, Adm.
Horchow™ catalog
Hormel™ meats
Hormuz, Strait of, or Ormuz
Horn, Cape
Horne, Lena
Horne, Marilyn
Hornie (the Devil)
Hornsby, Rogers
Horowitz, David
Horowitz, Vladimir
Horse Guard (Br.)

Horseback Knob (hill), OH
Horsley, Lee
Horticulture
Horton, Edward Everett
Horus (a god)
Hoskins, Bob
Hosni Mubarak, Pres.
Hostess™ Cupcakes
Hostess™ Ding Dongs
Hostess™ Ho Ho's
Hostess™ Sno Balls
Hostess™ Suzy Q's
Hostess™ Twinkies
Hot Lips Page
Hot Wheels™ toys
Hotchner, A. E.
Hottentot
Houdin, Jean (Fr. magician)
Houdini, Harry (US magician)
Houghton Mifflin Co.
House & Garden
House Beautiful
House of Burgesses
House of Commons
House of Lords
House of Parliament
House of Representatives
House of Usher
house of Tudor
Houseman, John
Housing and Urban Development
    (HUD)
Housman, A. E.
Houston Astros
Houston Chronicle
Houston Coast Guard Air Station, TX
Houston Oilers
Houston Post
Houston, Samuel, Gen.
Houston, TX
Houston, Whitney
Hovercraft™
Howard Carter
Howard Cosell
Howard Duff
Howard Hesseman
Howard Hughes
Howard Johnson Hotel/restaurant

Howard K. Smith
Howard University (DC)
Howard, Curly (1 of 3 Stooges)
Howard, Moe (1 of 3 Stooges)
Howard, Ron
Howdy Doody
Howdy Doody Show, The
Howe, Elias
Howe, Gordie
Howe, Julia Ward
Howie Mandell
Hsia dynasty
Hubba Bubba™ gum
Hua Guofeng, Premier
Hubbard, L. Ron
Hubbard, Mother
Hubble Space Telescope
Hubble, Edwin Powell
Hubble's law of expanding universe
Hubert de Givenchy
Hubert Horatio Humphrey, V.P.
Hubert van Eyck
Huckleberry Finn
Huckleberry Hound
Huddie 'Leadbelly' Ledbetter
Hudson Bay, Can.
Hudson Bay blanket
Hudson River, NY
Hudson River school
Hudson, Henry
Hudson, Rock
Hudson's Bay Co.
Huey Lewis And The News
Huey P. Long, Gov.
Huey P. Newton
Huggies™ diapers
Hugh Downs
Hugh Heffner
Hughes Aircraft Co.
Hughes Markets
Hughes, Howard
Hughes, John
Hugo Black, Justice
Hugo De Vries, or de Vries
Hugo Wolf
Hugo, Victor, Vicomte
Huguenots
Hula Hoop™, or Hula-Hoop

Hulce, Tom
Hulk Hogan
Hull House (Chicago)
Hull, Bobby
Hull, Cordell, Adm./Secy. State
Hull, Josephine
Hull, Québec, Can.
Humboldt Bay Coast Guard Air
    Station, CA
Humboldt Current, also Peru Current
Hume Cronyn
Hume, David
Hummel figurines
Humperdinck, Engelbert (Ger.
    composer)
Humperdinck, Engelbert (pop. singer)
Humphrey Bogart
Humphrey, Hubert Horatio, V.P.
Humpty Dumpty
Hunan province, China
Hunchback of Notre Dame, The
Hund, Friedrich
Hund's rule
Hundred Days (Napoleon I)
Hundred Years War (1337-1453)
Hungary
Hungnam, N. Korea
Hungry Jack™ pancake mix/biscuits
Hunkers vs. Barnburners
Huns, the
Hunt, Linda
Hunt's™ foods
Hunt's™ Manwich sloppy Joe mix
Hunter Army Airfield, GA
Hunter, Catfish
Hunter, Holly
Huntington, WV
Huntington Beach, CA
Huntington Library (L.A.)
Huntington Park, CA
Huntington, Collis Potter
Huntington, Henry (Library)
Huntington's chorea
Huntley, Chet
Huntsville, AL
Huron Indians
Huron, Lake
Huron-Manistee Nat. Forest

Hurt, William
Hush Puppies™ shoes
Husky Oil Ltd.
Husky, Ferlin
Hussein I, king of Jordan
Hussein, Saddam, Pres.
Hussey, Olivia
Hussey, Ruth
Hustler
Huston, Anjelica
Huston, John
Huston, Walter
Hutton, Timothy
Hutzler's Department Stores
Huxley, Aldous
Huygens, Christian
Hy Averback
Hyannis Port, MA, also Hyannisport
   (Kennedy Compound)
Hyatt Hotel
Hyatt Legal Services
Hyde Park (Lon.)
Hyde Park (NY)
Hydra (Sea Serpent) constellation
Hydrox™ cookies
Hydrus (Water Snake) constellation
Hyland, Diana
Hyman George Rickover, Adm.
Hyponex™ potting soil
Hyundai™ car

I (chem. sym. iodine)
I Can't Believe It's Not Butter™
I Ching (Book of Changes)
I. M. Pei
I. Magnin store
Iacocca, Lee

Iago (*Othello*)
Iams™ dog food
Ian Fleming
Iberia Airlines of Spain
Iberian Peninsula
Ibizan Hound, or hound
Iblis (the Devil)
IBM (International Business Machines
   Corp.)
Ibsen, Henrik
Ibuprin™ (not Ibuprofen)
Icarus
Iceland
Icelandair Airlines
Icelandic Pony
Icy™ vodka
Ida Lupino
Ida Minerva Tarbell
Idaho (ID)
Idaho Falls, ID
Idaho™ potato
Ideas for Better Living
Idi Dada Oumee Amin, Pres.
Iditarod Trail Sled Dog Race
Idol, Billy
Iglesias, Julio
Igloo™ cooler
Ignace Henri Fantin-Latour
Ignace Jan Paderewski
Ignat Solzhenitsyn
Igor Kipnis
Igor Stravinsky
Ikhnaton, or Akhenaton
Il Sorrento restaurant
Il Trovatore
Ildebrando Pizzetti
Ile-de-France, Fr.
Iliad (Homer's)
Ilka Chase
Illinois (IL)
Illinois Indians
Imelda Marcos
Imhotep
Immanuel Kant
Imodium A-D™
Imogene Coca
Imperial conference
Imperial™ Margarine

Imperial Valley, CA
Importance of Being Ernest, The
Impressionism art
Impulse™ body spray
In Business
In-N-Out Burger™ fast food
In-Sink-Erator™
Inc. magazine
Inca empire
Inchon, S. Korea
InCider magazine
Income Opportunities
Independence Day
Indcpendence Hall
Independence, American War of
Independence, Declaration of
Independence, MO
Index Expurgatorius (Catholic)
Index Liborum Prohibitorum (Cath.)
India
India paper
India-Pakistan Wars
India-rubber tree
Indian Affairs, Bureau of
Indian Mutiny, also Sepoy Rebellion
Indian Ocean
Indian Territory
Indiana (IN)
Indiana Jones
Indianapolis 500
Indianapolis News
Indianapolis Star
Indianapolis, IN
Indians, American
Indira Gandhi, P.M.
Individual Retirement Account (IRA)
Indo-Chinese
Indochina
Indonesia
Industrial Revolution
Industrial World
Industry Week
Industry, the (Hollywood movie biz)
Infinite, the
Infiniti™ (Nissan's)
Information Week
Infoworld
Inge, William

Ingels, Marty
Ingemar Johansson
Inglenook™ wine
Ingmar Bergman
Ingres, Jean Auguste
Ingrid Bergman
Ink Spots, The
Inner Hebrides
Innsbruck, Austria
Inouye, Daniel, Sen.
Instamatic™ camera
Intel™ computer
Intercoastal Waterway (SE U.S.)
Interior, U.S. Dept. of
Interlaken, Switz.
Internal Revenue Service (IRS)
International Business Monthly
International Flat Earth Society
International Harvester Co.
International Jewish Monthly
International Paper Co.
International Style
Interplak™ dental care
Interpol
Interview
Inverness, Scot.
INXS (rock group)
Io (Jupiter moon)
Io (Gr. myth)
Iolani Palace (HI)
Iolanthe
Ionesco, Eugene
Ionian Islands
Ionian Sea
Ionic order
Iowa (IA)
Iowa City, IA
Ipswich, Eng.
Ir (chem. sym. iridium)
Ira Frederick Aldridge
Ira Gershwin
Iran (was Persia)
Iran-Contra scandle
Iraq
Ireland, Jill
Ireland, Northern
Ireland, or Eire
Irene Castle

Irene Dunne
Irish coffee
Irish Gaelic
Irish Republican Army
Irish setter (dog)
Irish wolfhound (dog)
Irishman
Irma La Douce
Iron Age
Iron Chancellor (Prince Otto von
    Bismarck)
Iron Cross, the
Iron Maiden (rock group)
Iron, Ralph (pseud. Olive Schreiner)
Irons, Jeremy
Ironwood Trading Co.™
Iroquois Confederacy, or League
Iroquois Indians
Irrawaddy River
Irvine, CA
Irving Berlin
Irving 'Swifty' Lazar
Irving R. Levine
Irving Thalberg
Irving, John
Irving, Washington
Isaac Asimov
Isaac Asimov's Science Fiction
Isaac Newton, Sir
Isaac Pitman, Sir
Isaac B. Singer (author)
Isaac M. Singer (inventor)
Isaac Stern
Isaacs, Susan
Isaak Babel
Isabel Sanford
Isabella, Queen of Spain
Isabella Rossellini
Isadora Duncan
Isamu Noguchi
Iscariot, Judas
Isenheim Altarpiece (Grünewald)
Ish Kabibble
Isherwood, Christopher
Ishtar (fertility deity)
Ishtar (movie)
Isis
Islam

Islamabad, Pakistan
Islamic Republic of Mauritania
Isle of Guernsey
Isle of Man, U.K.
Isle of Wight, Eng.
Isley Brothers, The
Isolde, Tristran and, or Tristram
Isotoner™ gloves/slippers
Israel (country)
Israel, Tribes of
Israeli (residents of Israel)
Israelite (a Hebrew)
Istanbul, Turkey
Isuzu™ car
Isuzu™ I-Mark
Isuzu Motors Ltd.
Isuzu, Joe
Italian greyhound
Italy
Ithaca, MI, NY
Itsy Bitsy Spider
ITT (International Telephone and
    Telegraph Corp.)
Iturbi, Jose
Itzhak Perlman
Ivan Albright
Ivan F. Boesky
Ivan Ditmars
Ivan Lendl
Ivan Nagy
Ivan Pavlov
Ivan Tors
Ivana Trump
Ives, Burl
Ives, Currier and
Ives, James (of Currier & Ives)
Ivory Coast
Ivory Liquid™
Ivry-sur-Seine, Fr.
Ivy League
Iwo Jima
Ixtapa, Mex.
Iyar (Jewish mo.)
IZE™ software
Izmir, Turkey

J. A. Hansom (hansom cab)
J. B. Priestley
J. C. Penney
J. Crew (sportswear)
J. Carrol Naish
J. D. Salinger
J. Danforth Quayle, III, V.P.
J. Edgar Hoover (of FBI)
J. G. Ballard
J. J. Tissot
J. Joseph Thomson, Sir
J. P. Morgan & Co.
J. Paul Getty
J. Pierpont Morgan
J. R. Ewing
J. R. R. Tolkien
J. S. Bach (Johann Sebastian)
J. Thomas Talbot
J. Walter Thompson advertising
J. William Fulbright, Sen.
J. Z. Knight (& Ramtha)
Jack Benny (b. Benjamin Kubelsky)
Jack Daniels™ whiskey
Jack Dempsey
Jack Elam
Jack Haley
Jack-in-the-Box™ fast foods
Jack Klugman
Jack LaLanne
Jack Lemmon
Jack Lescoulie
Jack London
Jack Nicholson
Jack Nicklaus
Jack Oakie
Jack Paar

Jack Palance
Jack Pumpkinhead of Oz
Jack the Ripper
Jack Sharkey
Jack Teagarden
Jack Valenti
Jack L. Warner
Jack Webb
Jack Wrather
Jackie Collins
Jackie Coogan
Jackie Gleason
Jackie Joyner-Kersee
Jackie Mason
Jackie (John) Robinson
Jackson Browne
Jackson 5, The
Jackson Pollock
Jackson, Andrew, Pres.
Jackson, Bo
Jackson, Helen Hunt (aka H.H.)
Jackson, Keith
Jackson, Mahalia
Jackson, MS
Jackson, Reggie
Jackson, Stonewall (pop singer)
Jackson, Stonewall, Gen.
Jacksonville, FL
Jaclyn Smith
Jacob Marley, the ghost of
Jacobean style
Jacobites
Jacopo Bellini
Jacopo Robusti (aka Tintoretto)
Jacqueline Bisset
Jacqueline Bouvier Kennedy Onasis
Jacques Ange Gabriel
Jacques Callot
Jacques Charles
Jacques Cousteau
Jacques Lipchitz
Jacques Necker
Jacques Offenbach
Jacques Villon
Jacques-Louis David
Jacuzzi
Jaffe, Sam
Jagger, Dean

Jagger, Michael 'Mick'
Jaime Paz Zamora, Pres.
Jakarta, Indonesia, or Djakarta
Jake La Motta
Jakes, John
Jakob Bernoulli, or Jacques, or James
Jalisco, state, Mexico
Jamaica
Jamal, Ahmad
James Agee
James Arness
James A. Baker, III, Secy. State
James Baldwin
James Barrie
James M. Barrie, Sir
James Belushi
James 'Biggles' Bigglesworth
James Gillespie Birney
James G. Blaine, Secy. State
James Bond
James Boswell
James Bowie, Colonel
James Breasted
James Brudenell, Earl of Cardigan
   (cardigan sweater)
James Buchanan, Pres.
James Caan
James Cagney
James M. Cain
James 'Jimmy' Earl Carter, Pres.
James Coco
James Cook, Capt.
James Fenimore Cooper
James Dewar, Sir
James R. Doohan (*Star Trek*)
James Ellroy
James Ensor, Baron
James Forrestal, Secy. Def./Navy
James Galanos
James Galway
James A. Garfield, Pres.
James Garner
James Herriot
James R. Hoffa
James Hogg
James Ives (of Currier & Ives)
James Earl Jones (actor)
James Joule

James T. Kirk, Capt.
James Knox Polk, Pres.
James Longstreet, Gen.
James A. Lovell, Jr., Astronaut
James Madison, Pres.
James Mason
James McNeill Whistler
James A. Michener
James Monroe, Pres.
James E. Oglethorpe, Gen.
James Kirke Paulding
James A. Pike, Bishop
James Earl Ray (killed M. L. King)
James Russell Lowell
James S. Sherman, V.P.
James Johnson Shotwell
James Sikking
James Spader
James Steerforth
James Stewart
James Thurber
James 'Jimmy' Van Heusen
James Dewey Watson
James G. Watt, Interior Secy.
James Whitcomb Riley
James Whitmore
James, Frank
James, Jesse
Jamie Lee Curtis
Jamie Farr
Jamieson, Bob
Jan Bruegel, also Brueghel, or
   Breughel (aka 'Velvet Bruegel')
Jan Peerce
Jan Steen
Jan Swammerdam
Jan van Eyck
Jan Vermeer, or Johannes
Jane Addams
Jane Austen
Jane Curtin
Jane Eyre
Jane Fonda
Jane Froman
Jane Goodall
Jane Grey, Lady
Jane Pauley
Jane Russell

Jane Seymour (actress)
Jane Seymour, Queen Consort
Jane Wyatt
Jane Wyman
Jane, Calamity (Martha Jane Burke)
Janet Dailey
Janet Gaynor
Janet Leigh
Janet Suzman
Janet Waldo
Janis Joplin
Janis Paige
Janssen, David
Japan
Japan, Sea of
Japanese
Jarreau, Al
Jarriel, Tom
Jascha Heifetz
Jasmine Guy
Jason (Gr. myth)
Jason Robards
Jasper Johns
Java, Indonesia
Java Man
Jawaharlal Nehru, P.M.
Jaworski, Leon
Jaws of Life™
Jay C. Flippen
Jay Gatsby
Jay Gould
Jay Leno
Jay McInerney
Jay Sandrich
Jay Silverheels (played Tonto)
Jay, John, Ch. Justice
Jay's Treaty
Jayne Mansfield
Jayne Meadows
Jean Arp, or Hans
Jean M. Auel
Jean François Champollion
Jean Cocteau
Jean Baptiste Camille Corot
Jean Dubuffet
Jean Giraudoux
Jean Harlow
Jean Hersholt

Jean Houdin
Jean Auguste Ingres
Jean Kerr
Jean Laffite, or Lafitte
Jean Paul Marat
Jean François Millet
Jean Baptiste Molière
Jean Naté™ (toiletries)
Jean Picard (astronomer)
Jean Felix Piccard
Jean Baptiste Racine
Jean Jacques Rousseau
Jean Seberg
Jean Sibelius
Jean Stapleton
Jean Valjean
Jean Antoine Watteau
Jean-Baptiste-Siméon Chardin
Jean-Claude 'Doc' Duvalier
Jean-Claude Killy
Jean-Claude Van Damme
Jean-Honoré Fragonard
Jean-Luc Picard, Capt.
Jean-Paul Sartre
Jean-Philippe Rameau
Jean-Pierre Rampal
Jeane Kirkpatrick (U.S. Rep. UN)
Jeanette MacDonald
Jeanette Rankin
Jeanne Bécu Du Barry, Madame
Jeanne Crain
Jeanne Moreau
Jeanne Antoinette Pompadour, Mdm.
Jeanneret, Charles (aka Le Corbusier)
Jeannie C. Riley
Jeb Stuart Magruder
Jed Clampett
Jeeves, the butler
Jeff Goldblum
Jefferson, Thomas, Pres.
Jeffrey Amherst, General/Baron
Jeffrey Lyons
Jeffreys, Anne
Jehoshaphat, king of Judah
Jehovah's Witnesses
Jell-O™
Jell-O™ Pudding Pops
Jelly Belly™ beans

Jelly Roll Morton
Jellybean Benitez
Jemima Puddleduck
Jenkin's Ear, War of
Jenkins, Snuffy
Jenner, Edward
Jennifer Jason Leigh
Jennifer O'Neill
Jennings, Peter
Jenny Flinders
Jenny Lind
Jeno's™ pizza
Jeopardy!
Jeremy Bentham
Jeremy Irons
Jergens™ Skin Lotion
Jericho
Jerome Kern
Jerome Robbins
Jerry Brown, Gov. (Edmund Brown, Jr.)
Jerry Falwell, Rev.
Jerry Lee Lewis
Jerry Van Dyke
Jerry Wald
Jersey City, NJ
Jersey Joe Walcott
Jerusalem, Israel
Jerusalem artichoke
Jerzy Kozinski
Jesse Applegate
Jesse James
Jesse Owens
Jessel, George
Jessica Hahn
Jessica Lange
Jessica McClure
Jessica Savitch
Jesuit
Jesus, or Jesus Christ
Jesus freak
Jethro Clampett
Jethro Tull
Jewison, Norman
Jezebel
Jiang Zemin
Jif™ peanut butter
Jill Eikenberry
Jill Ireland

Jill St. John
Jill Trenary
Jillian, Ann
Jillie Mack
Jim Backus
Jim Bakker
Jim Crow (character)
Jim Fixx
Jim Henson (& Muppets)
Jim Kelly
Jim McKay
Jim Nabors
Jim Reeves
Jim Stafford
Jim Thorpe
Jimi Hendrix
Jimmy Breslin
Jimmy Buffett
Jimmy (James) Earl Carter, Pres.
Jimmy Connors
Jimmy Dean™ Sausage
Jimmy Durante
Jimmy Smits
Jimmy "The Greek" Snyder
   (Dimetrios Synodinos)
Jimmy Swaggart, Rev.
Jinx Falkenburg
Jo Baer
Jo Stafford
Jo Anne Worley
Joachim Murat, king of Naples
Joan Aiken
Joan of Arc, or Jeanne d'Arc, or Maid
   of Orleans
Joan Baez
Joan Benoit
Joan Blondell
Joan Caulfield
Joan Crawford
Joan Lunden
Joan Miró
Joan Rivers
Joan Sutherland
Joan Van Ark
Joanna Cassidy
Jobe's Spikes™ plant care
JoBeth Williams
Jocasta

Jockey™ underwear
Jodhpur, India
Jody Watley
Joe Blow (average guy)
Joe Clark, P.M.
Joe Cocker
Joe College (average college student)
Joe Di Maggio
Joe Garagiola
Joe Greene
Joe Isuzu
Joe Louis
Joe Montana
Joe (Joseph) William Namath
Joe Piscopo
Joe Slovo
Joel McCrea
Joel Siegel
Joel, Billy
Joey Bishop
Joey Heatherton
Joffrey Ballet
Joffrey, Robert
Johann Ambrosia Bach
Johann Christian Bach
Johann Christoph Bach
Johann Balmer
Johann Faust, or Faustus
Johann Gutenberg (Bible)
Johann Pachelbel
Johann Wolfgang von Goethe
Johann David Wyss (*Swiss Family Robinson*)
Johanna Spyri
Johannes Bach, or Hans
Johannes Brahms
Johannes Kepler
Johannesburg, S. Afr.
Johansson, Ingemar
John Adams, Pres. (2nd)
John Quincy Adams, Pres. (6th)
John Andre, Major
John Francis Appleby
John Jacob Astor
John Aubrey
John James Audubon
John Logie Baird
John the Baptist, Saint

John Barbirolli, Sir
John Barbour
John Barleycorn
John Barrymore
John Barrymore Jr.
John Bartlett
John Baskerville
John Belushi
John Biddle
John Birch Society
John Wilkes Booth
John C. Breckinridge, V.P.
John Brown (abolitionist)
"John Bull" pamphlets
John Bunyan
John Burgoyne, Gen.
John Cabot
John Cage
John C. Calhoun, V.P.
John Calvin
John Candy
John Cassavetes
John Chancellor
John Chapman (aka Johnny Appleseed)
John Cheever
John Cleese
John Coltrane
John Constable
John Singleton Copley
John Cotton (Puritan clergyman)
John Crowley
John Dalton
John Charles Daly
John Davidson
John Deere™ farm equip.
John Derek
John Dillinger
John Doe
John Donne
John Dos Passos
John Dryden
John Foster Dulles, Secy. State
John Falstaff, Sir
John Fowles
John Charles Fremont
John Kenneth Galbraith
John N. Garner, V.P.
John Gielgud, Sir

John Glenn, Astro./U.S. Sen.
John of Gaunt
John Hancock, Gov.
John Heard
John Hodiak
John Houseman
John Hughes films
John Irving
John Jakes
John Jay, Ch. Justice
John Keats
John Fitzgerald Kennedy, Pres.
John Kluge
John Knox
John La Farge
John Labatt Ltd.
John Larroquette
John Le Carre (pseud. David Cornwall)
John Lennon
John L. Lewis
John Lily, or Lyly
John Lindsay
John Lithgow
John Locke
John Madden
John Marshall, Ch. Justice
John Masefield
John Matuszak
John McEnroe
John F. McWethy
John Cougar Mellencamp
John Stuart Mill
John Paul Mitchell Systems
John Montagu, Earl of Sandwich
John Hunt Morgan, Gen.
John Morrell™ meats
John Muir
John Palmer
John J. Pershing, Gen.
John M. Poindexter
John Wesley Powell
John Q. Public
John Pym
John Ritter
John 'Jackie' Robinson
John D. Rockefeller, III
John D. Rockefeller, IV, Gov.
John D. Rockefeller, Jr.

John Singer Sargent
John Sayles
John Schneider
John Scopes (of 'monkey trial')
John Slidell, Sen.
John Smith (& Pocahontas)
John Philip Sousa
John Hanning Speke
John Steed
John Steinbeck
John Paul Stevens, Justice
John Stossel
John Sturges
John Suckling, Sir
John L. Sullivan
John H. Sununu, Chief of Staff
John Cameron Swayze
John M. Synge
John Tenniel, Sir
John Tesh
John Travolta
John Scott Trotter
John Trumbull (painter)
John Trumbull (poet)
John Tyler, Pres.
John Updike
John van Druten
John Wanamaker Dept. Store
John Wayne (aka 'the Duke')
John Greenleaf Whittier
John Winthrop, Gov.
John R. Wooden Award
John Wyclif, or Wycliffe, or Wickliffe
John Young (lst Space Shuttle flight)
John, Elton
Johnnie Ray
Johnnie Walker™
Johnny Appleseed (pseud. John Chapman)
Johnny Belinda
Johnny Cash
Johnny Depp
Johnny Mathis
Johnny Reb
Johnny Weissmuller (star of *Tarzan*)
Johnny-come-lately
Johnny-jump-up
Johnny-on-the-spot

Johns Hopkins University
Johns, Glynis
Johns, Jasper
Johnson & Johnson™ first aid
Johnson, Andrew, Pres.
Johnson, Arte
Johnson, Ben (Can. athlete)
Johnson, Claudia 'Lady Bird'
Johnson, Luci Baines
Johnson, Lynda Bird (now Mrs. Charles Robb)
Johnson, Lyndon Baines, Pres.
Johnson, Magic
Johnson, Richard M., V.P.
Johnson, Samuel
Johnson, Van
Johnson, Dr. Virginia E. (Masters & Johnson)
Johnson, Walter 'Big Train'
Johnston™ Yogurt
Johnstown, PA
Joint Chiefs of Staff
Joliet Army Ammunition Plant, IL
Joliet prison
Joliet, IL
Jolly Green Giant™
Jolly Roger (the pirate flag)
Jolly Time™ popcorn
Jolson, Al
Jomo Kenyatta, Pres.
Jon Bon Jovi
Jon Voight
Jonah in the whale
Jonathan Livingston Seagull
Jonathan Swift
Jonathan Wainwright, Gen.
Jones, Bobby
Jones, Casey (& *Cannon Ball* express)
Jones, Chuck
Jones, Ed 'Too Tall'
Jones, James Earl
Jones, Quincy
Jones, Tommy Lee
Jong, Erica
Joni Mitchell
Jonny Cat™
Jonny Quest
Jonquière, Québec, Can.

Jonson, Ben (dramatist)
Jooss Ballet, Kurt
Joplin, Janis
Joplin, MO
Joplin, Scott
Jordache™
Jordan, Hashemite, or Kingdom of Jordan
Jordan almonds
Jordan River
Jordan, Barbara, Rep.
Jordan, Michael
Jordan, Richard
Jorgensen, Christine
Jory, Victor
Jose Cuervo tequila™
Jose Napoleon Duarte, Pres.
José Eber
Jose Iturbi
José Limón Dance Company
Josef Albers
Josef Suk
Joseph Beuys
Joseph Bonaparte
Joseph Brodsky
Joseph Campanella
Joseph Cotten
Joseph Henry
Joseph Hirshhorn
Joseph Hooker, Gen.
Joseph Patrick Kennedy
Joseph Lister
Joseph L. Mankiewicz
Joseph McCarthy, Sen. ('Commie' hunter)
Joseph Mengele, Dr.
Joseph 'Joe' William Namath
Joseph Priestley
Joseph Pulitzer
Joseph Hayne Rainey, Rep.
Joseph Schildkraut
Joseph Smith (Mormon leader)
Joseph Vissarionovich Stalin
Joseph Stilwell, Gen.
Joseph Story, Justice
Joseph J. Thomson
Joseph Mallord Turner
Joseph Wambaugh

Joseph A. Yablonski
Joseph's coat of many colors
Josephine Baker
Josephine Hull
Josephine, Empress
Josh Billings (pseud. Henry Wheeler Shaw)
Joshua Lederberg
Joshua Logan
Joshua Reynolds, Sir
Joshua tree
Joshua Tree, CA
Josiah Willard Gibbs
Josiah Spode
Jotul™ wood stove
Joule, James
Joy of Cooking
Joyce Brothers, Dr.
Joyce Kilmer
Joyce Carol Oates
Joyce, James
Joyner, Al
Joyner, Florence 'Flo Jo' Griffith
Joyner-Kersee, Jackie
Ju-Jube™ candy
Juan Bautista de Anza
Juan de Fuca, Strait of
Juan Gris
Juan Domingo Perón, Pres.
Juan Ponce de León
Judaea, or Judea
Judaica (books, objects RE: Jewish religion)
Judaism (Jewish religion)
Judas Iscariot
Judas Priest (rock group)
Judas tree
Judd Hirsch
Judd Nelson
Judds, The (Naomi & Wynonna)
Jude, Saint
Judge Roy Bean
Judgment Day
Judith Anderson, Dame
Judith Bancroft
Judith Crist
Judy Blume
Judy Canova

Judy Garland
Judy Holliday
Juilliard School
Jules Feiffer
Jules Emile Massenet
Jules Verne
Julia Child
Julia Ward Howe
Julia, Raul
Julian Schwinger
Juliana, Queen of Netherlands
Julie Andrews
Julie Harris
Julie Newmar
Juliet (Capulet)
Juliet Prowse
Juliette Low (Girl Scouts)
Julio César Chávez
Julio Iglesias
Julius Caesar (Shakespeare)
Julius Caesar (Rom. statesman)
Julius 'Dr. J' Erving
Julius & Ethel Rosenberg
Julius La Rosa
Julius Streicher
July Revolution
'jumping Jehoshaphat'
June Allyson
June bug
June Havoc
June Valli
Juneau, AK
Jung, Carl Gustav
Junior Scholastic
Junipero Serra, Father
Junius Brutus Booth
Junot, Philippe
Jupiter (head god, Rom. myth.)
Jupiter (the planet)
Jupiter, FL
Jurassic period
Jurgens, Curt
Just For Men™ haircolor
Just My Size™ pantyhose
Just 'n Case™ baby potty
Justin™ cowboy boots
Justin Martyr, Saint
JVC™ audio equip.

K (chem. sym. potassium)
K Mart
K-Y™ lubricant
K. I. Sawyer Air Force Base, MI
Kaaawa, HI
Kaaba, or Caaba (in Islam)
Kabibble, Ish
Kabuki drama
Kabul, Afghanistan
Kadavy, Caryn
Kaddish
Kafka, Franz
Kahlil Gibran
Kahlúa™ liqueur
Kahn, Madeline
Kahn, Princess Yasmin
Kai-shek, Chiang, or Chiang Chung-
    cheng
Kai-shek, Chiang, Madame
Kaibab Nat. Forest
Kaifu, Toshiki, P.M.
Kailua, HI
Kain, Karen
Kaiser Aluminum & Chemical Corp.
Kaiser Permanente Foundation
Kaiser roll
Kaiser, Henry J.
Kakuei, Tanaka, P.M.
Kal Kan™ dog food
Kalachakra, or Wheel of Time
Kalakaua Ave., Honolulu, HI
Kalamazoo, MI
Kalaupapa leper colony
Kaliber™ Non-Alcoholic Brew
Kallen, Kitty

Kama Sutra, or Kamasutra
Kamakura, Jap.
Kamchatka peninsula
Kamchatka, Siberia
Kamchatka™ vodka
Kamehameha, King (of Hawaii)
Kampala, Uganda
Kampuchea, or Democratic
    Kampuchea
Kanaka (Hawaiian for native, also
    derisive for 'mainlander')
Kandinsky, Wassily
Kandy, Sri Lanka
Kaniksu Nat. Forest
Kano, school of painters
Kanpur, India
Kansas (KS)
Kansas City Chiefs
Kansas City Royals
Kansas City Star
Kansas City Times
Kansas City, KS, MO
Kansas-Nebraska Act
Kant, Immanuel
Kaopectate™
Kaplan, Gabriel
Kapton™
Karachi, Pakistan
Karajan, Herbert von
Karastan™ carpet
Kareem Abdul-Jabbar (b. Lew
    Alcindor)
Karen Kain
Karen Young
Karen, Donna
Kariba Lake/Dam
Karl Philipp Emanuel Bach, or Carl
Karl Baedeker
Karl Barth
Karl Czerny
Karl Goldmark
Karl Malden
Karl Marx
Karl A. Menninger, Dr.
Karl Millöcker
Karl Shapiro
Karl Wallenda
Karl-Marx-Stadt, E. Ger.

Karloff, Boris
Karnak, Egypt
Karnak, temple at
Karo™ syrup
Karolyi, Bela (gymnastics coach)
Karol Wojtyla (Pope John Paul II)
Karpov, Anatoly
Karras, Alex
Karsavina, Tamara
Kasdan, Lawrence
Kasem, Casey
Kashmir, Asia
Kasimir Malevich, or Casimir
Kaspar von Schwenkfeld
Katanga
Katarina Witt
Kate Greenaway
Kate Smith (Kathryn)
Katharine of Aragón
Katharine Cornell
Katharine 'Kitty' Dukakis
Katharine Hepburn
Käthe Kollwitz
Katherine Graham
Kathie Lee Gifford
Kathleen Sullivan
Kathleen Turner
Kathleen Woodiwiss
Kathryn Grayson
Kathryn Kuhlman
Katmandu, Nepal, or Kathmandu
Katowice, Poland
Katt, William
Katzenjammer Kids
Kauai, HI
Kaufman & Broad homebuilders
Kaufman, George S.
Kaukauna™ cheese spread
Kawasaki Heavy Industries Ltd.
Kawasaki, Japan
Kawasaki™ motorbikes
Kawasaki Steel Corp.
Kawasaki syndrome
Kay Kyser
Kay Kyser's Kollege of Musical
    Knowledge
Kaye Ballard
Kaye, Danny

Kaye, M. M.
Kaye, Stubby
Kaypro™
Kazan, Elia
Kazan, Lainie
Kazi Zafar Ahmed, P.M.
Kaznar, Kurt
Keach, Stacy
Kealakekua, HI
Kean, Edmund
Keanu Reeves
Keaton, Buster
Keaton, Diane
Keats, John
Keds™ shoes
Keebler™ cookies/crackers
Keebler elves
Keefe Brasselle
Keeler, Ruby
Keenan Wynn
Keene, Carolyn
Keeshan, Bob (Capt. Kangaroo)
Keeshond (dog), or keeshound
Keesler Air Force Base, MS
Kefauver, Estes, Sen.
Keillor, Garrison
Keith Carradine
Keith Jackson
Keller, Helen
Kelley, DeForest
Kelley, Kitty
Kellogg Co.
Kellogg's™ Frosted Flakes
Kellogg's™ Pop-Tarts
Kellogg's™ Special K
Kelly Air Force Base, TX
Kelly Girl™ temporary services
Kelly, Gene
Kelly, Jim
Kelthane™ pesticide
Kelvin scale
Kelvin, Lord Wm. Thomson
Kelvinator™
"Kemo-sabe" (Tonto's saying)
Ken Berry
Ken Follett
Ken Wahl
Kenmore™

Kennebunkport, ME (Pres. Bush' summer house)
Kennedy Compound at Hyannis Port, MA
Kennedy Space Center
Kennedy, Edward Moore, Sen.
Kennedy, Ethel
Kennedy, John Fitzgerald, Pres.
Kennedy, Joseph Patrick
Kennedy, Patrick
Kennedy, Robert Francis, Sen.
Kennedy Schlossberg, Caroline
Kenneth Grahame
Kenneth Millar (aka Ross Macdonald)
Kenneth Roy Thomson
Kennington™ menswear
Kenny Loggins
Kenny Rogers
Kenpo Karate
Kent County, Eng.
Kent Family Chronicles
Kentucky (KY)
Kentucky Fried Chicken™
Kenworth™ trucks
Kenya, Afr.
Kenya, Mt., or Kirinyaga
Kenyatta, Jomo, Pres.
Kepler, Johannes
Kepler's laws
Keri™ Lotion
Kerkorian, Kirk
Kermit the Frog
Kern, Jerome
Kerr Jel'n Jam™
Kerr, Deborah
Kerr, Graham, the Galloping Gourmet
Kerr, Jean
Kerr, Walter
Kerry blue terrier
Kerry County, Ireland
Keshia Knight Pulliam
Kessel, Barney
Ketchikan Coast Guard Base, AK
Ketchikan, AK
Ketterley, Digory (Narnia)
Kettle Chips™
Kevin Bacon
Kevin Costner

Kew Gardens, London
Kewpie doll
Key Largo, FL
Key Biscayne, FL
Key lime pie
Key West Naval Air Station, FL
Key West, FL
Key, Francis Scott
Keyes, Evelyn
Keystone Kops, or Cops
Keystone State (Pennsylvania)
Khachaturian, Aram Ilich
Khadafy, Gadhafi, Gaddafi, or Qaddafi, Moammar, Muammar, or Muammar-al
Khafre, Pyramid of
Khamenei, Ali, Pres.
Khan, Chaka
Khan, Genghis
Khan, Kublai
Khan, Princess Yasmin
Khartoum, Sudan
Khashoggi, Adnan
Khayyam, Omar (*Rubaiyat*)
Khios Island, or Chios
Khirbat Qumran
Khmer Empire (ancient Cambodia)
Khmer Rouge
Khomeini, Ayatollah Ruhollah
Khrunov, Yevgeny, Cosmonaut
Khrushchev, Nikita S. Prem.
Khufu, Pyramid of, or Cheops
Khyber Pass
Kiam, Victor
Kiangsu, prov., Ch.
Kibbee, Guy
Kibbee, Roland
Kibbles And Chunks™
Kibbles 'N Bits™
Kickapoo Indians
Kid Ory
Kid, Thomas, or Kyd
Kidd, Captain (William)
Kidder, Peabody & Co.
Kidder, Margot
Kiefer Sutherland
Kierkegaard, Sören, or Søren
Kiev, Soviet Union (Ukraine)

Kikkoman™ soy sauce
Kilauea crater, Mauna Loa
Kilbride, Percy
Kiley, Richard
Kilgallen, Dorothy
Kilimanjaro, Mt.
Kilkenny, Ireland
Killarney, Lakes of
Killian's Red™ beer
Killy, Jean-Claude
Kilmer, Joyce
"Kilroy was here" (WWII)
Kim Basinger
Kim Il Sung, Prem.
Kim Novak
Kim Zimmer
Kimball™ pianos
Kimberley Heffner (Mrs. Hugh)
Kinco™ weed control
Kindergarten
King Arthur
King Charles spaniel
King Ethelred II (aka 'the Unready')
King Fahd of Saudi Arabia
King Faisal I & II, of Iraq, or Feisal
King Farouk of Egypt
King Camp Gillette
King of Glory (God)
King Hammurabi of Babylon
King Hussein I, of Jordan
King James Bible
King Kamehameha of Hawaii
King of Kings (God)
King Kong
King Kuts™ dog food
King Lear
King Ludd
King Menelaus
King Midas
King Minos
King Nebuchadnezzar
King Saul
King Solomon
King Thrushbeard
King Tutankhamen, Tutenkhamon, or
   'King Tut'
King Vidor
King, B. B.

King, Billie Jean
King, Coretta Scott
King, Larry
King, Martin Luther, Jr., Dr.
King, Pee Wee
King, Rufus
King, Stephen
King, William R., V.P.
Kingman, AZ
Kings Bay Naval Submarine Base,
   GA
Kings Canyon Nat. Pk. (CA)
King's (or Queen's) Counsel
King's Court™ menswear
Kings Road Entertainment
Kings, Book of
Kingston Trio
Kingston, Jamaica
Kingston, Ont., Can.
Kingsville Naval Air Station, TX
Kinko's™ Copies
Kinks, The
Kinsey, Dr. Alfred C. (*Kinsey Report*)
Kinshasa (Léopoldville), Zaire
Kinte, Kunta
Kiowa Indians
Kipling, Rudyard
Kipnis, Igor
Kirbati, nation, Oceania, or Kiribati
Kirby™ vacuum
Kirby, Bruno
Kirby, Durward
Kirin™ beer
Kirk Douglas
Kirk Gibson
Kirk Kerkorian
Kirk, James T., Capt.
Kirkland, Gelsey
Kirkpatrick, Jeane, U.S. Rep. to UN
Kirk-Stieff™
Kirlian photography
Kiron™ lens
Kirov Ballet
Kirsch™ blinds
Kirstie Alley
Kirtland Air Force Base, NM
Kisatchie Nat. Forest
Kishinev, Moldavia

Kislev (Jewish mo.)
Kismet
KISS (heavy metal band)
Kissimmee, FL
Kissinger, Dr. Henry A., Secy. State
Kissle™ Yogurt
Kit™ car wax
Kit Carson
Kit Kat™ bar
Kitakyushu, Japan
Kitaro
Kitchen Cabinet (unofficial presidential
    advisers)
KitchenAid™ appliances
Kitchener, Ont., Can.
Kitt Peak Nat'l Observatory, AZ
Kitt, Eartha
Kitten Dinners™
Kittrich™ contact paper
Kitty Carlisle
Kitty Carruthers
Kitty Diggin's™
Kitty Hawk, NC
Kitty Kallen
Kitty Kelley
Kitty Litter™
Kiwanis Magazine
Kix™ cereal
KKK, for Ku Klux Klan, also Klan
Klamath Falls, OR
Klaus Fuchs
Klaus Maria Brandauer
Klaxon horn™
Klee, Paul
Kleenex™
Klein, Anne
Klein, Calvin
Klemperer, Otto
Klerk, Frederik W. de, Pres.
Kliban, B., cats
Klimt, Gustav
Kline test
Klingon (*Star Trek*)
KLM™ Royal Dutch Airlines
Klondike™ ice cream
Klondike River
Klondike, region, Yukon
Klopfenstein's™ clothes

Kluge, John
Klugman, Jack
Klute (movie)
Knesset (Israeli parliament)
Knickerbocker Hotel
Knickerbockers ('knickers')
Knievel, Evel
Knievel, Robbie
Knight Rider (TV show)
Knight, Gladys
Knight, J. Z. (& Ramtha)
Knight, Ted
Knight-Ridder Inc.
Knights of Columbus
Knights of Labor
Knights of Pythias
Knights of the Apocalypse
Knights of the Round Table
Knights Templar
Knightsbridge, Lon.
Knokke-Heist, Belgium
Knopf, Alfred A.
Knorr Swiss™ soup
Knossos, or Cnossus
Knossos, palace at
Knots Landing (TV show)
Knott's Berry Farm
Knotts, Don
Know-Nothing movement
Knox™ gelatine
Knox, John
Knoxville, TN
Knudsen™ foods
Knute Rockne, Coach
Koala Blue™ sportswear
Koala Springs™ drink
Koasati Indians
Kobe, Japan
Kobo, Abe
Koch, Edward, Mayor
Kodacolor™
Kodak™
Kodamatic™
Kodály, Zoltán
Kodiak bear
Kodiak Island
Kodiak, AK
Koenig, Walter

Kohinoor diamond, or Kohinur
Kohl, Helmut, Chancellor
Kohler™ plumbing fixtures
Kojak (TV cop)
Kokomo, IN
Kokoschka, Oskar
Kolchak, the Night Stalker
Kollwitz, Käthe
Komodo dragon
Komondor (dog), or komondor
Kon Tiki raft (Thor Heyerdahl)
Konica™ photo.equip.
Konrad Adenauer, Chanc.
Konrad Emil Bloch
Konstantin Chernenko, Gen. Secy.
Koo Stark
Kool-Aid™ Koolers
Kooning, Willem de
Koontz, Dean R.
Koop, C. Everett, Surgeon Gen.
Kootenai Nat. Forest
Kootenay River
Kopechne, Mary Jo (Chappaquiddick
    tragedy)
Koppel, Ted
Koran, or Quran
Korat cat
Korbel™ champagne
Korbut, Olga
Kordite™ trash bags
Korea Strait
Korea, North, or Democratic People's
    Republic of Korea
Korea, South
Korean Air
Korean War
Koret™
Korla Pandit
Korman, Harvey
Kornberg, Arthur
Kosciusko, Mt.
Kostelanetz, Andre
Kosygin, Aleksei N., Prem.
Kotex™
Koubassov, Valery, Cosmonaut
Koufax, Sanford 'Sandy'
Kouros figures
Koussevitzky, Sergel 'Serge'

Kovacs, Ernie
Kowloon, Hong Kong
Kozinski, Jerzy
Kozlowski, Linda
KozyKitten™ cat food
Kr (chem. sym. krypton)
Krackel™ candy
Kraft, or Dart and Kraft Inc.
Kraft™ foods
Kraft™ Miracle Whip
Krakatoa volcano, or Krakatau
Kraków, Poland, or Cracow
Kramer, Stanley
Krantz, Judith
Kravis, Henry
Krazy Glue™
Krebs cycle
Krebs, Hans, Sir
Kreisler, Fritz
Kremlin, the
Kris Kristofferson
Krishna (Hinduism)
Kriss Kringle, or St. Nicholas, or
    Santa Claus
Kristofferson, Kris
Kristy McNichol
Kroc, Ray (founder McDonalds)
Kroch's & Brentano's
Kroft, Steve
Kronborg Castle (Hamlet's)
Kropotkin, Piotr, Prince
Krueger, Freddy
Kruger, Otto
Krugerrand
Krupa, Gene
Krups™ appliances
Krushchev, Nikita S.
Krusteaz™ foods
Krypton
Ku Klux Klan, or KKK, or the Klan
Ku Kluxer (Klan member)
Kuala Lumpur, Malaysia
Kublai Khan
Kübler-Ross, Elisabeth
Kubota™ riding mower
Kubrick, Stanley
Kuhlman, Kathryn
Kukla, Fran & Ollie

Kung Fu (martial art)
Kung Fu (TV series)
Kunta Kinte
Kuomintang political party
Kupka, Frank
Kuralt, Charles
Kurosawa, Akira
Kurt Adler
Kurt Jooss Ballet
Kurt Kaznar
Kurt Schwitters
Kurt von Schuschnigg, Chanc.
Kurt Vonnegut, Jr.
Kurt Waldheim, Pres./UN Secy. Gen.
Kurt Weill
Kurtz, Swoosie
Kuvasz (dog), or kuvasz
Kuwait (country)
Kuwait, Kuwait, or al-Kuwait (city, country)
Kwakiutl Indians
Kwangju, South Korea, or Kwangchu
Kwik-Kopy™ Printing
Ky, Nguyen
Kyd, Thomas, or Kid
Kyle MacLachlan
Kyoto, Japan
Kyrie eleison, or Kyrie eleison (Lord have mercy)
Kyser, Kay

L. A.™ beer
L. A. Business Journal
L. A. Gear™ shoes
L. A. Law (TV show)
L. A. Weekly
L. Frank Baum

L. L. Bean catalog
L. Ron Hubbard
La (chem. sym. lanthanum)
La Bamba
La Boheme
La Brea Tar Pits
La Choy™ Chinese foods
La Cote Basque (restaurant)
La Crosse, WI
La Dolce Vita
La Farge, John
La Forge, Geordi, Lt. Cmdr. (of *Star Trek*)
La Gioconda, or *Mona Lisa* (Da Vinci)
La Guardia Airport
La Guardia, Fiorello, Mayor
La Motta, Jake
La Paz, Bolivia
La Paz™ margarita mix
La Paz, Mex.
La Petite Marmite (restaurant)
La Prairie™
La Rosa, Julius
La Salle, Québec, Can.
La Salle, Robert Cavelier
La Scala opera
La Scala (restaurant)
La Sylphide
La Traviata
La Victoria™ Salsa
La-Z-Boy™ chair
Laarne, Belgium
LaBelle, Patti
Labor Day
Labour party (Br.)
Labrador
Labrador retriever
Lachaise, Gaston
Lachine, Québec, Can.
Lackland Air Force Base, TX
Lacsa Airlines™
Ladd, Alan
Ladd, Cheryl
Ladies' Home Journal
Lady Abracadabra
Lady Baltimore cake
Lady Bountiful

Lady Bracknell
Lady Chatterley's Lover
Lady Day
Lady Godiva
Lady Kenmore™
Lady of the Lake
Lady Macbeth (*Macbeth*)
Lady Macduff (*Macbeth*)
Lady Mitchum™
Lady Pepperrell™ linens
Lady of Shalott
Lady Speed Stick™
Lady or the Tiger, The
Laertes (*Hamlet*)
Lafayette, LA
Lafayette, Marie Joseph, Gen., or La Fayette
Laffite, Jean, or Lafitte
Lagos, Nigeria
Laguna Beach, CA
Lahr, Bert
Lainie Kazan
L'Air du Temps™ perfume
Lake Arrowhead, CA
Lake Balkhash
Lake Baykal
Lake Charles, LA
Lake Clark Nat. Pk. (AK)
Lake Erie (US)
Lake Eyre (Australia)
Lake Forest, IL
Lake Geneva
Lake Havasu City, AZ
Lake Louise
Lake Malawi
Lake Manitoba
Lake Mead
Lake Michigan
Lake Nipissing
Lake Okeechobee
Lake Ontario
Lake Placid, NY
Lake Superior
Lake Tahoe
Lake Tanganyika
Lake Titicaca
Lake Wobegon
Lake of the Woods

Lake, Veronica
LaLanne, Jack
Lalique crystal
Lalo, Édouard Victor
Lamarr, Hedy
Lamas, Fernando
Lamas, Lorenzo
Lamaze method
Lamb of God (Jesus)
Lamb, Charles
Lamborghini™ car
Lamour, Dorothy
L'Amour, Louis
Lana Turner
Lanacort™ ointment
Lanai, HI
Lancashire Co., Eng.
Lancaster New Era
Lancaster, Burt
Lancaster, house of
Lancaster, PA
Lanchester, Elsa
LanChile™ Airlines
Lancia™ car
Lancôme™ skincare
Land of Beulah
Land O' Lakes™ butter
Land Rover™
Land's End cape, Eng.
Lands' End™ catalog
Landau, Martin
Landers, Ann (Eppie Lederer)
Landis, Carole
Landon, Michael
Landrum-Griffin Act.
Landry, Tom
Lane Smith
Lang, Fritz
Lange, Hope
Lange, Jessica
Langella, Frank
Langford, Frances
Langley Air Force Base, VA
Langtry, Lillie, or Lily
Lanier™ business prod.
Lansbury, Angela
Lansing, MI
Lansing, Robert

Lansing, Sherry
Lanson, Snooky
Lao-tze, or Lao-tzu
Laocoön sculpture
Laos
Laotse, or Laotzu, or Laotaze
Lapland
Lapps, or Laplanders
Lapsang souchong tea
Laputa Island (Gulliver's)
Laramie, WY
Lardner, Ring
Laredo, TX
Largo Entertainment
Largo, Key
Larroquette, John
Larry Adler
Larry Joe Bird
Larry Fine (1 of 3 Stooges)
Larry Hagman
Larry Holmes
Larry King
Larry Mahan
Larry Poons
Larson, Gary
Las Cruces, NM
Las Vegas, NV
Las Vegas Review-Journal
Las Vegas Sun
Lascaux cave paintings, Fr.
LaserWriter™ printer
Lasorda, Tommy
Lassen Peak volcano
Lassen Volcanic Nat. Pk.
Lassie
Last Judgment
Last of the Mohicans, The
Last Supper (Da Vinci)
Last Supper (Jesus' last meal)
Lastex™ (not latex)
Latakia, Syria
Lateran basilica, or Basilica of the
    Savior
Lateran Treaty
Latin America
Latin cross
Latino (slang)
Latrobe, Benjamin Henry

Latter Day Saints (Mormons)
Latvia
Laughlin Air Force Base, TX
Laughton, Charles
Laughtrack
Laundromat™
Lauper, Cyndi
Laura Ashley™ clothes/decorating
Laura Branigan
Laura San Giacomo
Laura Scudder's™ foods
Laura Ingalls Wilder
Laurance S. Rockefeller
Laurel & Hardy (Stan & Oliver)
Laurel, Stan
Lauren Bacall
Lauren, Ralph
Laurence Harvey
Laurence Luckinbill
Laurence Olivier, Sir/Lord
Laurence Sterne
Laurentiis, Dino De
Laurie, Piper
Lauritz Melchior
Laval, Quebec, Can., or Ville de
    Laval
Laver, Rod
Lavin, Linda
Lavoisier, Antoine Laurent
Lavoris™ mouthwash
Law of Moses
Lawrence of Arabia (T. E. Lawrence)
Lawrence Berkeley Laboratory
Lawrence Durrell
Lawrence Kasdan
Lawrence Livermore Laboratory
Lawrence Tibbett
Lawrence Welk And His Orchestra
Lawrence, D. H. (David Herbert)
Lawrence, Gertrude
Lawrence, KS, MA
Lawrence, Steve
Lawrence, Vicki
Lawry's™ foods
Lawton, OK
Lazar, Irving 'Swifty'
Lázaro Cárdenas, Pres.
Lazarus (raised from dead)

Lazarus, Emma
Le Bain Deneuve™ perfume
Le Carre, John (pseud. David Cornwell)
Le Chantilly (restaurant)
Le Corbusier (pseud. Charles Jeanneret)
Le Duc Tho
Le Gallienne, Eva
Le Guin, Ursula K.
Le Havre, Fr.
Le Journal de Montreal
Le Journal de Quebec
Le Mans, France
Le May, Curtis, Gen.
Le Misanthrope
Le Mond, Greg
Le Perroquet restaurant
Le Tartuffe
Le, Thuy Thu
Lea & Perrins™ sauce
Lea Thompson
Leach, Robin
League of Nations
League of Women Voters
Leakey, Louis S. B.
Leakey, Mary
Lean Cuisine™
Leaning Tower of Pisa
Lear, Norman
Learjet™
Learned Hand, Judge
Leary, Timothy
Leavenworth prison
Leavenworth, KS
Lebanon
Lebedev, Valentin, Cosmonaut
Lebniz, Gottfried, or Leibnitz
Lech Walesa (Solidarity)
Lectric Shave™
Led Zeppelin
Ledbetter, Huddie 'Leadbelly'
Lederberg, Joshua
Lee Atwater (Rep. Chair)
Lee J. Cobb
Lee De Forest (radio)
Lee Horsley
Lee Iacocca
Lee™ jeans
Lee Majors

Lee Harvey Oswald
Lee™ Press-On Nails
Lee Radziwill, Princess
Lee Remick
Lee Strasberg
Lee Trevino
Lee, Bruce
Lee, Francis 'Lightfoot'
Lee, Gypsy Rose
Lee, Light-Horse Harry
Lee, Michele
Lee, Robert E., General
Lee, Stan (Marvel Comics)
Lee, Spike
Lee/Rowan™ hangers
Leeds, Eng.
Leeuwenhoek, Antony van
Leeza Gibbons
Left Bank, Paris
Lefty Grove
L'eggs™
Legion of Honor (Fr.)
Legion of Merit (U.S.)
Legionnaire (member Am. Legion)
Legionnaire's Disease, or disease
Lego™ toys
Legree, Simon
Lehar, Franz
Leibman, Ron
Leica™ camera
Leicester County, Eng.
Leicester Square (Lon.)
Leif Ericsson
Leigh, Janet
Leigh, Jennifer Jason
Leigh, Vivien
Leinsdorf, Erich
Leipzig, E. Ger.
Lem, Stanislaw
Lemmon, Chris
Lemmon, Jack
LeMond, Greg
Lemoore Naval Air Station, CA
Lena Horne
Lender's™ Bagels
Lendl, Ivan
L'Engle, Madeleine
Lenin Library (Moscow)

Lenin Peak (USSR)
Lenin, Vladimir Ilyich
Leningrad, USSR (was St. Petersburg)
Lenni-Lenape Indians
Lennie Tristano
Lennon Sisters, The
Lennon, John
Lennon, Julian
Lennox™ china/crystal
Lenny Bruce
Leno, Jay
Lens Magazine
Lens On Campus
Lens Plus™ saline
Lent
L'Entrecote (restaurant)
Lenz, Heinrich
Leo Carillo
Leo F. Buscaglia
Leo G. Carroll
Leo Durocher
Leo Gorcey
Leo Rossi
Leo Rosten
Leo Szilard
Leo Tolstoy, or Tolstoi
Leon Ames
Leon Bakst
Leon Fromkess
Leon Jaworski
Leon Spinks
Leon Trotsky, or Trotski
Leon Uris
León, Mexico
León, Ponce de
Leona Helmsley
Leonard Bernstein
Leonard Bloomfield
Leonard 'Bones' McCoy, Dr. (of *Star Trek*)
Leonard Nimoy
Leonard Slatkin
Leonard, Sheldon
Leonard, Sugar Ray
Leonardo da Vinci
Leonardo Fibonacci
Leoncavallo, Ruggiero
Leonid I. Brezhnev, Pres.

Leonids meteor shower (Nov.)
Leonine Wall (Vatican)
Leonov, Aleksei, Cosmonaut
Leonova, Mariana
Leontyne Price
Leopold Stokowski
Lepus (Hare) constellation
Lerner & Loewe (Alan Jay & Frederick)
Lerner, Alan Jay
Leroy 'Satchel' Paige
Leroy, Mervyn, or LeRoy
Les Fauves
Les Misérables
Les Paul & Mary Ford
Les Sylphides
Les Tremayne
Lesbos Island
Lescoulie, Jack
Lesley Ann Warren
Leslie Caron
Leslie Stahl
Leslie Uggams
Lesotho, country, Africa
Lesser Antilles, W.I.
Lessing, Doris
Lester Flatt
Lestor Maddox, Gov.
Letterkenny Army Depot, PA
Letterman, David
Lettermen, The
Levant, Oscar
Levar Burton
Lever Brothers Co.
Levertov, Denise
Levi Strauss Co.
Levi-Strauss, Claude
Levi, tribe
Levi's™ jeans
Leviathan
Levine, Irving R.
Levites
Leviticus
Levittown, NY
Levolor™ blinds
Lew Alcindor (Kareem Abdul-Jabbar)
Lew Ayres
Lew Wasserman
Lewis and Clark Expedition

Lewis Carroll (pseud. Chs. Dodgson)
Lewis F. Powell, Jr., Justice
Lewis, C. S.
Lewis, Jerry Lee
Lewis, John L.
Lewis, Meriwether
Lewis, Shari (& Lambchop)
Lewis, Sinclair
Lexington Herald-Leader
Lexington, battle of
Lexington, KY
Lexington-Bluegrass Army Depot
Lexus™ car
Lhasa Apso, or apso
Lhasa, Ch.
Li (chem. sym. lithium)
Li Peng, Premier
Li Tai Po, or Li Po
Liaoning, prov., Ch.
Libbey™ Glassware
Liberace (b. Wladziu Valentino)
Liberal party (Br.)
Liberal Republican party (U.S.)
Liberia
Libermann, Max
Liberty Bell (in Philadelphia)
Liberty Bell 7, or *Mercury
     Redstone 3*
Liberty Island (Statue Lib.)
Liberty, Statue of
Libra (zodiac sign)
Library of Congress (DC)
Libya, or Socialist People's Libyan
     Arab Jamahiriyah
Libyan Desert
Lichtenstein, Roy
Liddy, G. Gordon
Lidice, Czech.
Lie, Trygve H., Secy. Gen.
Lieberman, Nancy
Liebfraumilch wine
Liechtenstein
Liederkranz cheese
Life Guards (Br.)
Lifebuoy™ soap
LifeSavers™ candy
Lifestyle magazine
Lifetime Cable Network

Light n'Lively™ cheese
Light of the World (God)
Lightfoot, Gordon
Light-Horse Harry Lee
Li'l Abner
Liliuokalani, Queen of Hawaii
Lille, France
Lilli Palmer
Lillian Gish
Lillian Hellman
Lillian Russell
Lillian Vernon catalog
Lillie Langtry, or Lily
Lillie Rubin™ clothes
Lillie, Beatrice
Lilliput (Gulliver's)
Lilliputian
Lilly, John, or Lyly
Lilt™ perm
Lily Pons
Lily Tomlin
Lima, Peru
Limbo
Limehouse district, Lon.
Limelight
Limerick, Ireland
Limoges™ china
Limoges, France
Limón, José, Dance Company
Limousin, Fr.
Limousine Liberals
Lincoln Center for the Performing
     Arts
Lincoln™ Continental
Lincoln Memorial
Lincoln™ Town Car
Lincoln, Abraham, Pres.
Lincoln, Mary Todd
Lincoln, NE
Lincoln, Robert Todd
Lincoln-Douglas debates
Lind, Jenny
Linda Darnell
Linda Ellerbee
Linda Fratianne
Linda Gray
Linda Hunt
Linda Kozlowski

Linda Lavin
Linda Ronstadt
Lindal Cedar™ Homes
Lindbergh kidnapping
Lindbergh, Anne Spencer
Lindbergh, Charles A.
Linden, Hal
Lindsay™ olives
Lindsay Wagner
Lindsay, John
Lindy Hop
Linear Link™ power saw
Linotype™
Linus C. Pauling, Dr.
Lionel Barrymore
Lionel de Rothschild, Baron
Lionel Richie
Lions Club
Lions, Gulf of
Lipari Island, Italy
Lipchitz, Jacques
Lipizzaner horse/stud farm
Lippi, Filippino
Lippi, Fra Filippo
Lippmann, Walter
Lipton™ Cup-A-Soup
Lipton™ tea
Liquid Paper™
Liquid Plumr™
Liquitex ™ art products
Lisa Bonet
Lisa Lynn Gregory
Lisbon, Portugal
Lister, Joseph
Listerine™
Listermint™
Liston, Sonny
Liszt, Franz
Literary Magazine Review
Lithgow, John
Lithuania
Little Bighorn
Little Bo-Peep
Little Corporal (Napoleon B.)
Little Creek Naval Amphibious Base, VA
Little Dipper (Ursa Minor)
Little Jimmy Dickens

Little John (R. Hood's)
Little League
Little Leaguer
Little Lord Fauntleroy
Little Orphan Annie
Little Rock, AR
Little Rock Air Force Base, AR
Little Turtle, Chief (Miami In.)
Little Women (Meg, Jo, Beth & Amy March)
Little, Clevon
Little, Stuart
Litton Industries Incorporated
Litton™ stove
Liturgy of the Hours
Liv Ullmann
Livermore, CA
Livermore, Lawrence
Liverpool, Eng.
Living Strings, the
Living Theater (Europe)
Living Theater (NYC)
Livingstone, Dr. David
Livonia, MI
Liz Claiborne™ clothes
Liza Minnelli
Lizabeth Scott
Lizwear™ clothes
Lizzie Borden
Lladró porcelain
Lloyd Bentsen, Sen.
Lloyd Bridges
Lloyd 'Pete' Bucher, Commander
Lloyd, Christopher
Lloyd, Emily
Lloyd, Harold
Lloyd's™ VCR
lobster Newburg
Loc, Tone
Loch Lomond, Scot.
Loch Ness, Scot.
Loch Ness monster
Lochinvar, young
Locke, John
Lockheed Corp.
Locklear, Heather
Locus
Lodge, Henry Cabot, Sen.

Lodge, Henry Cabot, Jr., Sen.
Lodi, CA
Lodovico Carracci
Loewe, Frederick
Logan, Joshua
Loggia, Robert
Loggins & Messina
Loggins, Kenny
Logitech HiRez™ mouse
Logoya, Alexandre
Lohengrin
Loire River
Lola Montez
Lolita
Loman, Willy
Lombard, Carole
Lombardi, Vince
Lombardo, Guy
Lon Chaney
Lon Chaney, Jr.
London Bridge (now in AZ)
London broil
London Fog™ raincoat
London Free Press
London, Eng.
London, Jack
Londonderry, N. Ire.
Lone Ranger & Tonto
Lone Star State (Texas)
Long Beach, CA
Long Beach Naval Shipyard, CA
Long Island Expressway (NYC)
Long Island Journal
Long Island, NY
Long Island Sound
Long March, Mao's
Long, Huey P., Gov.
Long, Shelley
Longboat Key, FL
Longfellow, Henry Wadsworth
Longs Drugs™
Longstocking, Pippi
Longstreet, James, Gen.
Longueuil, Québec, Can.
Longview, TX
Lonnie Shorr
Loomis™ armored-car
Looney Tunes

Loos, Anita
Lopez, Nancy
Lorado Taft
Lord & Taylor
Lord High Chancellor (Br.)
Lord of the Flies (novel)
Lord of the Flies (the Devil)
Lord Greystoke
Lord of Lords (God)
Lord of the Rings
Lord Peter Wimsey
Lord of Vermin (the Devil)
Lord's Prayer, or "Our Father"
Lord's Supper
Lords, Traci (actress/former porn queen)
L´Oréal™ cosmetics
L´Oréal™ Plénitude skincare
L´Oréal™ Studio Line haircare
Loren, Sophia
Lorenzo dé Medici, the Magnificant
Lorenzo Ghiberti
Lorenzo Lamas
Lorenzo, Frank
Loretta Lynn
Loretta Swit
Loretta Young
Lorimar Films
Loring Air Force Base, ME
Loring, Eugene
Loring, Gloria
Lorna Doone
Lorna Doone™ socks
Lorna Luft
Lorne Greene
Lorraine, Fr.
Lorre, Peter
Lorus™ watch
Los Alamos Scientific Laboratory
Los Alamos, NM
Los Angeles Basin
Los Angeles, CA
Los Angeles County Museum
Los Angeles Dodgers
Los Angeles Herald-Examiner
   (defunct)
Los Angeles Kings
Los Angeles Rams
Los Angeles Times

Los Angeles Times Book Review
Lot (Biblical)
Lotophagi (lotus-eaters)
Lotos-Eaters, The
Lotta Crabtree
Lotus™ car
Lotus™ computer
Lotus Magazine
Lotusland
Lou Brock
Lou Costello
Lou Ferrigno
Lou Gehrig
Lou Gehrig's disease
Lou Diamond Phillips
Lou Rawls
Louella Parsons
Louganis, Greg
Louis Agassiz
Louis 'Satchmo' Armstrong
Louis Bonaparte
Louis Botha, P.M. (Unionist Party)
Louis Braille
Louis Brandeis, Justice
Louis Calhern
Louis Daguerre
Louis de Bougainville
Louis deBroglie
Louis Gossett, Jr.
Louis Moreau Gottschalk
Louis L´Amour
Louis S. B. Leakey
Louis Napoleon (Napoleon III)
Louis Pasteur
Louis Quatorze style (Louis XIV)
Louis Quinze style (Louis XV)
Louis Rich™ coldcuts
Louis S. St. Laurent, P.M.
Louis Seize style (Louis XVI)
Louis Stanton Auchincloss
Louis Tiffany
Louis Treize style (Louis XIII)
Louis Vuitton™ luggage
Louis XIII style (baroque)
Louis XIV style (classic)
Louis XV style (rococo)
Louis XVI style (classic revival)
Louis, Joe

Louisa May Alcott
Louise Bourgeois
Louise Dresser
Louise Mandrell
Louisiana (LA)
Louisiana Purchase
Louisville Courier-Journal
Louisville, KY
Lourdes miracle
Lourdes, France
Lournay™ skincare
Louvre Museum (Paris)
Love-A-Bye Baby™ doll
Lovelace, Richard
Lovell, James A., Jr., Astronaut
Lovell, Sir Bernard
Lovepats™ panties
Love's Labour Lost
Low Church
Low Countries, reg., Europe
Low Sunday
Low, Juliette (Girl Scouts)
Lowe, Rob
Lowell, Amy
Lowell, James Russell
Lowell, Percival
Löwenbräu™ beer
Lower California, or Baja Calif.
Lower Saxony, W. Ger.
Lowestoft porcelain
Lowestoft, Eng.
Loy, Myrna
Loyal Order of Moose
Loyola University
Loyola, Saint
Lr (chem. sym. lawrencium)
Lu Wang
Luanda, Angola
Lubbock, TX
Lubitsch, Ernst
Lubriderm™ Lotion
Lucas Industries Ltd.
Lucas Samaras
Lucas Tanner
Lucas, George
Lucci, Susan
Luce, Clare Booth
Luce, Henry Robinson

Lucerne, Switz., or Luzern
Luci Baines Johnson
Luciano Pavarotti
Lucie Arnaz
Lucien Bonaparte
Lucien Piccard™ watch
Lucifer (the Devil)
Lucille Ball
Lucite™
Luckinbill, Laurence
Lucknow, India
Lucky Charms™ cereal
Lucky Dog™ dog food
Lucretia Borgia
Lucretia Coffin Mott
Lucretius (poet)
Lucullus (Roman general)
Lucy Stone
Ludd, King
Ludden, Allen
Ludgate Circus (Lon.)
Ludlum, Robert
Ludwig Boltzmann
Ludwig van Beethoven
Luft, Lorna
Lufthansa™ German Airlines
Luftwaffe
Luger™ gun
Lugosi, Bela
Luigi Boccherini
Luigi Pirandello
Luis Walter Alvarez
Luke Air Force Base, AZ
Luke Skywalker
Lum and Abner
Lumet, Sidney
Lumumba, Patrice, P.M.
Luna space probe
Lunar Excursion Module
Lunar Orbiter
Lunar Rover
Lunch Bucket™ meals
Lunchables™ snacks
Lunden, Joan
Lundgren, Dolph
Lunt, Alfred
Lupino, Ida
Lurex™ fabric

Lusaka, Zambia
Lusitania, S.S.
Luther Adler
Luther Burbank
Luther Vandross
Luther, Martin
Lutheranism
Luvs™ diapers
Lux™ soap
Luxembourg (country), or Luxemburg
Luxembourg, Luxembourg (city, country), or Luxemburg
Luxman™ audio system
Luxor, Egypt
Luzern, Switzerland
Luzon, Philippines
Lyceum, the
Lycopodiophyta
Lycra
Lydia Pinkham (patent medicine)
Lydia Sokolova
Lyle Waggoner
Lyman Abbott
Lyme disease
Lyn Nofziger
Lynch, David (*Twin Peaks*)
Lynda Benglis
Lynda Bird Johnson (now Mrs. Charles Robb)
Lynde, Paul
Lyndon B. Johnson Space Center, TX
Lyndon Baines Johnson, Pres.
Lynette 'Squeaky' Fromme
Lynn Fontanne
Lynn Redgrave
Lynn, Loretta
Lyonel Feininger
Lyonnesse (legend. Arthurian country)
Lyons, Jeffrey
Lyons, Fr.
Lyons, Council of
Lysander (Spartan leader)
Lysippos (sculptor)
Lysol™ cleaner
Lytell, Bert

M-14 automatic rifle
M & M's™ candy
M. H. de Young Museum
M. J. Divine, Major, or Father Divine
M. M. Kaye
Ma & Pa Kettle
Ma Maison restaurant
Ma, Yo-Yo
Maalox™
Mab, Queen
Macao, Portugal prov., China
MacArthur, Douglas, Gen.
MACazine
Macbeth (Shakespeare)
Macbeth, king of Scotland
Maccabees
Macchio, Ralph
MacDill Air Force Base, FL
MacDonald, Jeanette
Macdonald, Ross (pseud. Kenneth
   Millar)
MacDowell, Andie
Mace™
Macedonia rep., Yugoslavia
MacGraw, Ali
MacGyver (TV show)
MacGyverism (from TV character)
Mach number
Mach, Ernst
Machiavelli, Niccolò
Machiavellian deed
Machu Picchu (Peru)
MacInnes, Helen
Macintosh™ computer
Mack Sennett Studios (old Hollywood)
Mack, Jillie

Macke, August
Mackenzie river (Canada)
MacKenzie, Gisele
Mackenzie, Alexander, P.M.
Mackenzie, Sir Alexander (explorer)
Mackie, Bob
Mackinac, Straits of
Mackinaw blanket
Mackinaw boat
Mackinaw coat
Mackintosh, Charles Rennie
MacLachlan, Kyle
MacLaine, Shirley
Maclean's Magazine
MacLeish, Archibald
MacLeod, Gavin
MacMillan and Wife
Macmillan, Harold, P.M.
MacMurray, Fred
Macnee, Patrick
MacNeil/Lehrer Report
Macon, GA
Macon Telegraph & News
MacPherson™ struts
MacRae, Gordon
Macready, George
MacUser
Macworld
Macy's department store
Mad Hatter, the
Mad Magazine
Mad Tea Party
Madagascar
Madalyn Murray O'Hair
Madam Tussaud's Wax Museum
Madame Jeanne Antoinette Pompa-
   dour
Madame Bovary
Madame Jeanne Bécu Du Barry
Madame Helena Blavatsky, or Helena
   Petrovna Hahn Blavatsky
Madden, John
Maddox, Lester, Gov.
Madeira Island
Madeira wine
Madeleine L'Engle
Madeline Kahn
Mademoiselle

Madigan, Amy
Madison Avenue (slang for adv. biz)
Madison Avenue (NYC)
Madison, Dolley (not Dolly)
Madison, James, Pres.
Madison, WI
Madonna (Virgin Mary)
Madonna (singer)
Madras cloth
Madras, India
Madrid, Spain
Madsen, Virginia
Madwoman of Chaillot, The
Mae West (actress)
Mae West (life jacket)
Maelstrom
Maeterlinck, Count Maurice
Mafia
Mafia princess
Mafioso
Mag Lite™ flashlight
Magdalene, Mary
Magdeburg, E. Ger.
Magee, Patrick
Magellan, Ferdinand
Magellan, Strait of
Magellanic clouds (galaxies)
Magen David, or Mogen David (Star of David)
Maggie and Jiggs
Magi (the wise men)
Magic Johnson
Magic Marker™
Magilla Gorilla
Maginot Line, or line
Magna Carta, or Magna Charta
Magnani, Anna
Magnavox™ electronics
Magnificat
Magnificent Ambersons
Magnoliophyta
Magnum, P.I.
Magritte, René
Magruder, Jeb Stuart
Magyar (Hungary ethnic group)
Mahalia Jackson
Mahan, Larry
Maharishi Mahesh Yogi

Mahatma Mohandas Gandhi
Mahican Indians
Mah-Jong™, also mah jongg
Mahler, Gustav
Mahre, Phil
Mahre, Steve
Mai Tai (cocktail)
Maid Marian (R. Hood's)
Maid of Orleans, also Jeanne d'Arc, or Joan of Arc
Maidenform™ bra
Mailer, Norman
Maillol, Aristide
Main Street (central street of any town)
Main, Marjorie
Mainbocher
Maine (ME)
Maine Coon cat
Maine Sunday Telegram
Mairzy Doats
Maison Blanche
Majestic™ binder
Majolica table wine
Majolica tablewear
Major Bowes
Major Bowes' Original Amateur Hour
Major Grey's chutney
Majorca™ pearls
Majorca, Spain
Majors, Lee
Makarova, Natalia
Makita™ power tools,
Malabo, Equitorial Guinea
Malacca, Strait of
Malachi, or Malachy, or Malachias (Old Test.)
Malaga grapes
Malaga, Spain
Malaga wine
Malawi, Lake
Malawi republic
Malay Archipelago
Malay Peninsula
Malaysia, Federation of
Malaysia Airlines
Malcolm Forbes
Malcolm McDowall

Malcolm X
Malcolm-Jamal Warner
Malden, Karl
Maldives republic
Malevich, Kasimir, or Casimir
Mali republic
Malibu, CA
Malibu™ cigarettes
Malikites
Mallomar™ candy
Malmaison, France
Malmstrom Air Force Base, MT
Malory, Sir Thomas
Malt-O-Meal™ cereal
Malta
Maltese dog
Maltese Falcon, The
Malthusianism (population theory)
Mamas, The & The Papas
Mamie Van Doren
Mammoth Cave Nat. Pk. (KY)
Mammoth Lakes, CA
man Friday/girl Friday
Man From U.N.C.L.E.
Man of Galilee (Jesus)
Man of God (saint, clergyman,
   priest, etc.)
Man of La Mancha
Man of Sorrows (Jesus)
Man O'War (race horse)
Man Ray
Man, Isle of
Managua, Nicaragua
Manassas, VA
Manaus, Brazil
Manchego cheese
Manchester terrier (dog)
Manchester Union Herald
Manchester, Eng.
Manchester, NH
Manchester, Melissa
Manchu (people of Manchuria)
Manchuria
Manchurian Candidate, The
Mancini, Henry
Mancini, Ray 'Boom Boom'
Manco Capac
Mandalay, Burma

Mandan Indians
Mandarin (high official)
Mandarin Chinese (language)
Mandela, Nelson
Mandela, Winnie
Mandell, Howie
Manderley (on the road to)
Mandrell, Barbara
Mandrell, Louise
Mandy Patinkin
Manet, Edouard
Manganin™
Mangas Coloradas, Chief
Mangione, Chuck
Manhattan clam chowder
Manhattan cocktail
Manhattan Project
Manhattan Transfer, The
Manhattan, or Manhattan Island
Manhattans, The
Manifest Destiny
Manila hemp/rope
Manila paper
Manila, Philippines
Manila rope
Manilow, Barry
Manischewitz™ kosher foods/wines
Manitoba, Can.
Manitoba, Lake
Mankiewicz, Joseph L.
Mann Act
Mann, Herbie
Mann, Horace
Mann, Thomas
Mann's Chinese Theater
Manne, Shelly
Mannerheim Line
Mannerheim, Baron Carl Gustav
Mannheim School
Mannheim, W. Ger.
Mannington™ flooring
Mannix
Manowar (rock group)
Manpower™ Employment Agency
Mansard roof (François Mansard)
Mansard, François, or Mansart
Mansfield, Jayne
Mansfield, OH

Manson, Charles
Mantle, Mickey
Mantoux test (for TB)
Mantovani
Mantua, Italy
Manuel De Falla
Manuel A. Noriega, Gen.
Manwich™ sloppy Joe (Hunt's)
Manx cat
Manzanillo, Mex.
Mao Tse-tung, Chairman, or Zedong
Maoism (political ideal)
Maori people
Maples, Marla
Mapp vs. Ohio
Maputo, Mozambique
Maracaibo, Lake
Maracaibo, Venezuela
Marat, Jean Paul
Marathon (ancient plain)
Marc Antony, or Mark
Marc Chagall
Marc, Franz
Marcel Breuer
Marcel Duchamp
Marcel Marceau
Marcel Proust
Marcello Mastroianni
March Air Force Base, CA
March hare
March, Fredric
Marchand, Nancy
Marciano, Rocco 'Rocky'
Marco Polo
Marconi, Guglielmo (telegraph)
Marcos, Ferdinand E., Pres.
Marcos, Imelda
Marcus Andronicus
Marcus Tullius Cicero
Marcus Welby, M.D.
Mardi Gras
Mare Island Naval Station, CA
Margaret of Anjou
Margaret Atwood
Margaret of Austria
Margaret Bourke-White
Margaret Fox (occult)
Margaret Maid of Norway

Margaret Mead
Margaret Mitchell
Margaret of Parma
Margaret Rutherford
Margaret Sanger
Margaret Chase Smith, Sen.
Margaret Sullivan
Margaret Thatcher, P.M.
Margaret Trudeau
Margaret Truman
Margaret Tudor
Margaret of Valois
Margaret Whiting
Margaux Hemingway
Margery Daw
Margot Fonteyn, Dame
Margot Kidder
Maria Callas
María de Perón
Maria Montessori
Maria Schell
Maria Shriver
Maria Taglioni
Maria Tallchief
Maria Theresa of Austria
Maria von Trapp
Mariachi music
Marian Anderson
Mariana Islands
Mariana Leonova
Marianas trench, or trough, or deep
Marie Antoinette
Marie Henri Beyle (aka Stendhal)
Marie Callender's restaurant
Marie Curie, Madam
Marie dé Medici
Marie Dressler
Marie Joseph Lafayette, Gen., or La
   Fayette
Marie Louise of France (empress)
Marie Osmond
Marie Tussaud (waxworks)
Marie, Rose
Marilu Henner
Marilyn Horne
Marilyn Monroe (b. Norma Jean Baker)
Marilyn Quayle
Marin, Cheech

Marina del Rey, CA
Marinaro, Ed
Marine Corps, U.S.
Mariner space probe
Mario Andretti
Mario M. Cuomo, Gov.
Marion Zimmer Bradley
Marion Francis (aka 'the Swamp Fox')
Marion Ross
Maris, Roger
Maritime Provinces
Marjorie Kinnan Rawlings
Marjorie Main
Mark Antony, or Marc
Mark di Suvero
Mark Goodman
Mark Hellinger
Mark Hopkins hotel
Mark Spitz
Mark Taper Forum (in L.A.)
Mark Twain (pseud. Samuel Clemens)
Marks & Spencer (aka 'Marks & Sparks')
Marks-A-Lot™
Marla Gibbs
Marla Maples
Marlboro Man (Marlboro cigarettes)
Marlboro Music Festival
Marlene Dietrich
Marlin Fitzwater
Marlon Brando
Marlowe, Christopher
Marlowe, Philip
Marple, Miss, of St. Mary Mead
Marquette University
Marquis de Lafayette
Marquis de Sade, or Marquis Donatien de Sade
Marquis of Queensberry Rules
Marrakech, Morocco, or Marrakesh
Marriner, Neville
Marriott Hotel(s)
Marriott's Essex House (NYC)
Mars (god of war)
Mars™ candy
Mars space probe
Mars, Forest E.
Marsala wine

Marsala, Italy
Marseille, Fr.
Marseilles (cotton material)
Marshal Tito, P.M.
Marshall Field's store
Marshall Islands
Marshall Plan, or European Recovery Program
Marshall Space Flight Center, AL
Marshall, George Catlett, Gen.
Marshall, Ch. Justice John
Marshall, Penny
Marshall, Peter
Marshall, Thoman R., V.P.
Marshall, Justice Thurgood
Martha & the Vandellas
Martha Jane Burke (aka Calamity Jane)
Martha Graham
Martha Plimpton
Martha Quinn
Martha Raye
Martha 'Sunny' von Bülow
Martha's Vineyard (MA)
Marthinus Pretorius
Martin Bormann
Martin Frobisher, Sir
Martin Gabel
Martin Landau
Martin Luther King, Jr., Dr.
Martin Luther
Martin Scorsese
Martin Sheen
Martin Van Buren, Pres.
Martin, Dean
Martin, Steve
Martina Navratilova
Martinelli's™ cider
Martini & Rossi Asti Spumante
Martinique, W.I.
Martinmas
Marty Ingels
Marty Robbins
Marvin Gaye
Marvin Hagler
Marvin Mitchelson, Atty.
Marx Brothers, the Three (Chico, Groucho, Harpo)
Marx, Chico (Leonard)

Marx, Groucho (Julius)
Marx, Gummo (Milton)
Marx, Harpo (Arthur)
Marx, Karl (Ger. philosopher)
Marx, Richard
Marx, Zeppo (Herbert)
Marxism (philosophy)
Mary Astor
Mary of Burgundy
Mary Cassatt
Mary Baker Eddy
Mary Elizabeth Coleridge
Mary Elizabeth Mastrantonio
Mary Ann Evans, or Marian (aka
    George Eliot)
Mary Fickett
Mary Ford (Les Paul &)
Mary Frann
Mary Gross
Mary of Guise
Mary Janes™ shoes
Mary Jo Kopechne (Chappaquiddick
    tragedy)
Mary Leakey
Mary Todd Lincoln
Mary Magdalene
Mary McCleod Bethune
Mary Montagu, Lady
Mary Pickford
Mary Poppins
Mary Quant
Mary Lou Retton
Mary Roberts Rinehart
Mary Shelley
Mary Decker Slaney
Mary Steenburgen
Mary Stolz
Mary Stuart, or Mary Queen of Scots
Mary Tudor, or Mary I
Mary Tyler Moore
Maryland (MD)
Maryknoll School of Theology
Masaccio (painter)
Masada fortress
Masai people
Masayoshi, Ohira, P.M.
Mascagni, Pietro
Masefield, John

Maserati™ car
MASH, also M*A*S*H
Mashhad, Iran
Masland™ carpet
Mason™ jar
Mason, Jackie
Mason, James
Mason, Perry
Mason-Dixon line
Masonite™
Masport™ wood stove
Mass (Catholic ceremony)
Massachuset Indians, or Massachusett
Massachusetts (MA)
Massachusetts Bay Company
Massachusetts Institute of
    Technology (MIT)
Massapequa, NY
Massasoit, Chief
Massenet, Jules Emile
Massengill™ douche
Masserer, Asaf
Massey, Raymond
Massey-Ferguson Ltd.
Massif Central plateau
Massys, Quentin, or Matsys, or
    Messys, or Metsys
MasterCard™
Masters and Johnson, Drs.
Masters golf tournament
Masters, Edgar Lee
Masters, William H., Dr.
Masterson, Bat
Mastiff (dog)
Mastrantonio, Mary Elizabeth
Mastroianni, Marcello
Mastroianni, Umberto
Mata Hari
Matabele (Zulu tribe)
Matamoros, Mexico
Matchbox™ cars
Match-Light™ charcoal
Mather Air Force Base, CA
Mather, Rev. Cotton
Mathew B. Brady
Mathew, Saint
Mathewson, Christy (Christopher)
Mathias Grünewald

Mathis, Johnny
Matisse, Henri
Mats Wilander
Matt Biondi
Matt Dillon, Marshall
Mattel™ toys
Matterhorn
Matthau, Walter
Matthew Ridgway, Gen.
Matthias, Saint
Mature, Victor
Matuszak, John
Mau Mau (secret society Kikuyu tribe)
Maud Frizon
Maude Adams
Maugham, W. Somerset
Maui, HI
Mauldin, Bill (William)
Mauna Kea volcano (inactive)
Mauna Kea volcano (dormant)
Mauna Loa volcano (active)
Maundy Thursday
Maupassant, Guy de
Maupin, Bennie
Maureen "Little Mo" Connolly
Maureen O'Hara
Maureen Stapleton
Maurice Barres
Maurice Barrymore
Maurice Chevalier
Maurice de Vlaminck
Maurice Evans
Maurice Maeterlinck, Count
Maurice Prendergast
Maurice Ravel
Maurice 'The Rocket' Richard
Maurice Sendak
Maurice Utrillo
Maurier, Daphne Du
Mauritania, or Islamic Republic of
    Mauritania
Mauritius nation
Maury Povich
Mauser™ rifle/pistol
Mausoleum at Halicarnassus
Maverick (Bret Maverick)
Max Baer, Jr.
Max Beckmann

Max Beerbohm, Sir
Max Born
Max Ernst
Max Factor™ cosmetics
Max Headroom
Max Libermann
Max Planck
Max Reinhardt
Max Schmeling
Max Shulman
Max von Sydow
Max Weber (artist)
Max Weber (sociologist)
Max Wertheimer
Maxell™ audio cassettes
Maxfield Parrish
Maximilien Robespierre, `the
    Incorruptible´
Maxithins™
Maxwell Anderson
Maxwell Bodenheim
Maxwell House™ Coffee
Maxwell Smart
Maxwell Davenport Taylor, Gen.
May apple
May Company, store
May Day (holiday)
May queen
May wine
Maya Angelou
Maya Indians
Mayan ruins
Maybelline™ cosmetics
Mayberry R.F.D.
Mayday (signal for help)
Mayfair district, Lon.
Mayfell™ saw
Mayflower
Mayflower Compact
Mayflower Transit™
Maynard Ferguson
Mayo Clinic
Mayor of Casterbridge, The
Maypo™ cereal
Maypole, also maypole
Mayron, Melanie
Mays, Willie (Howard)
Maytag™

Maytag repairman, the
Mayumi Moriyama, Cabinet Secy.
Mazarin Bible, or Gutenberg Bible
Mazatlán, Mex.
Mazda™ car
Mazda™ Miata
Mazda™ Protege
Mazola™ margarine/oil
Mazowiecki, Tadeusz, P.M.
Mazurka (dance)
MBA Magazine
Mbala, Zambia
MCA Incorporated
McAlester Army Ammunition Plant,
  OK
McAuliffe, Christa (*Challenger*
  teacher)
McCall's magazine
McCallum, David
McCambridge, Mercedes
McCann, Specs
McCarthy, Eugene, Sen.
McCarthy, Joseph, Sen. ('Commie'
  hunter)
McCarthyism
McCartney, Paul
McChord Air Force Base, WA
McClanahan, Rue
McCleery, Albert
McClellan Air Force Base, CA
McClellan, George B., Gen.
McClure, Jessica
McClure, Sir Robert John
McConnell Air Force Base, KS
McCormick harvester
McCormick™ vodka
McCormick, Cyrus
McCormick/Schilling™ seasonings
McCoy, Dr. Leonard 'Bones' (*Star
  Trek*)
McCrea, Joel
McCullers, Carson
McCulloch™ saw
McCulloch vs. Maryland
McCullough, Colleen
McD.L.T.™ (McDonald's)
McDonald House, Ronald
McDonald's restaurant

McDonaldland™ cookies
  (McDonald's)
McDonnell Douglas Co.
McDowall, Roddy
McDowall, Malcolm
McEnroe, John
McEntire, Reba
McFerrin, Bobby
McGarrett, Steve, of Five-O
McGee, Fibber and Molly
McGill University (Que.)
McGovern, George S., Sen.
McGraw, Charles
McGraw-Edison Co.
McGraw-Hill Inc.
McGuire Air Force Base, NJ
McGuire Sisters, The
McGuire, Dorothy
MCI Communications Corp.
McInerney, Jay
McIntosh apple
McKay, Jim
McKenzie, Spuds
McKids™ boyswear
McKinley, Mt.
McKinley, William, Pres.
McKuen, Rod
McLaglen, Victor
McLean Stevenson
McMahon, Ed
McNamara, Robert, Secy. Def.
McNichol, Kristy
McPherson, Aimee Semple
McQueen, Steve
McRae, Carmen
McRaney, Gerald
McWethy, John F.
MD Magazine
Mead™ stationery
Mead, Lake
Mead, Margaret
Meade, George, Gen.
Meadows, Audrey
Meadows, Jayne
Meany, George
Mecca, Saudi Arabia
Mecham, Evan, Gov. (impeached)
Mechanix Illustrated

Medal of Honor
Medea
Medellin cartel
Medellin, Columbia
Medfly (Mediterranean fruit fly)
Medford, MA, OR
Medgar Evers
Medicaid health insurance
MediCal health insurance
Medicare health insurance
Medici Chapel
Medici family (Italy)
Medici, Catherine dé
Medici, Lorenzo dé, also Lorenzo, the
  Magnificent
Medicine Hat, Alberta, Can.
Medina, Saudi Arabia
Medipren™
Medi-Quik™
Mediterranean fruit fly (Medfly)
Mediterranean Sea
Medusa (myth)
Medvedev, Vadim
Meeker, Ralph
Meese, Edwin, III, Atty. Gen.
Meg Foster
Meg Ryan
Meg Tilly
Mehta, Zubin
Mein Kampf
Meineke™ mufflers
Meir, Golda, P.M.
Meissen, E. Ger.
Meissen™ porcelain
Meister Bräu™ beer
Meistersinger, or meistersinger
Mekong Delta, Vietnam
Mekong River
Mel Allen
Mel Blanc
Mel Brooks
Mel Ferrer
Mel Gibson
Mel Tillis
Mel Torme
Melanesia
Melanesian
Melanie Griffith

Melanie Mayron
Melba Moore
Melba toast
Melba, Dame Nellie (Melba toast)
Melbourne, Australia
Melcher, Terry
Melchior (1 of Magi)
Melchior, Lauritz
Melina Mercouri
Melissa Gilbert
Melissa Manchester
Melitta™ coffeemaker
Mellencamp, John Cougar
Mello Yello™ cola
Mellon, Andrew W.
Melrose Avenue (in L.A.)
Melville, Herman
Melvin Belli, Atty.
Memorex™
Memorial Day (formerly Decoration
  Day)
Memphis (ancient Egypt)
Memphis, TN
Menachem Begin, P.M.
Menander (Gr. dramatist)
Mencius (Chinese philosopher)
Mencken, H. L.
Mendel, Gregor Johann
Mendelism, or Mendelianism, or
  Mendel's laws
Mendelssohn, Felix
Mendes, Sergio
Menelaus, King (Gr. myth)
Menem, Carlos Saul, Pres.
Mengele, Dr. Joseph
Menjou, Adolphe
Menlo Park, CA
Mennen Speed Stick™
Menninger Clinic
Menninger, Dr. Karl A.
Menninger, Dr. William Claire
Mennonite Church
Mennonites
Menotti, Gian Carlo, or Gian-Carlo
Mensa (I.Q. group)
Mensa constellation
Mente Alban Mezcal™
Mentholatum™ rub

Menuhin, Yehudi
Meow Mix™ cat food
Mephistopheles
Mercator map projection
Mercator, Gerardus, or Gerhard
  Kremer
Merced River
Mercedes McCambridge
Mercedes Ruehl
Mercedes-Benz™
Mercouri, Melina
Mercury (messenger of gods)
Mercury (planet)
Mercury Space Project
Mercury-Atlas
Mercury-Redstone
Meredith Baxter-Birney
Meredith, Burgess
Mérida, Mex.
Meridian Naval Air Station, MS
Meriwether Lewis
Merkel, Una
Merksamer Jewelers
Merkur™
Merle Haggard
Merle Norman™ cosmetics
Merle Oberon
Merle Travis
Merlin (Arthurian)
Merlin Olsen
Merman, Ethel
Merovingian art/architecture
Merriam-Webster Dictionary
Merrick, David
Merrie Olde England
Merrill Lynch & Co.
Merrill, Dina
Merrimack (*Monitor* &)
Mersey River
Merseyside Co., Eng.
Merv Griffin
Mervyn Leroy, or LeRoy
Mervyn's department store
Meryl Streep
Mesa Verde ruins & Nat. Park
Mesa, AZ
Mesdames
Mesmer, Franz

Mesolithic period, or Middle Stone
  Age
Mesopotamia (ancient region, Asia)
Mesozoic era
Mesquite, TX
Messalina, Empress Valeria
Messenia region, Greece
Messerschmitt plane
Messerschmitt, Willy
Messiah (Handel's)
Messiah, the
Messier catalog (astronomy)
Messieurs
Messina, Italy
Messina, Strait of
Mesta, Pearl
Metalious, Grace (*Peyton Place*)
Metamorphosis (Kafka)
Metamucil™ laxative
Metaxa™ brandy
Methedrine™
Metheny, Pat
Methodism (doctrines)
Methodist
Methuselah
Metonic cycle (astronomy)
Metrazol™
Metrocolor™
Metropolitan Home
Metropolitan Museum of Art (NYC)
Metropolitan Opera Co.
Metternich, Age of
Metternich, Clemens Wenzel
Meursault wine
Meuse river, or Maas
Mexene™ seasoning
Mexicali, Mex.
Mexican hairless, dog
Mexican stand-off
Mexican War
Mexicana Airlines
Mexico
Mexico City, Mex.
Mexico, Gulf of
MexSp (abbrev. Mexican-Spanish)
Meyer Schapiro
Meyerbeer, Giacomo
Mg (chem. sym. magnesium)

MGM Grand Hotel (Las Vegas)
MGM/UA Communications Co.
MGM/UA films
Mia Farrow
Miami, FL
Miami Beach, FL
Miami Dolphins
Miami Herald
Miami Indians
Miami Sound Machine
Miata™ car
Micatin™ ointment
Michael Balfe
Michael Caine
Michael Chang
Michael Cimino
Michael Conrad
Michael Crichton
Michael Douglas
Michael Dukakis, Gov.
Michael Eisner
Michael Faraday
Michael J. Fox
Michael 'Mick' Jagger
Michael Jordan
Michael Landon
Michael Milken
Michael O'Keefe
Michael Redgrave, Sir
Michael Sarrazin
Michael Spinks
Michael Tippett, Sir
Michael Tucker
Michael Wigglesworth
Michael, George
Michaelmas
Michaels, Al
Michelangelo (Michelangelo
   Buonarroti)
Michelangelo da Caravaggio
Michele Greene
Michele Lee
Michelin Guide
Michelin™ tire
Michelle Pfeiffer
Michelob™ beer
Michelozzo Michelozzi
Michelson, Albert

Michener, James A.
Michigan (MI)
Michigan, Lake
Mick Jagger
Mickey Cohen
Mickey Mantle
Mickey Mouse
Mickey Rooney
Mickey Spillane
Micmac Indians
Micronesia, Federated States of
Micronta Road Patrol™
Microsoft™
Midas™ Muffler Shop
Midas, King
Middle Ages
Middle America
Middle American Indians
Middle Atlantic States (US)
Middle East (Asia/Africa)
Middle English
Middle French
Middle Greek
Middle High German
Middle Irish
Middle Kingdom (China)
Middle Latin
Middle Low German
Middle Stone Age, or Mesolithic
Middlesex, Eng.
Midget Man missile
Midget Pony
Midi-Pyrénées, Fr.
Midianites (Biblical)
Midler, Bette
Midol™
Midori™ liqueur
Midori Susuki
Midsummer Day (June 24)
Midsummer-Night's Dream, A
Midway Islands
Midwest, or Middle West (US)
Miës van der Rohe (Ludwig)
Mifune Toshiro
MIG jet fighter, or MiG
Miguel de Cervantes Saavedra
Mikado, The
Mike Ditka

Mike Farrell
Mike Hammer
Mike Nesbitt
Mike Teevee
Mike Tyson
Mike Wallace
Mikhail Bakunin
Mikhail Baryshnikov
Mikhail Ivanovitch Glinka
Mikhail S. Gorbachev, Pres.
Mikhail Mordkin
Mikhail Aleksandrovich Sholokhov
Miklos Nemeth, P.M.
Miklos Rozsa
Milan, Italy
Milan, Victor
Milanov, Zinka
Mildred Natwick
Mildred Pierce
Milenkovic, Stefan
Miles Davis
Miles Standish, or Myles
Milford, CT
Milhaud, Darius
Mili Alekseyevich Balakirev
Milk Duds™ candy
Milk, Harvey
Milk-Bone™ dog biscuits
Milken, Michael
Milky Way™ candy
Milky Way galaxy
Mill, John Stuart
Milland, Ray
Millar, Kenneth (aka Ross Macdonald)
Millard Fillmore, Pres./V.P.
Millay, Edna St. Vincent
Miller™ beer
Miller, Arthur
Miller, Daisy
Miller, Glenn
Miller, Henry
Miller, Mitch
Miller's Outpost store
Millerand, Alexandre, Pres.
Millet, Jean François
Millikan, Robert
Millöcker, Karl
Mills Brothers, The

Mills, Hayley
Milne, A. A. (*Winnie-the -Pooh*)
Milos Forman
Milos, Greece, or Milo
Milquetoast, Casper
Milquetoast, or milquetoast (a timid person)
Milsap, Ronnie
Milton Berle ('Uncle Miltie')
Milton Caniff
Milton Hershey
Milton Obote, Pres.
Milton Byron Babbit
Milton, John
Milton-Bradley™
Milwaukee Brewers
Milwaukee Journal
Milwaukee Sentinel
Milwaukee, WI
Milwaukee's Best ™
Mimas (Saturn moon)
Mimetics™ software
Mimiya™ photo. equip.
Minamata disease (mercury poisoning)
Mindanao, Philippines
Mineo, Sal
Minerva (Rom. myth)
Ming dynasty
Mingus, Charlie
Minimal Art
Mink Difference™ Hair Spray
Minneapolis City Pages
Minneapolis, MN
Minneapolis Star and Tribune
Minnehaha (Indian maiden)
Minnelli, Liza
Minnelli, Vincente
Minnesota (MN)
Minnesota Twins
Minnesota Vikings
Minnie Maddern Fiske, or Mrs. Fiske
Minnie Pearl
Minoan civilization
Minolta™ electronics
Minor Prophets
Minorca Island, or Menorca
Minorities and Women in Business
Minos, King of Crete

Minot Air Force Base, ND
Minotaur, the (Gr. myth)
Minseito (Jap. politics)
Minsk, USSR
Minuit, Peter
Minute Maid™ juice
Minute™ Rice
Miocene epoch
Mirabeau, Honoré Gabriel
Mirabella magazine
Miracle of Fatima
Miracle Whip™
MiraFlow™
Miramax Films
Miranda (Uranus moon)
Miranda vs. Arizona
Miranda warnings (Miranda warnings)
Miranda, Carmen
Miró, Joan
Mirro™ cookware
Mischa Elman
Mishima Yukio
Miskolc, Hungary
Miss America
Miss Breck™ hairspray
Miss Clairol™ haircoloring
Miss Marple of St. Mary Mead
Miss Piggy
Mission Viejo, CA
Missionary Ridge, TN
Mississauga, Ont., Can.
Mississippi (MS)
Mississippi River
Missoula, MT
Missouri (MO)
Missouri Compromise
Missouri Fox Trotter
Missouri River
Mister Roger's Neighborhood
Mister Salty™ pretzels
Misty Harbour™ rainwear
Mita™ copier
Mitch Miller
Mitchell, Joni
Mitchell, Margaret
Mitchelson, Marvin, Atty.
Mitchum™ Anti-Perspirant
Mitchum, Robert

Mitsotakis, Constantine
Mitsubishi Chemical Industries Ltd.
Mitsubishi Electric Corp.
Mitsubishi™ electronics
Mitsubishi Heavy Industries Ltd.
Mitsukoshi restaurant (NYC)
Mittermaier, Rosi
Mitterrand, François, Pres.
Mitty, Walter
Mitzi Gaynor
Mix, Tom
Mixtec Indians
MJB™ coffee
Mn (chem. sym. manganese)
Mo (chem. sym. molybdenum)
Mo Ti
Moab (ancient nation)
Moabite stone
Moabites
Moammar, Muammar, or Muammar-
   al, Khadafy, Gadhafi, Gaddafi, or
   Qaddafi
Mobile, AL
Mobile™ gas
Mobile Press-Register
Möbius strip
Mobuto Sese Seko, Pres.
Moby Dick
Mocha Mix™
Model A Ford
Modern Electronics
Modern English
Modern Greek
Modern Hebrew
Modern Latin
Modest Moussorgsky, or Mussorgsky
Modesto, CA
Modesty Blaise
Modigliani, Amedeo
Modjeska, Helena
Modoc Indians
Moe Howard (1 of 3 Stooges)
Moët & Chandon champagne
Moffet Field Naval Air Station, CA
Mogadisho, Somali
Mogen David™ kosher foods
Mogul, or Mughal (Muslim empire)
Mogul art/architecture

Mohammad Zia-ul-Haq, or 'Pres. Zia'
Mohawk hair style
Mohawk Indians
Mohawk River
Mohegan Indians
Mohs' scale
Moi, Daniel arap, Pres.
Moira Shearer
Moise Tshombe, Pres.
Moiseyev Dance Company
Mojave Desert, or Mohave
Moldavia, or Moldavian Soviet
    Socialist Republic
Molière, Jean Baptiʌe
Molina, Rafael Trujillo, Pres.
Moll Flanders
Mollweide projection
Molly Maguires, or Mollies
Molly McButter™
Molly Pitcher
Molly Ringwald
Molokai, Hawaii
Molotov cocktail
Molotov, Vyacheslav M., Vice
    Premier
Moluccas, or Spice Islands
Mom & Dads, The
Mombasa, Kenya
MOMA, or Museum of Modern Art
    (NYC)
Mona Lisa, or *La Gioconda* (Da Vinci)
Mona Lisa smile
Monaco principality
Mond, Greg Le
Mondale, Walter F., V.P.
Mondi (designer)
Mondrian, Piet
Monet™ jewelry
Monet, Claude
Moneysworth
Mongolia region, Asia
Mongolian (native of Mongolia)
Mongoloid, or Mongolian idiot (now
    Down's syndrome)
Monica de Greiff, Jus. Minister
Monitor & Merrimac
Monk, Thelonious
Monkees, The

Monmouth Beach, NJ
Monmouth, battle of
Mono Lake
Monongahela Nat. Forest
Monopoly™
Monotheletism, or Monothelitism
Monotype™
Monroe Doctrine
Monroe™ shocks
Monroe, James, Pres.
Monroe, Marilyn (b. Norma Jean
    Baker)
Monsanto Acrilan™ carpet
Monsanto Co.
Monseigneur (French title)
Monsieur (French for Mr.)
Monsignor (Catholic title)
Mont Blanc (Alps)
Mont-Royal, Québec, Can.
Montagnais Indians
Montagu, Lady Mary
Montalban, Ricardo
Montana (MT)
Montand, Yves
Montauk, NY
Monte Carlo method
Monte Carlo, Monaco
Monte Cristo sandwich
Montego Bay, Jamaica
Montenegro
Monterey Bay, CA
Monterey Jack cheese
Monterey, CA
Monterrey, Mex.
Montessori method
Montessori, Maria
Monteverdi, Claudio
Montevideo, Uraguay
Montez, Lola
Montezuma, Emperor, or Moctezuma
Montezuma's revenge
Montgolfier brothers
Montgomery Clift
Montgomery Ward
Montgomery, AL
Montgomery, Robert
Montgomery, Ruth
Montgomery 'Scotty' Scott (Star Trek)

Monticello (Jefferson's home)
Montmartre area, Paris
Montparnasse area, Paris
Montpelier, VT
Montrachet cheese
Montrachet wine
Montreal Expos
Montreal Gazette
Montreal La Presse
Montréal, Quebec, Can.
Montréal-Nord, Québec, Can.
Montreux International Jazz Festival
Montserrat, British colony
Monty Hall
Monty Python
Monty Python's Flying Circus
Monty Woolley
Moody Air Force Base, GA
Moody, Helen Wills
Moody, Dr. Raymond
Moog synthesizer
Moon Mulligan
Moon, Rev. Sun Myung
Moonie (follower of Rev. Moon)
Moor, the (*Othello*)
Moore, Clayton (played Lone Ranger)
Moore, Demi
Moore, Dudley
Moore, Henry
Moore, Mary Tyler
Moore, Melba
Moore, Roger
Moore, Thomas (Ir. poet)
Moore, Victor
Moorehead, Agnes
Moors (nomadic people)
Moose Jaw, Saskatchewan, Can.
Moosehead Lake
Mootsies Tootsies™
Mop & Glo™
Moral Majority
Moran, 'Bugs'
Moranis, Rick
Moravia region, Czech.
Moravian Church
Mordecai (Biblical)
Mordkin, Mikhail
More, Sir Thomas

Moreau, Jeanne
Morehouse™ mustard
Moreno, Rita
Morey Amsterdam
Morey Boogie™ Boogieboard
Morgan Freeman
Morgan horse
Morgan, Sir Henry
Morgan, J. Pierpont
Morgan, John Hunt, Gen.
Morgenthau, Henry Jr., Secy. Treas.
Moriarty, Professor
Morisot, Berthe
Morita, Pat
Moriyama, Mayumi, Cabinet Secy.
Morley Safer
Morley, Robert
Mormon Tabernacle Choir
Mormon, Book of
Mormons, or Latter Day Saints
Mornay sauce
Morocco
Moroni (Mormon angel)
Morpheus (Gr. myth)
Morris K. Udall, Rep.
Morris, William, Agency
Morro Bay, CA
Morse code
Morse, Carlton E.
Morse, Samuel
Mort Sahl
Mort Zuckerman
Morte Darthur
Morton Dean
Morton Downey
Morton Downey, Jr.
Morton™ salt
Morton, Gary
Morton, Jelly Roll
Morton, Levi P., V.P.
Mosaic law
Moscow Art Theater
Moscow Moffia (writers' group)
Moscow, ID
Moscow, USSR
Moses (Bib. leader)
Moses Lake, WA
Moses, Edwin

Moses, Grandma (Anna Mary)
Moshe Dayan, Def. Min.
Moslem, or Muslim
Mosquito Coast
Moss Hart
Mössbauer effect
Mostel, Zero
Moten, Bennie
Mother Cabrini, also St. Frances
  Cabrini
Mother Earth
Mother Earth News
Mother Goose Tales
Mother Goose and Grimm
Mother Holle
Mother Hubbard
Mother Jones
Mother Lode (Calif. gold rush)
Mother Nature
Mother Niddity Nod
Mother of God
Mother Seton, or St. Elizabeth Ann
  Seton
Mother Teresa
Mother Twitchett
Mother Widdle Waddle
Mother's Day
Mothers Today
Motherwell and Wishaw, Scot.
Motherwell, Robert
Mötley Crüe
Motor Trend
Motorland
Motorola Inc.
Motown (Detroit)
Motown Records
Motrin™ pain reliever
Mott, Lucretia Coffin
Mott's™ foods
Motta, Jake La
Moulin Rouge (in Paris)
Moulin Rouge (movie)
Moulins, France
Moulson Companies Ltd., The
Mound Builders Indians
Mounds™ candy
Mount of Olives, or Olivet
Mount Vernon (Washington's home)

Mountain Dew™ drink
Mountain Home Air Force Base, ID
Mountain Standard Time
Mountain States
Mountbattan, Philip, Duke of
  Edinburgh
Mountie, or Mounty (Royal Canadian
  Mounted Police)
Mountie Dudley Do-Right
Mouskouri, Nana
Moussorgsky, Modest, or
  Mussorgsky
Movie Tone news
Mow Sang™ egg rolls
Moxie magazine
Moyers, Bill
Moynihan, Daniel Patrick, Sen.
Mozambique
Mozart, Wolfgang Amadeus
Mr. Blackwell
Mr. Bubble™ bubble bath
Mr. Charlie ('Black' slang)
Mr. Clean (slang)
Mr. Clean™ cleaner
Mr. Coffee™
Mr. Fixit (slang)
Mr. Goodbar™ candy
Mr. Goodwrench™
Mr. Magoo
Mr. Peppe French Cuisine (restaurant -
  Dallas)
Mr. Spock (*Star Trek*)
Mr. Store-It™
Mr. T
Mr. Tumnus
Mrs. America
Mrs. Butterworth's™
Mrs. Dash™
Mrs. Malaprop ('malapropism')
Mrs. Paul's™ frozen fish
Mrs. Tiggy-Winkle
Mrs. Tittlemouse
Ms. magazine
Mt. Ararat
Mt. Baker-Snoqualmie Nat. Forest
Mt. Blackburn
Mt. Elbrus
Mt. Etna

Mt. Everest
Mt. Fairweather
Mt. Fuji, or Fujiyama
Mt. Holyoke College (MA)
Mt. Hopkins Observatory (AZ)
Mt. Kilimanjaro
Mt. Kosciusko
Mt. McKinley Nat. Park
Mt. Palomar Observatory
Mt. Popocatepetl
Mt. Rainier Nat. Pk. (WA)
Mt. Rushmore Nat. Memorial (SD)
Mt. Saint Helens
Mt. Shasta
Mt. Sinai
Mt. Suribachi (marine flag raising)
Mt. Vesuvius
Mt. Whitney
Mt. Zion
Muammar, Muammar-al, or Moam-
    mar, Khadafy, Gadhafi, Gaddafi,
    or Qaddafi
Mubarak, Hosni, Pres.
Much Ado About Nothing
Mudd Mask™
Mudd, Roger
Muenster cheese
Muesli™ cereal
Müeslix™ cereal
Muggs, Fred J. (TV chimp)
Mughal, or Mogul (Muslim empire)
Muhammad (Prophet of Islam)
Muhammad Ali (Cassius Clay, Jr.)
Muhammad Ali (pasha of Egypt)
Muhammad Mussadegh
Muir, John
Muir Woods Nat. Monument
Muldoon, Robert, P.M.
Mulhare, Edward
Mulholland Drive (in L.A.)
Mulligan, Moon
Mulligan, Richard
Mulroney, Brian, P.M.
Multigraph™
Multilith™
Munch, Edvard
Munchkin of OZ
Munchos™ chips

Muncie, IN
Muni, Paul
Munda languages
Munich Pact, or Agreement
Munich, W. Ger., or München
Munro, Alice
Munsel, Patrice
Munson, Ona
Muppets, the
Murat, Joachim, king of Naples
Murata™
Murdoch, Rupert
Muriel Hemingway
Muriel Rukeyser
Murine™ eye drops
Murjani™ clothes
Murnau, F.W.
Murphy bed
Murphy Man
Murphy, Eddie
Murphy's Law
Murray™ bike
Murray Perahia
Murray, Arthur
Murray, Bill
Murray, Philip
Murrow, Edward R.
Musburger, Brent
Muscadet wine
Muscle Beach (in L.A.)
Muscovite
Muscovy Co., or Russia Company
Muse (source of inspiration)
Muses (myth. nine goddesses)
Museum of Fine Art (Boston)
Museum of Modern Art, or MOMA
    (NYC)
Musial, Stan 'the Man'
Muskegon, MI
Muskie, Edmund, Sen.
Muskogee, OK
Muskol™
Muslim, or Moslem
Muslim League
Mussadegh, Muhammad
Mussolini, Benito, also *El Duce*
Mussorgsky, Modest, or Mous-
    sorgsky

Mustardseed (a fairy)
Muti, Riccardo
Mutt & Jeff
Mutual Radio Network
Muybridge, Eadweard
Muzak™
MX missile (aka 'Peacemaker')
My Fair Lady
My Lai massacre, or Mi Ly
My-Te-Fine™ foods
Myadec™ Multivitamins
Mycenae, Greece
Mycenaean civilization
Myerson, Bess
Mykonos Isl., Greece, or Mikonos Isl.
Mylanta™ Antacid
Mylanta-II™ Antacid
Myles Standish, or Miles
Myrna Loy
Myrtle Beach, SC
Myrtle Beach Air Force Base, SC
Mystic, CT
Mystic Mint™ cookies
Mystic Pizza

N (chem. sym. nitrogen)
N'ICE™
Na (chem. sym. sodium)
Nabis art
Nabisco Brands, Inc.
Nabisco™ Ritz crackers
Nabisco™ Shredded Wheat
Nabisco™ Triscuit crackers
Nabors, Jim
Nacogdoches, TX
Nader, Ralph
Nadia Boulanger

Nadia Comaneci
Nagasaki, Japan
Nagel, Conrad
Nagy, Ivan
Nair™ hair remover
Nairobi, Kenya
Naish, J. Carrol
Nakasone, Yasuhiro, P.M.
Nalley™ foods
Namath, Joseph 'Joe' William
Namibia, or South West Africa
Nana Mouskouri
Nanaimo, B.C., Can.
Nancy Drew mysteries
Nancy Dussault
Nancy Etticoat
Nancy Lieberman
Nancy Lopez
Nancy Marchand
Nancy Reagan
Nancy, France
Nanette Fabray
Nanjing, China (was Nanking)
Nansen bottle (oceanographic
    instrument)
Nantucket, MA
Naomi Judd
Napa, CA
Naples, FL
Naples, Italy, or Napoli
Napoleon (pastry)
Napoleon Bonaparte
Napoleon III, Louis
Napoleonic Code
Napoleonic Wars
Narcissus (Gr. myth)
Narnia
Narragansett Bay
Narragansett Indians
Nash, Beau
Nash, Ogden
Nashe, Thomas, or Nash
Nashville Network
Nashville Tennessean
Nashville, TN
Naskapi Indians
Nassau, Bahamas
Nassau, W. Ger.

Nasser, Gamal Abdal, Pres.
Nast, Thomas
Nat 'King' Cole
Nat Turner
Natalia Makarova
Natalie Cole
Natasha Fataly, or Badenov
Natasha Zvereva
Natchez Trace
Natchez, MS
Natchitoches settlement
Nathan Bailey
Nathan Hale
Nathan, George Jean
Nathaniel Bacon
Nathaniel Currier
Nathaniel Hawthorne
Natick Research and Development
  Center (MA)
Nation, Carrie, or Carry
National Academy of Sciences
National Aeronautics & Space Adm.,
  or NASA
National Archives
National Association for the
  Advancement of Colored People,
  or NAACP
National Audubon Society
National Ballet of Canada
National Bureau of Standards
National Business Woman
National Christian Network
National City Bank of NY
National Enquirer
National Gallery of Art (DC)
National Gallery (Eng.)
National Geographic magazine
National Geographic Society
National Guard
National Lampoon
National League
National Organization for Women,
  or NOW
National Public Radio
National Republican party
National Review
National Security Council
National Socialism, or Nazism

National Theatre of Great Britain
National Wildlife
Native American, or American Indian
Naturalizer™ shoes
Nature Made™ vitamins
Natwick, Mildred
Naugahyde™
Naughty Marietta
Naum Gabo
Nautilus™
Navajo Indians, or Navaho
Naval Construction Battalion Center,
  MS
Naval Jelly™
Naval Medical Command, Bethesda,
  MD
Naval Surface Weapons Center, VA
Navarre region, Spain
Navarro, Fats
Navigation Acts
Navistar International Corp.
Navratilova, Martina
Navy Cross
Nazarene, the (Jesus)
Nazarenes
Nazareth, Israel, or Nazerat
Nazarite, or Nazirite
Nazca, or Nasca (ancient) Indian
  culture
Nazi (member Nazi party)
Nazi party
Nazism, or National Socialism
Nb (chem. sym. niobium)
NBC Radio
NBC Talknet
NBC-TV
Nd (chem. sym. neodymium)
Ndjamena, Chad, or Fort-Lamy
Ne (chem. sym. neon)
Neanderthal man
Neapolitan (Naples citizen)
Neapolitan ice cream
NearEast™ rice mix
Nebraska (NE)
Nebuchadnezzar, King
Necchi™ sew. mach.
Necker, Jacques
Needles, CA

Neet™ hair remover
Nefertiti, Queen of Egypt
Neff, Hildegarde
Negev region of Israel, or Negeb
Negri, Pola
Negro (singular)
Negro Modelo™ beer
Negroes (plural)
Negroid
Nehru jacket
Nehru, Jawaharlal, P.M.
Nehru, Pandit, P.M.
Neidlinger, Buell
Neil A. Armstrong, astronaut
Neil Diamond
Neil Sedaka
Neil Simon
Neiman-Marcus store
Nell Gwyn, or Gwynn
Nellie Bly
Nellie Melba, Dame (Melba toast)
Nellis Air Force Base, NV
Nelly Sachs
Nelson Mandela
Nelson Riddle Orchestra
Nelson A. Rockefeller, V.P.
Nelson, Harriet
Nelson, Horatio, Adm.
Nelson, Judd
Nelson, Ozzie
Nelson, Willie
Nembutal™
Nemean lion (Hercules killed)
Nemesis
Nemeth, Miklos, P.M.
Neo-Dada school
Neolithic period, or New Stone Age
Neoplatonism
Neosporin™ antiseptic
Nepal
Neptune (planet)
Neptune (Rom. god)
Nereid (Neptune moon)
Nero Wolfe
Nero, Emperor of Rome
Nervi, Pier Luigi
Nesbitt, Cathleen
Nesbitt, Mike

Nescafé™ coffee
Ness, Eliott
Ness, Loch
Nesselrode mix
Nestea™ instant tea
Nestlé™ Quik
Nestlé™ Toll House cookies
Netherlands Antilles
Netherlands, Dutch, or Holland
Netzahualcóyotl, Mexico
Neuchâtel, Switz.
Neufchâtel cheese
Neutra, Richard
Neutrogena™ skincare
Nevada (NV)
Never-Never Land
Nevil Shute
Neville Chamberlain, P.M.
Neville Marriner
New Age
New Age Journal
New American Bible
New Amsterdam
New Balance™ shoes
New Bedford, MA
New Britain Island
New Brunswick, Can.
New Brunswick, NJ
New Caledonia
New Castle, PA
New Cumberland Army Depot, PA
New Deal (FDR's)
New Delhi, India
New England boiled dinner
New England clam chowder
New England Confederation
New England Journal of Medicine
New England Patriots
New England Primer
New England region
New English Bible
New General Catalog (astronomy)
New Granada
New Guinea
New Hampshire (NH)
New Hampshire Sunday News
New Haven, CT
New Hebrides

New Jersey (NJ)
New Kowloon, Hong Kong
New London, CT
New Mexico (NM)
New Orleans, LA
New Orleans Saints
New Providence Isl., Bahamas
New Republic magazine
New Rochelle, NY
New Scotland Yard, or Scotland Yard
New South Wales, Austl.
New Stone Age, or Neolithic period
New Testament
New Thought
New Westminster, B.C., Can.
New Woman
New Year's Day
New Year's Eve
New York (NY)
New York City (NYC)
New York City Ballet
New York Daily News
New York Giants
New York Jets
New York Mets
New York Post
New York Public Library
New York Review of Books
New York Shakespeare Festival
New York steak
New York Stock Exchange
New York Times
New York Times Book Review
New York Yankees
New Yorker
New Zealand
Newark Air Force Station, OH
Newark Star Ledger
Newark, NJ
Newburg, lobster
Newcastle disease
Newcastle, Australia
Newcastle, Eng.
Newell Convers Wyeth
Newfoundland Standard Time
Newfoundland, Can.
Newfoundland dog
Newgate prison (old Lon.)

Newhart, Bob
Newhouse, Donald E.
Newhouse, Samuel I., Jr.
Newman, Edwin
Newman, Paul
Newmar, Julie
Newmarket district, Lon.
Newport Beach, CA
Newport Jazz Festival, RI
Newport News, VA
Newport, RI
Newsday magazine
Newsweek magazine
Newton, Huey P.
Newton, MA
Newton, Sir Isaac
Newton-John, Olivia
Newton's laws of motion, or
    Newtonian law
Newtownabbey, N. Ireland
NeXt Inc.
Nexus™ hair care
Nez Perce Indians
Nezperce Nat. Forest
Ngo Dinh Diem, Pres.
Nguyen Van Thieu, Pres.
Nguyen, Dustin
Nguyen, Ky
Ni (chem. sym. nickel)
Niagara Falls, NY
Niagara Falls, Ont., Can.
Niagara River
Niamey, Niger
Niaux cave paintings
Nicaea
Nicaea, Councils of
Nicaragua
Niccolo Paganini
Niccolò Machiavelli
Nice, France
Nice'n Easy™ haircare
Nicene Council (Christian)
Nicene Creed (Christian)
Nicholas Biddle
Nicholas Copernicus
Nicholas Nickleby
Nicholas, Saint, or Santa Claus, or
    Kriss Kringle

Nicholson, Jack
Nichrome™
Nick Carter
Nick Chopper, the tin woodman
  of Oz
Nick Nolte
Nickelodeon channel
Nicklaus, Jack
Nicks, Stevie
Nicolai Rimsky-Korsakov
Nicolai, Otto
Nicolas Cage
Nicolas Poussin
Nicollette Sheridan
Nicosia, Cypress
Niddity Nod, Mother
Niels Bohr
Nielsen Media Research
Nielsen ratings
Nielsen, Brigitte
Nielsen, Carl
Niemeyer, Oscar
Nietzsche, Friedrich Wilhelm
Nigel Bruce
Niger, Afr.
Niger river
Nigeria, Afr.
Night Ranger
Nightingale, Florence
Nightlife
Nijinsky, Vaslav
Nike (myth. goddess of victory)
Nike missile
Nike™ shoes
Nikita S. Krushchev
Nikkei Average, or Index
Nikki Sixx
Nikko, Jap.
Nikko Nat. Park, Jap.
Nikko™ stereo
Nikkor™ lens
Nikola Tesla
Nikolai A. Bulganin, Prem.
Nikolai I. Ryshkov, Prem.
Nikolay Sokoloff
Nikolayev, Andriyan, Cosmonaut
Nikon™ camera
Nikor™ camera equipment

Nile River (Egypt)
NIMH, Rats of
Nimitz, Chester W. Adm.
Nimoy, Leonard
Nimrod
Nimslo™ 3-D camera
Nina Blackwood
Nina Foch
Nina Ricci™ clothing
9 Lives™ cat food
Nineveh (capitol Assyrian empire)
Ninotchka
Nintendo™ games
Nipissing, Lake
Nipon, Albert
Nippon Electric Co. Ltd.
Nippon Steel Corp.
Niro, Robert De
Nisan (Jew. mo.)
Nisei (Jap. American)
Nissan™ Infiniti
Nissan™ Stanza
Nissen hut
Nissin™ Cup O' Noodles
Nitty Gritty Dirt Band, The
Niue Island, N.Z.
Nivea™ lotion
Niven, David
Nixon, Agnes
Nixon, Pat
Nixon, Richard Milhous, Pres.
  (resigned)
Nixon, Tricia
No (chem. sym. nobelium)
No nonsense™ pantyhose
No Problem™ clothes
No. 10 Downing St. (Lon.)
Noah Beery, Jr.
Noah Webster
Noah's ark
Nob Hill (S.F.)
Nobel Peace Prize
Nobel Prize for Chemistry
Nobel Prize for Literature
Nobel Prize for Medicine
Nobel Prize for Physics
Nobel Prizes (all)
Nobel, Alfred B. (funded prizes)

Noël Coward, Sir
Nofziger, Lyn
Nogales, Mexico
Noguchi, Isamu
Noh drama
Nolan Ryan
Nolde, Emil
Nolte, Nick
None Such™ mincemeat
Nonoxynol-9™ spermicide
Nonpartisan League
Noodle Roni™
noodles Romanoff
Nord-Pas-de-Calais, Fr.
Nordica™ ski boots/skis
NordicTrack™
Nordstrom store
Norelco™ appliances
Norell™ perfume/clothes
Norfolk County, Eng.
Norfolk Island pine
Norfolk Island, Austl.
Norfolk Jacket
Norfolk Naval Air Station, VA
Norfolk Naval Shipyard, VA
Norfolk terrier
Norfolk, VA
Norge™ appliances
Noriega, Manuel A., Gen.
Noritake™ china
Norm Van Brocklin
Norma Kamali™ clothes
Norma Quarles
Norma Talmadge
Normal, IL
Norman architecture
Norman Bel Geddes
Norman Conquest
Norman Cousins
Norman Fell
Norman Jewison
Norman Lear
Norman Mailer
Norman Vincent Peale, Rev.
Norman Rockwell
Norman, Merle
Normandy campaign
Normandy region, France

Normerel™ printer
Norris, Chuck
Norse, Old
Norseman, or Northman
North America
North Atlantic Drift
North Atlantic Treaty Organization,
    or NATO
North Carolina (NC)
North Cascades Nat. Pk. (WA)
North Dakota (ND)
North Dartmouth, MA
North Korea, or Democratic People's
    Republic of Korea
North Platte River
North Platte, NE
North Pole
North Sea
North Star, or Polaris, or Pole Star
North York Co., Eng.
North York, Ont., Can.
North, Oliver 'Ollie', Col.
Northampton Co., Eng.
Northampton, MA
Northeast Passage (Europe/Asia)
Northern Hemisphere
Northern Ireland
Northern Marianas, or Mariana Is.
Northern Rhodesia (now Zambia)
Northerner
Northumberland Co., Eng.
Northumbria (Anglo-Saxon kingdom)
Northwest Airlines
Northwest Passage (North Am.)
Northwest Territories (Can)
Northwest Territory (U.S.)
Norton Simon Museum
Norville, Deborah
Norvo, Red
Norwalk, CT
Norway
Norway maple
Norway pine
Norway spruce
Norwegian elkhound (dog)
Norwegian people
Norwegian Sea
Norwich terrier

Norwich, Eng.
NoSalt™
Noskote™ sunblock
Nostradamus
Nosy Parker (slang)
Notre Dame Cathedral, or
    Notre-Dame de Paris
Notre Dame University
Nottingham (Robin Hood's)
Nottingham Co., Eng.
Nottingham, Sheriff of
Nottinghamshire, Eng.
Nouakchott, Mauritania
Noumea, New Caledonia
Nouriche™ skincare
Nova Scotia
Novak, Kim
Novarro, Ramon
Novato, CA
Novocain™, or Novocaine
Novosibirsk, USSR
Noxzema™ skincare
Noyes, Alfred
Np (chem. sym. neptunium)
Nubia (Africa)
Nubian Desert
Nubian goat
Nucleus™ shoes
Nucoa™ Margarine
Nude Descending a Staircase
    (Duchamp)
Nuevo Leon, state, Mexico
Nunn Bush™ shoes
Ñuñoa, Chile
Nuprin™
Nuremberg Trials
Nuremberg, W. Ger.
Nureyev, Rudolf
Nut & Honey Cruncho O's™
Nutcracker Ballet
Nutcracker Suite
NutraSweet™
Nutri-Grain Nuggets™ cereal
Nutri/System™ Weight Loss
Nutter Butter™ cookies
NY Talk
Nyad, Diana
Nyasa, Lake, or Lake Malawi

Nylint™ toys
NyQuil™
Nytol™

O (chem. sym. oxygen)
O cedar Angler™ broom
O Sole Mio
O Tannenbaum
o. b.™ tampons
O. H. Platt, Sen.
O. Henry (pseud. Wm. Sydney Porter)
O. J. Simpson
Oahu, HI
Oak Lawn, IL
Oak Park, IL
Oak Ridge Boys, The
Oak Ridge, TN
Oakie, Jack
Oakland A's
Oakland Raiders
Oakland, CA
Oakley, Annie
Oates, Joyce Carol
Oatmeal Goodness™ bread
Oaxaca, Mexico
Oberon (Uranus moon)
Oberon, King of the Fairies
Oberon, Merle
Oberti™ olives
Obidos, Portugal
Oboler, Arch
Obote, Milton, Pres.
Ocasek, Ric
O'Casey, Sean
Occident (Europe + W. Hemisphere
    countries)
Occidental Petroleum Corp.

Occupational Safety and Health
   Adm., or OSHA
Ocean Spray™ juices
Ocean, Billy
Oceania, or Oceanica
Oceanic art
O'Cello™ sponge
Oconee Nat. Forest
O'Connor, Carroll
O'Connor, Donald
O'Connor, Justice Sandra Day
O'Connor, Sinéad
October Revolution (Rus.)
Ocu Clear™ eye drops
Odessa, TX
Odessa, USSR
Odets, Clifford
Odilon Redon
Odin (Norse god)
Odio, Rodrigo Carazo, Pres.
Odor-Eaters™
Odysseus (hero of Odyssey)
Odyssey, The
Oedipus at Colonus
Oedipus complex
Oedipus Rex
Oersted, Hans
off-Broadway
off-off Broadway
Offenbach, Jacques
Offenbach, W. Ger.
OffEzy™
Ogden Nash
Ogden, UT
Ogilvie™ hair prod.
Ogilvy, David
Oglethorpe, James E., Gen.
O'Grady's™ potato chips
Oh Boy!™ pizza
Oh! Calcutta!
O'Hair, Madalyn Murray
O'Hara, Maureen
O'Hara, Scarlett
O'Hare International Airport
O'Herlihy, Dan
Ohio (OH)
Ohio River
Ohira Masayoshi, P.M.

Ohm, Georg
Ohm's law
Oil of Olay™
Oingo Boingo
Ojai, CA
Ojibwa Indians, or Chippewa
Okeechobee, FL
Okeechobee, Lake
O'Keefe, Claudia
O'Keefe, Dennis
O'Keefe, Michael
O'Keefe, Walter
O'Keeffe, Georgia
Okefenokee Swamp
Okhotsk, Sea of
Okidata™
Okie (slang)
Okinawa
Oklahoma (OK)
Oklahoma City, OK
Oklahoman
Oktoberfest
Olaus Roemer, or Ole
Old Bailey court
Old Body (the Devil)
Old Boy (Br. slang)
Old Dominion (Virginia state)
Old El Paso™ foods
Old English sheepdog
Old Faithful geyser
Old Glory
Old Harry (the Devil)
Old Ironsides
Old Man River (Mississipi R.)
Old Mother Shuttle
Old Nick (the Devil)
Old One (the Devil)
Old Rinkrank (the Devil)
Old Scratch (the Devil)
Old Spice™ men's cologne
Old Stone Age, or Paleolithic period
Old Testament
Old Vic theatre, or Royal Victoria
   Hall
Old World
Old-House Journal
Oldfield, Barney
Oldsmobile™ Cutlass Supreme

Oldsmobile™ 'Olds' Rocket 88
Olduvai Gorge (Tanganyika)
Oleg Cassini
Olestra (fat substitute)
Olga™ clothing
Olga Korbut
Olga Petrova
Oligocene epoch
Olive Oyl
Olive Schreiner (aka Ralph Iron)
Oliver Cromwell
Oliver Goldsmith
Oliver Hardy
Oliver Wendell Holmes (author/ physician)
Oliver Wendell Holmes, Jr., Justice
Oliver 'Ollie' North, Col.
Oliver Twist
Olives, Mount of, or Mt. Olivet
Olivia De Havilland
Olivia Hussey
Olivia Newton-John
Olivier, Sir Laurence
Olly Took
Olmsted Act
Olsen, Merlin
Olvera Street (in L.A.)
Olympia Dukakis
Olympia (Gr. center worship)
Olympia, WA
Olympiad (celebration of games)
Olympian (participant in games)
Olympian (Gr. god)
Olympic games
Olympic Mts., WA
Olympic Nat. Pk.
Olympic Penisula, WA
Olympus™ camera
Olympus, Mt.
Omaha Indians
Omaha World Herald
Omaha, NE
O'Malley, Walter
Oman (Sultanate)
Omar Bradley, Gen.
Omar Torrijos Herrera
Omar Khayyam, Rubaiyat of
Omar Sharif

Omarr, Sydney
Omega™ watch
Omni
Omnibus
Omnifax ™ fax
Omnipotent (God)
Omniscient (God)
On Cable Magazine
Ona Munson
Onassis, Aristotle Socrates
Onassis, Jacqueline Bouvier Kennedy
Onassis, Christina
Ondine
O'Neal, Ryan
O'Neal, Tatum
Oneida Indians
Oneida Lake
Oneida™ silverware
O'Neill, Eugene
O'Neill, Jennifer
O'Neill, Thomas 'Tip', Speaker of House
Oni (the Devil)
Onkyo™ stereo
Online Access Guide
Ono, Yoko
Onondaga Indians
Onondaga Lake
Ontario, CA
Ontario, Lake
Ontario, prov., Can.
Oort, Jan H.
Op Art, or op art
Open Door policy
Open Pitt™ BBQ sauce
Ophelia (Hamlet's)
Opium War
Oppenheimer, J. Robert
Oprah Winfrey
Opti-Clean™
Opti-Free™
Opti-Zyme™
Oracle of Delphi
Orajel™ pain reliever
Oral-B™ toothbrush
Orange Pekoe tea
Orangemen
Orbison, Roy

Order of Lenin
Order of the Bath
Order of the Garter
Ordovician period
Ore-Ida™ Tater Tots
Oregon (OR)
Oregon fir
Oregon grape
Oregon myrtle
Oregon Trail
Orel Hershiser
Oreo™ cookies
Orestes (Gr. myth)
Orff, Carl
Organic Gardening
Organization of Odd Fellows, or Odd
　Fellows
Organization of Petroleum Exporting
　Countries, or OPEC
Oriental rug, or carpet
Oriental shorthair cat
Orinoco River
Orion constellation
Orion Pictures
Orizaba, Mt.
Orkin™ Exterminating Co.
Orkney Is.
Orlando Sentinel
Orlando, FL
Orlando, Tony (and Dawn)
Orléans, Fr.
Orly, Fr.
Ormandy, Eugene
Ormazd (Zoroastrianism deity)
Ormuz, Strait of, or Hormuz
Ornette Coleman
Oroweat™ bread
Orpheus (Gr. myth)
Orr, Bobby
Orser, Brian
Orson Welles
Ortega™ Salsa/Mex. foods
Ortega, Daniel, Pres.
Ortho™ pest control
Orthodox Eastern Church
Orthodox Judaism
Orvieto, Italy
Orvieto wine

Orville Redenbacher™ popcorn
Orville Wright
Orwell, George (pseud. Eric A. Blair)
Ory, Kid
Os (chem. sym. osmium)
Osage Indians
Osage River
Osaka, Japan
Osbert Sitwell, Sir
Osborne, John
Osbourne, Ozzy
Os-Cal™ calcium tablets
Oscar (film award)
Oscar de la Renta
Oscar the Grouch
Oscar Hammerstein
Oscar Levant
Oscar Mayer™
Oscar Niemeyer
Oscar Peterson
Oscar Pettiford
Oscar Arias Sanchez, Pres.
Oscar Wilde
Osceola Nat. Forest
Osco Drug (now Sav-On Drug)
Osgood, Charles
Oshawa, Ont., Can.
Oshkosh, WI
OshKosh B'Gosh™ overalls
Osho (formerly Bhagwan Shree
　Rajneesh)
Osiris (Eg. god)
Oskar Kokoschka
Oskar Werner
Oslo Fjord
Oslo, Norway
Osmond, Donny
Osmond, Marie
Ostade, Adriaen van
Ostend Manifesto
Ostend, Belgium
Osterizer™ blender
Ostrava, Czech.
Ostrogoths, or East Goths
Oswald, Lee Harvey
Oswego River
Oswego tea
Othello, the Moor of Venice

Otis™ elevator
Otis Skinner
Otis, Elisha (elevator safety device
  inventor)
O'Toole, Peter
Ottawa Citizen
Ottawa Indians
Ottawa, Ontario, Can.
Ottawa River
Otto Dix
Otto Klemperer
Otto Kruger
Otto Nicolai
Otto Preminger
Otto von Bismarck, Prince ('Iron
  Chancellor')
Ottoman Empire
Ottorino Respighi
Ottumwa, IA
Oud, Pieter
Ouija™ Board
Oujda, Morocco
Our Father (prayer)
Our Lady (Virgin Mary)
Ouse River, or Great Ouse
Outdoor Life
Outer Hebrides
Outer Mongolia (now Mongolian
  People's Rep.)
Outremont, Québec, Can.
Ouzo apéritif
Oval Office (US Pres. office)
Overeaters Anonymous
Ovid (poet)
Owens, Jesse
Owens-Corning Fiberglas Corp.
Oxford Co., Eng.
Oxford, Eng.
Oxford University
Oxnard, CA
Oxy 10™ skincare
Oyl, Olive
oysters Rockefeller
Oyvind Fahlstrom
Oz, Land of
Oz, Queen of (Tippetarius)
Ozalid™
Ozark Mts., or the Ozarks

Ozarks, Lake of the
Ozawa, Seiji
Ozma of Oz
Ozymandias
Ozzie & Harriet Nelson
Ozzy Osbourne

P (chem. sym. phosphorus)
P. D. Q. Bach (pseud. Peter Schickele)
P. G. T. Beauregard, General
P. G. Wodehouse, Sir (Pelham
  Grenville)
P. L. Travers (*Mary Poppins*)
Paar, Jack
Pablo Casals
Pablo Picasso
Pace™ Picante Sauce
Pachelbel Canon, The
Pachelbel, Johann
Pacific Bell™ telephone
Pacific Missile Test Center, Point
  Mugu, CA
Pacific Northwest
Pacific Ocean
Pacific Rim
Pacific scandal
Pacific Standard Time
Pacific, War of the
Pacino, Al
Packard Bell™
Paddington
Paddy (slang, Irishman)
Paddy Chayefsky
Paderewski, Ignace Jan
Padua, Italy
Paducah, KY
Paganini, Niccolo

Page Boy™ maternity clothes
Page, Hot Lips
Page, Patti
Pagliacci
Pago Pago, American Samoa
Paige, Janis
Paige, Leroy 'Satchel'
Paine Webber stock broker
Paine, Thomas
Painted Desert, AZ
Paisley, Scot.
Paiute Indians
Pakistan (country)
Pakistani (native)
palace at Knossos, or Cnossus
Paladin
Palais Mendoub
Palance, Jack
Paleocene epoch
Paleolithic period, or Old Stone age
Paleozoic era
Palermo, Italy
Palestine
Palestine Liberation Organization, or
    PLO
Paley, William S.
Pall Mall™ cigarettes
Palladian style
Palladio, Andrea
Pallas Athena (asteroid)
Palm Beach, FL
Palm Springs, CA
Palm Sunday
Palma, Brian De
Palmdale, CA
Palmer House (Chicago)
Palmer, AK
Palmer, Arnold
Palmer, John
Palmer, Lilli
Palmolive™ soap
Palmyra (ancient city)
Palmyra, NY
Palo Alto, CA
Palo Mayombe
Palomar Observatory (CA)
Palomar, Mt.
Palomino horse

Palos Verdes Estates, CA
Palwick, Susan
Pam™ Cooking Spray
Pam Dawber
Pam Shriver
Pampers™ diapers
Pamprin™ pain reliever
Pan (mythical god)
Pan, Peter
Pan Am™ airline
Pan-American Union
Panadol™ pain reliever
Panama Canal (waterway)
Panama Canal Zone (area)
Panama City, FL
Panama hat
Panama (country)
Panama, Panama (city, country)
Panasonic™
Panavision™
Pancaldi™ shoes
Pancho Gonzalez
Pancho Villa
Pandemonium (capital of Hell)
Pandit Nehru, P.M.
Pandit, Korla
Pandora (Gr. myth)
Pandora's box
Pangloss, Dr.
Panhellenism
Pankhurst, Emmeline
Panmunjom, Korea
Pansa, House of (Pompeii)
Pantages Theater (L.A.)
Pantaloon (character)
Pantene™ haircare
Pantheon (Rome)
Panza, Sancho
Panzer Division
Paolo Soleri (Arcosanti)
Paolo Uccello
Pap test
Papadopoulos, George, Prem.
Papago Indians
Papal States
Papandreou, Andreas, P.M.
Papandreou, George, P.M.
Papua New Guinea

Papuan
Paracel Islands
Parade
Paradigm™ speakers
Paradise Regained
Paradise, or Heaven
Paraguay
Paramaribo, Suriname
Paramount Communications
Paramount™ Pictures
Parcheesi™
Parents Magazine
Paris, or Alexander (myth.)
Paris, France
Paris green
Paris Opéra
Paris Pacts (1954)
Paris Peace Conference (1919)
Paris Review
Paris, Treaty of (1763)
Paris, TX
Paris, University of, or Sorbonne
Parisian
Park Avenue
Park Chung Hee, Pres.
Parkay™ Margarine
Parke-Bernet Gallery
Parker Brothers™ games
Parker House Hotel, Boston
Parker House roll
Parker Stevenson
Parker, Charlie 'Bird'
Parker, Dorothy
Parkinson's disease, or Parkinsonism
Parkinson's Law (economics)
Parliament (Gr. Britain)
Parma, OH
Parmesan cheese
Parnassus, Mt.
Parrish, Maxfield
Parry, Sir William Edward
Parsee, or Parsi, Parsees or Parsis
Parsifal, or Sir Percivale
Parsons table
Parsons, Alan
Parsons, Estelle
Parsons, Gram
Parsons, Louella

Parthenon (on Acropolis)
Parton, Dolly
Partridge Family
Partridge, Eric
Party of God, or Hezbollah
Pasadena, CA, TX
Pasadena Playhouse
Pasadena Tournament of Roses, or
    Rose Parade
Pascal, Francine
Pasha, Ali
Paslode™ power tools
Paso Fino horse
Passaic, NJ
Passamaquoddy Bay
Passion play
Passion Sunday
Passos, John Dos
Passover, or Pescah
Pasternak, Boris
Pasteur treatment
Pasteur, Louis
Pat Benatar
Pat Boone
Pat Buchanan
Pat Buttram
Pat Garrett, Sheriff (shot Billy, the Kid)
Pat Harrington
Pat Metheny
Pat Morita
Pat Nixon
Pat Paulsen
Pat Sajak
Pat Summerall
Paterson, NJ
Patagonia region, S. Am.
Pathe' Gazette newsreel
Pathé, Charles
Patinkin, Mandy
Patrice Lumumba, P.M.
Patrice Munsel
Patricia 'Patty' Hearst
Patrick Air Force Base, FL
Patrick Maynard Blackett, Baron
Patrick Duffy
Patrick Henry
Patrick Kennedy
Patrick Macnee

Patrick Magee
Patrick Swayze
Patrick, Saint
Patsy Cline
Patterson, Floyd
Patti LaBelle
Patti Page
Patti, Adelina
Patton, George S., Gen.
Patty Berg
Patty Duke Astin, or Patty Duke
Paul Bunyan (& Babe, the Blue Ox)
Paul Cézanne
Paul Cheneau™ wine
Paul Delaroche
Paul Delvaux
Paul Dukas
Paul Ehrlich
Paul Feely
Paul Gallico
Paul Gann (intro. CA Prop. 13)
Paul Gauguin
Paul Gleason
Paul Harvey
Paul Hindemith
Paul Klee
Paul Lynde
Paul Masson™
Paul McCartney
Paul Mitchell™ hair prod.
Paul Muni
Paul Newman
Paul Prudhomme
Paul Revere
Paul Revere And The Raiders
Paul Robeson
Paul A. Samuelson
Paul Scofield
Paul Signac
Paul Simon (musician)
Paul Simon, Sen.
Paul Volcker
Paul Whiteman Band
Paul Junger Witt
Paul Zindel
Paul, Don Michael
Paul, Les (&Mary Ford)
Paula Abdul

Paula Zahn
Paulding, James Kirke
Paulette Goddard
Pauley, Jane
Paulina Porizkova
Pauline Collins
Pauline Frederick
Pauline Trigère
Pauling, Linus C.
Paulsen, Pat
Pavarotti, Luciano
Pavel Popovich, Cosmonaut
Pavlov, Ivan
Pavlova, Anna
Pawnee Indians
Pawtucket, RI
Pax Romana (political peace)
Payday™ candy
Payette Nat. Forest
Payless Super Drug
Pays de la Loire, region, Fr.
PBS-TV
PC Magazine
PC World
Pd (chem. sym. palladium)
Peabo Bryson
Peabody, MA
Peace Corps
Peacemaker (MX missile)
Peale, Rev. Norman Vincent
Peanuts
Pearl Bailey
Pearl S. Buck
Pearl Harbor, HI
Pearl Mesta
Pearl, Minnie
Pearly Gates, the
Peary, Robert E.
Pease Air Force Base, NH
Peaseblossom (a fairy)
Peavy, Queenie
Peck, Gregory
Peck's bad boy
Peckinpah, Sam
Pecos Bill
Pecos River
Pedro Antonio Alarcón
Pee-Chee™ folders

Pee Wee King
Pee-Wee Herman
'Pee Wee' Reese (Harold)
Pee-Wee's Playhouse
Peel, Emma
Peele, Sir Robert, P.M.
Peeping Tom
Peer Gynt
Peer Gynt Suite
Peerage
Peerce, Jan
Pegasus, the Winged Horse
Pegboard™
Peggy Fleming
Pegler, Westbrook
Pei, I. M.
Peking duck
Peking man, or Sinanthropus
Peking, China (now Beijing)
Pekingese (dog)
Pelagian
Pele´ (soccer player)
Pelée (volcano)
Peloponnesian War
Peloponnesus, Grc.
Peltier effect (electricity)
Pendaflex™ files
Pendragon, Uther (Arthurian)
Peng, Li, Premier
Penn™ tennis balls
Penn, Sean
Penn, William
Pennine Alps
Pennsylvania (PA)
Pennsylvania Dutch
Penny Marshall
Penny Singleton (played Blondie)
Pennzoil™
Penobscot Bay
Penobscot River
Pensacola Air Force Station, FL
Pensacola, FL
Pentagon, the
Pentateuch (1st 5 books Bible)
Pentax™
Pentecost (religious feast)
Pentecostalism (sect)
Pentel™ pen

Penthouse magazine
Pentothal Sodium™, or Pentothal
Penzance, Eng.
People magazine
People's Court
People's party
Peoria Journal Star
Peoria, IL
Pepe Le Pew
Peppard, George
Pepper, Claude, Rep.
Pepperdine University
Pepperidge Farm™ foods
Pepsi™
Pepsi-Cola™
PepsiCo Incorporated
Pepsodent™ toothpaste
Pepto-Bismol™
Pepys's Diary
Pepys, Samuel
Pequot Indians
Perahia, Murray
Perc Westmore
Percheron draft horse
Percival Blakeney, Sir (aka Scarlett
   Pimpernel)
Percival Lowell
Percy Bysshe Shelley
Percy Kilbride
Pereira, Columbia
Perelman, S. J.
Perez, Carlos Andres, Pres.
Perez, Shimon
Pericles (statesman)
Perils-of-Pauline
Perkins, Anthony
Perlman, Itzhak
Perlman, Rhea
Perlman, Ron
Perma Soft™
Perma Tweeze™
Perma-Prest™
Permian period
Pernell Roberts
Pernod™
Perón, Eva Duarte de, Pres.
Perón, Juan Domingo, Pres.
Perón, María de

Perrault, Charles (wrote *Mother Goose*)
Perrier™ water
Perrine, Valerie
Perry Como
Perry Ellis™
Perry Mason
Perseids meteor shower (July-Aug.)
Persepolis (cap. ancient Persian empire)
Perseus (Gr. myth)
Perseus, king of Macedon
Pershing, John J., Gen.
Persia (now Iran)
Persian cat
Persian Empire
Persian Gulf
Persian Gulf States
Persian lamb
Persian rug, or carpet
Persian Wars
Persius, the poet
Personal Finance
Persephone, or Proserpine
Perspex™
Persus constellation
Pert Plus™ haircare
Perth, Australia
Perth, Scotland
Peru
Peruvian Paso horse
Pesach, or Passover
Pet Inc.
Pet Ritz™ foods
Pet Rock™
Pete Rose (aka 'Charlie Hustle')
Peter Abelard, or Pierre
Peter Arno
Peter Behrens
Peter Bogdanovich
Peter Boyle
Peter Carl Fabergé
Peter Carruthers
Peter the Cruel (Spain)
Peter Damian, Saint (Pope Gregory VII)
Peter Fonda
Peter Frampton
Peter Gallagher
Peter Golfinopoulos

Peter Graves
Peter the Great (Russ.)
Peter Gunn
Peter Lind Hayes
Peter Jennings
Peter Lorre
Peter Marshall
Peter Minuit
Peter O'Toole
Peter Pan
Peter Pan collar
Peter Pan™ peanut butter
Peter Paul Almond Joy™
Peter Paul Mounds™
Peter Piper
Peter Piper's™ pickles
Peter Principle
Peter Roget (Thesaurus)
Peter Paul Rubens
Peter Schickele (aka P.D.Q. Bach)
Peter Straub
Peter Stuyvesant
Peter Ilyich Tchaikovsky
Peter Ueberroth
Peter Ustinov
Peter Vidmar
Peter Wimsey, Lord
Peter, Paul and Mary
Peter, Saint (at Heaven's Gate)
Peterbilt™ truck
Peterborough, Ont., Can.
Peter's Church, Saint
Peters, Bernadette
Petersburg, VA
Peterson, Oscar
Petit Trianon
Petit, Roland
Petition of Right (Eng.)
Petri dish
Petrie, Sir William
Petrified Forest, The
Petrified Forest National Park
Petronius (satirist)
Petrova, Olga
Petruchio (Kate's suitor)
Petticoat Lane market
Pettiford, Oscar
Peugeot™ car

Pevensie's, the (Peter, Susan, Edmund, Lucy)
Pevsner, Antoine
Peyton Place
Pfaff™ sewing machine
Pfeiffer, Michelle
Pfister, Andrea
Pfizer Incorporated
Phaedo
Phaedra (Gr. myth)
Phaëthon, or Phaëton
Pham Van Dong, Prem.
Phantom of the Opera
Phar Lap
Pharaoh (title)
Pharisees & Sadducees
Pharos lighthouse at Alexandria (1 of 7 Wonders)
Pheromone™ perfume
Phi Beta Kappa (honorary U.S. college society)
Phi Beta Kappa key
Phidias, or Pheidias
Phil Bacolod
Phil Donahue
Phil Harris
Phil Mahre
Phil Spitalny and his All Girl Orchestra
Philadelphia Athletics
Philadelphia Daily News
Philadelphia Eagles
Philadelphia Inquirer
Philadelphia lawyer (slang)
Philadelphia Museum of Art
Philadelphia Naval Shipyard, PA
Philadelphia Phillies
Philadelphia, PA
Philbin, Regis
Philip Barry
Philip the Bold
Philip Chesterfield, Lord
Philip the Fair
Philip the Good
Philip Marlowe
Philip Morris Incorporated
Philip Mountbattan, duke of Edinburgh

Philip Murray
Philip Roth
Philip John Schuyler, Gen.
Philip Henry Sheridan, Gen.
Philip the Tall
Philippe Junot
Philippians (Biblical)
Philippine Airlines
Philippine mahogany
Philippines, or Philippine Is.
Phillip A. Waxman
Phillips curve (inflation/unemployment)
Phillips Petroleum Co.
Phillips™ screwdriver
Philo T. Farnsworth
pHisoDerm™
Phnom Penh, Cambodia
Phobos (Mars' moon)
Phoebe (Saturn moon)
Phoebe Cates
Phoenicia
Phoenician art
Phoenix Gazette
Phoenix, AZ
Phone-Mate™
Photorealism art
Photostat™
Phyfe, Duncan
Phylicia Rashad
Phyllis Diller
Phyllis Schlafly
Phytin™
Pia Zadora
Piaf, Edith
Picard, Jean (astronomer)
Picard, Jean-Luc, Capt. (*Star Trek*)
Picardie, Fr.
Picasso, Pablo
Picatinny Arsenal, NJ
Piccadilly Circus (Lon.)
Piccard, Auguste
Piccard, Jean Felix
Piccone, Robin
Pickens, T. Boone, Jr.
Pickering, William H.
Pickfair mansion
Pickford, Mary
Pickles, Christina

Pickwick Papers
Pickwick, Mr. Samuel
Pico Rivera, CA
Pictionary™
Picts (ancient Scots)
Picture of Dorian Gray
Pidgeon, Walter
Pidgin English
Pied Piper of Hamelin
Pied Pipers, The
Piedmont™ Airlines
Piedmont region (east U.S.)
Pier Luigi Nervi
Pierce Brosnan
Pierce, Franklin, Pres.
Pierpont Morgan Library (NYC)
Pierre Bonnard
Pierre Boulez
Pierre Curie
Pierre Auguste Renior
Pierre Salinger
Pierre Elliott Trudeau, P.M.
Pierrefonds, Québec, Can.
Piers Anthony
Piet Mondrian
Pietà (Michelangelo's)
Pieter Bruegel, the Elder, also
    Brueghel, or Breughel
Pieter Bruegel, the Younger, also
    Brueghel, or Breughel
Pieter Oud
Pieter W. Botha, Pres. (National Party)
Pietro Mascagni
pig Latin
Piglet (*Winnie-the-Pooh*)
Pigling Bland
Pike, James A., Bishop
Pik-Nik™ snacks
Pikes Peak
Pilate, Pontius
Pilgrim Fathers
Pilgrim's Progress
Pillars of Hercules
Pillsbury™ foods
Pillsbury's Best™
Pilobolus Dance Theater
Piltdown man
Pima Indians

Pimlico Race Course
Pimm's Cup
Pinafore, H.M.S.
Pinchas Zuckerman
Pindar, the poet
Pine Bluff, AR
Pine Bluff Arsenal, AR
Pine™ cleaner
Pine-Sol™ cleaner
Ping-Pong™, or Ping Pong
Pink Floyd
Pinkerton Nat. Detective Agency
Pinkerton, Allan
Pinkham, Lydia (patent-medicine)
Pinocchio
Pinochet, Ugarte Augusto, Pres.
Pinot Noir wine
Pinter, Harold
Pinza, Ezio
Pioneer Electronic Corp.
Pioneer™ audio
Pioneer space probe
Piotr Kropotkin, Prince
PIP™ Printing
Piper Cherokee™ plane
Piper-Heidsieck™ champagne
Piper Laurie
Pippi Longstocking
Pirandello, Luigi
Pirates of Penzance, The
Pirelli SpA
Pisa, Italy
Pisa, Council of
Pisa, Leaning Tower of
Piscataway, NJ
Pisces (zodiac sign)
Pisces (Fish) constellation
Piscopo, Joe
Pismo Beach, CA
Pissarro, Camille
Pitcairn Island (H.M.S. Bounty)
Pitcher, Molly
Pithecanthropus erectus
Pitkin, Walter
Pitman shorthand
Pitman, Sir Isaac
Pitney Bowes Incorporated
Pitney Bowes™ office machines

Pitot tube
Pitt, William, P.M.
Pitti Palace
Pitts, ZaSu
Pittsburg, CA
Pittsburgh, PA
Pittsburgh Pirates
Pittsburgh Steelers
Pittsburgh Post Gazette
Pittsburgh Press
Pizza Hut™
Pizzetti, Ildebrando
place de la Concorde
Placido Domingo
Plain People (Mennonites, Amish,
    Dunker sects)
Plains Indians
Plains of Abraham
Planck, Max
Planck's constant
Planned Parenthood™
Plant, Robert
Plantagenet ruling dynasty
Plantagenet, Richard, Duke of York
Planters™ Cheez Balls
Planters™ Cheez Curls
Planters™ Nuts
Plantronics™
plaster of Paris
Plasticine™
Plateau Indians
Plath, Sylvia
Plato
Platonism
Platt, O. H., Sen.
Platte River
Platters, The
Plattsburgh Air Force Base, NY
Plautus (Titus Maccius)
Plax™ mouthwash
Play-Doh™
Playboy Entertainment
Playboy magazine
Playboy Mansion
Playboy of the Western World, The
Playgirl magazine
Playskool™ toys
Playtex™ Living Gloves

Plaza Hotel (NYC)
Plaza Suite
Plazzo Vecchio (in Italy)
Pleiades (7 daughters of Atlas)
Pleiades (star cluster)
Pleistocene epoch
Pleshette, Suzanne
Plexiglas™
Plimpton, George
Plimpton, Martha
Pliny the Elder
Pliny the Younger
Pliocene epoch
Pliofilm™
Plochman's™ mustard
Plummer, Christopher
Plummer, Polly
Plutarch (Gr. writer)
Pluto (god of Hades)
Pluto (planet)
Plymouth™ car
Plymouth, Eng.
Plymouth, MA
Plymouth Colony
Plymouth™ Road Runner
Plymouth Rock (chicken)
Plymouth Rock (Pilgrims landed)
Po (chem. sym. polonium)
Po, Li Tai, or Li
Pocahontas
Pocatello, ID
Pocono Mts.
Podunk (any 'dull' town)
Poe, Edgar Allan
Pogo
Pohl, Frederik
Poindexter, Buster
Poindexter, John M.
Point Barrow, AK
Point Mugu, CA
Pointe-à-Pitre, Guadeloupe
Pointe-aux-Trembles, Québec, Can.
Pointe-Claire, Québec, Can.
Pointe-Noire, Congo
Pointilism
Poirot, Hercule
Poison (rock group)
Poitier, Sidney

Poitou-Charente, Fr.
Pol Pot, P.M.
Pola Negri
Poland
Polanski, Roman
Polaris, or North Star, or Pole Star
Polaroid™ camera/film
Polaroid Corp.
Poli-Grip™ denture fix.
Police Gazette
Polish Corridor
Politburo (Soviet)
Polk™ Audio
Polk, James Knox, Pres.
Pollock, Jackson
Pollux (Castor and)
Polly Plummer
Pollyanna (foolishly optomistic person)
Pollyanna (the novel)
Polo Lounge (Beverly Hills Hotel)
Polo, Marco
Polonaise, the, or the polonaise
Polonius (in *Hamlet*)
Poltergeist
Poly Shield™
Polycarp, Saint
Polydorus
Polyester™
PolyGram Records
Polynesia
Polynesian
Polyphemus (Cyclops)
Polypodiophyta
Pom Poms™ candy
Pomerania, region, Poland
Pomeranian (dog)
Pomo Indians
Pomona, CA
Pompadour, Madame Jeanne
    Antoinette
Pompano Beach, FL
Pompeian red
Pompeii (ancient city, Italy)
Pompey the Great
Pompidou, Georges, Pres.
Ponce de León, Juan
Ponchielli, Amilcare
pons Varolii

Pons, Lily
Pont Neuf bridge
Ponti, Carlo
Pontiac™ car
Pontiac Indians
Pontiac, MI
Pontiac™ Trans Am
Pontiac, Chief
Pontiac's Rebellion, or Conspiracy
Pontius Pilate
Pony Express
Pony of the Americas, or POA
Pony™ shoes
Ponzi scheme, or game (investment
    scheme)
Poole, Eng.
Poona, India, or Pune
Poons, Larry
Poor Richard's Almanack
Pop Art
Pop 'n Snak™ popcorn
Pop-Tarts™
Pope Air Force Base, NC
Pope John Paul II (b. Karol Wojtyla)
Pope, Alexander
Popeye Doyle
Popeye the Sailor
Popkin, Harry M.
Popocatépetl volcano
Popov™ vodka
Popovich, Pavel, Cosmonaut
Poppins, Mary
Popsicle™
Popular Mechanics
Popular Photography
Popular Science
Populist party
Porcelana™ skincare
Porch of the Caryatids
Porcupine River
Porizkova, Paulina
Porgy and Bess
Porky Pig
Porsche™ car
Port Angeles Coast Guard Air
    Station,WA
Port Angeles, WA
Port Arthur, TX

Port Authority of New York Piers
Port du Salut cheese
Port of Spain, Trinidad &Tobago
Port Richey, FL
Port Royal, Jamaica
Port Said, Egypt
Port Townsend, WA
Port-au-Prince, Haiti
Porter, Cole
Porter, Wm. Sydney (aka O.Henry)
Portinari, Beatrice (maiden name
   Dante's love)
Portland Hoffa
Portland Oregonian
Portland, OR, ME
Portmeirion™
Portnoy's Complaint
Portobello Road market, Lon.
Portofino, Italy
Portsmouth, Eng.
Portsmouth, NH, VA
Portsmouth Naval Shipyard, NH
Portugal
Portuguese
Portuguese man-of-war
Pos-A-Traction™ tire
Poseidon (Gr. god)
Post™ cereals
Post Exchange, or PX
Post™ Grape-Nuts
Post, Emily
Post, Wiley
Post-impressionism art, or
   post-impressionism
Post-it™ Notes
Post-modernism art, or
   post-modernism
Postman Always Rings Twice, The
Postum™ beverage
Posturepedic™ mattress
Pot, Pol, P.M.
Potemkin, Grigori Aleksandrovich,
   Prince
Potomac, MD
Potomac River
Potsdam Conference
Potsdam, E. Ger.
Potsdam, NY

Pott's disease
Potter, Beatrix
Potts, Annie
Poughkeepsie, NY
Pouilly Blanc Fume wine
Pouilly-Fuisse wine
Pound, Ezra Loomis
Poussin, Nicolas
Povich, Maury
Powder Puff Derby
Powell, Adam Clayton, Jr.
Powell, John Wesley
Powell, Justice Lewis F., Jr.
Powell, William
Power House™ candy
Powers, Gary Francis (U-2 pilot)
Powhatan Confederacy
Powhatan Indians
Pozzi™ windows
Prado Museum (Madrid)
Praemium Imperiale awards
Praetorians (Roman bodyguards)
Prague, Czech.
Praia, Cape Verde
Prairie Provinces, Can.
Praise the Lord Network, or PTL
Pravda
Praxiteles (sculptor)
pre-Columbian art
Pre-Raphaelites
Preakness Stakes
Precambrian era
Preemption Act
Prego™ sauce
Prell™
Preminger, Otto
Premium™ saltines
Prendergast, Maurice
Prentice-Hall Inc.
Preparation H™
Preppy (slang)
'Pres. Zia', or Mohammad Zia-ul-
   Haq, Pres.
Presbyterian (member)
Presbyterianism (church group)
Presidential Medal of Freedom
Presidio of San Francisco
Presley, Elvis

Preston Sturges
Prestone™ coolant
Pretoria, S. Africa
Pretorius, Andries
Pretorius, Marthinus
Previn, André
Priam (Gr. myth)
Price Waterhouse accounting firm
Price, Leontyne
Pride, Charley
Priestley, J. B. (author)
Priestley, Joseph (chemist)
Prime Mover (God)
Primo Carnera
Prince Albert, Sask., Can.
Prince Caspian
Prince of Darkness (the Devil)
Prince Edward Island
Prince Ellidyr
Prince Lionheart™ baby furn.
Prince of Peace (Jesus)
Prince Rainier III of Monaco
Prince William Sound, AK (Exxon
    spill)
Princess Grace, Consort of Monaco
Princess Summerfall Winterspring
Princess Yasmin Khan
Princeton, NJ
Princeton University
Principal, Victoria
Pringles™ chips
Prinze, Freddie
Pritikin diet
Privacy Act of 1974
Prizzi's Honor
Procter & Gamble Co.
Proctor Silex™ coffeemaker
Product 19™ cereal
Professional Builder
Professor Branestawm
Professor Moriarty
Progressive Grocer
Progressive party
Progressive Radio Network
Progressive, The
Progresso™ Soup
Prokofiev, Sergei, or Sergey
Prometheus (Gr. myth)

Promised Land
Propa pH™ skincare
Prophet, The (Gilbran)
Proserpine, or Persephone
Prospero (*The* Tempest)
Protagoras (philosopher)
Proterozoic era
Protestant
Protestant Union
Protestant work ethic
Protestantism
Proteus (Gr. myth)
Proton™ electronics
Protozoa
Proust, Marcel
Provence reg., France
Provence-Alpes-Côte d'Azur, Fr.
Proverbs, Book of
Providence (God, as guiding power)
Providence Journal-Bulletin
Providence, RI
Provincetown Players (NYC)
Provo, UT
Prowse, Juliet
Proxmire, William, Sen.
Prudential-Bache Securities
Prudhoe Bay, AK
Prudhomme, Paul
Prussia region, Ger.
Pryor, Richard
Psalms, or Psalter
Psyche
Psyche knot
Psycho (Robert Bloch)
Psychology Today
PT boat
Pt (chem. sym. platinum)
PTL Club ('Praise the Lord')
Ptolemaic system
Ptolemy (astronomer)
Ptolemy (14 kings of Egypt)
Pu (chem. sym. plutonium)
Public Works Administration
Publishers Weekly
Pucci, Emilio
Puccini, Giacomo
Puck, or Robin Goodfellow (*A
    Midsummer Night's Dream*)

Puck of Pook's Hill
Puck, Wolfgang
Puddleduck, Jemima
Puddleglum the Marsh-wiggle
Pueblo Indians
Pueblo, CO
Puerto Rico
Puerto Vallarta, Mex.
Puget Sound Naval Shipyard, WA
Puget Sound, WA
Pugwash, Captain
Pulitzer, Joseph (Pulitzer Prizes)
Pulliam, Keshia Knight
Pullman™ car
Pullman kitchen
Pulsar™ watch
Puma™ shoes
Puma™ sweats
Pumpernickel
Pumpkinhead, Jack
Punch-and-Judy show
Punchinello
Punic Wars
Punjab region, India
Punky Brewster
Punta Gorda, Belize
Punxsutawney Phil (groundhog)
Puppis constellation
Purcell, Henry
Purdue University
Pure Jeanswear™
Pure Sweat™
Purina™ Cat Chow
Purina™ Dog Chow
Purina™ Goat Chow
Purina™ Grrravy™
Puritan work ethic
Puritanism movement
Purolator™
Purple Heart
Pusan, S. Korea
Pushkin Square (Russia)
Pushkin, Aleksander (or Aleksandr) Sergeyevich
Pushmi-Pullyu
Puyallup, WA
Pygmalion (Galatea statue sculptor)
Pygmalion (Shaw play)

Pygmy
Pyle Driver™ car stereo
Pyle, Ernest 'Ernie'
Pyle, Gomer
Pym, John
Pyongyang, N. Korea
Pyramid of Khafre
Pyramid of Khufu, or Cheops
Pyramus and Thisbe
Pyrenees Mts.
Pyrex™
Pyrrophta
Pythagoras
Pythagorean theorem
Pythian games
Pythias (Damon and)
Python, Monty
Pyxis (Mariner's Compass) constellation

Q (pseudo. Sir Arthur Quiller-Couch)
Q clearance (highest nuclear security clearance)
Q Test™
Q-tips™
Qaddafi, Gadhafi, Gaddafi, or Khadafy, Moammar, Muammar, or Muammar-al
Qamdo, Ch.
Qantas™ Airline
Qatar, Arab Emirate
Qingdao, China, or Tsingtao
Qinghai province, China
Qom, Iran
Quaalude™
Quadruple Alliance
Quaid, Dennis

Quaker Oats Co.
Quaker Oh!s™ cereal
Quakers, or Religious Society of
  Friends
Quakertown, PA
Quamran (Dead Sea Scrolls)
Quant, Mary
Quantaray™ camera filters
Quantico Marine Corps Air Station,
  VA
Quantrill, William Clarke
Quantrill's guerrillas
Quantum theory, or quantum
Quarles, Francis
Quarles, Norma
Quarter Horse
Quarter Pounder™ (McDonald's)
Quartermaster Corps
Quasar ™ electronics
Quasimodo, Salvatore
Quasimodo, the hunchback
Quayle, J. Danforth, III, V.P.
Quayle, Marilyn
Québec, prov., Can.
Québec Le Soleil
Québec, Québec, Can.
Queen Anne style
Queen Anne's lace
Queen Charlotte Isl.
Queen Elizabeth II
Queen Guinevere (Arthurian)
Queen Hatshepsut
Queen of Hearts
Queen Hecuba of Troy
Queen Isabella of Spain
Queen Liliuokalani of Hawaii
Queen Mab
Queen Nefertiti, or Nefretete
Queen of Oz, Tippetarius
Queen of Sheba
Queen of Sweden, Christina
Queen Victoria
Queen, Ellery
Queenie Peavy
Queen's Bench, or Queen's Counsel
Queens Tribune
Queens, NYC
Queensberry, Marquis of, Rules

Queensborough Bridge (NYC)
Queensland, Australia
Quentin, Massys, or Matsys, or
  Messys, or Metsys
Quentin, San (CA prison)
Quetzalcoatl (Toltec deity)
Quezon City, Luzon, Phil.
quiche Lorraine
Quick Draw McGraw
Quickie™ mop
Quicksilver™ menswear
Quik Print™
QuikRef™ Publishing
Quikut knives
Quiller-Couch, Sir Arthur (aka 'Q')
Quincy Jones
Quincy, MA
Quincy Patriot Ledger
Quinn Yarbro, Chelsea
Quinn, Anthony
Quinn, Martha
Quintana Roo, state, Mexico
Quisling, Vidkun
Quito, Ecuador
Quixote, Don, or Don Quixote de la
  Mancha
Quo Vadis
Quonset™ hut
Quran, or Koran

R. Buckminster Fuller
R. J. Reynolds Industries Inc.
R. J. Reynolds Tobacco Co.
Ra (chem. sym. radium)
Ra Expeditions (T. Heyerdahl)
Ra, or Re (Egypt. god)
Rabat, Morocco

Rabbitt, Eddie
Rabelais, François
Rabindranath Tagore, Sir
Rabinowitz, Shalom (aka Sholom
   Aleichem)
Rachel Carson
Rachins, Alan
Rachmaninoff, Sergei V.
Racine, Jean Baptiste
Radcliffe College
Radio America
Radio City Music Hall
Radio Free Europe
Radisson Hotel (chain)
Radner, Gilda
Radziwill, Princess Lee
Rae Dawn Chong
Rafael L. Callejas, Pres.
Rafael Trujillo Molina, Pres.
Rafferty, Scruff
Raffin, Deborah
Rafsanjani, Hashemi, Pres.
Raggedy Ann & Andy
Ragu™ sauce
Rahal, Bobby
Raid™ bug killer
Raiders of the Lost Ark
Rainbow Bridge (UT)
Rainer Werner Fassbinder
Raines, Ella
Rainey, Joseph Hayne, Rep.
Rainier III, Prince of Monaco
Rainier™ beer
Rains, Claude
Rain-X™ windshield treat.
Raisa Gorbachev
Raisinets™
Raitt, Bonnie
Rajiv Gandhi, P.M.
Rajneesh, Bhagwan Shree (now called
   Osho)
Raleigh News & Observer
Raleigh, NC
Raleigh, Sir Walter, or Ralegh
Ralph Abernathy
Ralph Bellamy
Ralph J. Bunche
Ralph Waldo Emerson

Ralph Iron (pseud. Olive Schreiner)
Ralph Lauren™
Ralph Macchio
Ralph Meeker
Ralph Nader
Ralph Vaughan Williams
Ralston Purina Co.
Ramada Inn Hotel
Ramadan (Muslim holy month)
Rambo (Stallone)
Rameau, Jean-Philippe
Ramis, Harold
Ramon Novarro
Rampal, Jean-Pierre
Ramses™ condoms
Ramses, or Rameses, or Ramesses,
   (12 kings of Egypt)
Ramsgate, Eng.
Rancho Cordova, CA
Rancho Mirage, CA
RAND Corp.
Rand McNally World Atlas
Randall, Tony
Randolph Caldecott
Randolph, Edmund, or "Randolph of
   Roanoke"
Random House publishers
Randy Travis
Range Rover™
Ranger Rick magazine
Ranger space probe
Rangerbred horse
Rangoon, Burma
Rankin, Jeanette
Raoul Dufy
Rape of the Sabine Women
Raphael (b. Raphael Santi, or Sanzio)
Raphael, Sally Jessy
Rapid City, SD
Rappahannock River
Rapunzel
Raquel Welch
Rashad, Ahmad
Rashad, Phylicia
Rashomon
Rasputin, Grigori
Rastafarian
Rathbone, Basil

Rather, Dan
Rats of NIMH
Ratt (rock group)
Rattigan, Terence
Raul Julia
Ravel, Maurice
Ravenna, Italy
Ravi Shankar
Rawalpindi, Pakistan
Rawlings, Marjorie Kinnan
Rawls, Lou
Ray Bloch
Ray Bolger
Ray Bradbury
Ray Charles
Ray Conniff Orchestra
Ray Kroc (founded McDonald's)
Ray 'Boom Boom' Mancini
Ray Milland
Ray 'Sugar Ray' Robinson
Ray, James Earl
Ray, Man
Ray, Johnnie
Ray-Ban™ sunglasses
Ray-O-Vac™ batteries
Rayburn, Sam, Speaker of House
Raye, Martha
Raymond Burr
Raymond Chandler
Raymond Ditmars
Raymond Duchamp-Villon
Raymond Massey
Raymond Moody, Dr.
Raymonde Armitage
Rb (chem. sym. rubidium)
RC™ Cola
RCA™ electronics
RCA Corp.
Re (chem. sym. rhenium)
Reader's Digest
Reading, PA
Reading Railroad
Ready Crust™
Ready Mix™ Concrete
Reagan, Nancy
Reagan, Ronald Wilson, Pres.
Real-Kill™ Ant & Roach Killer
ReaLemon™ juice

Realtor™
Reasoner, Harry
Reb, Johnny
Reba McEntire
Récamier carpet
Recife, Brazil
Record, The
Record-A-Call™
Red Angus cattle
Red Badge of Courage, The
Red Barber
Red Bluff, CA
Red Carpet™ Realty
Red Cloud, Chief (Sioux leader)
Red Cross International
Red Delicious apple
Red Foley
Red Grange (Harold)
Red Grooms
Red Jacket (Seneca Indian leader)
Red Light Bandit (Caryl Chessman)
Red Norvo
Red River Army Depot, TX
Red River Rebellion (Can.)
Red River Settlement (Can.)
Red Sea
Red Skelton
Redbook magazine
Redd Foxx
Redding, CA
Reddi-wip™
Reddy, Helen
Redenbacher, Orville
Redfield, Robert (anthropologist)
Redford, Robert (actor)
Redgrave, Lynn
Redgrave, Sir Michael
Redgrave, Vanessa
Redkin™ Hair Care
Redmond, WA
Redon, Odilon
Redondo Beach, CA
Redwood City, CA
Redwood Nat. Park (CA)
Reebok™ shoes
Reed & Barton™ silver
Reed Smoot, Sen.
Reed, Donna

Reed, Dr. Walter
Reed, Sir Carol
Reepicheep
Reese Air Force Base , TX
Reese, Harold 'Pee Wee'
Reese's™ Peanut Butter Cups
Reese's™ Pieces
Reeve, Christopher
Reeves, Jim
Reeves, Keanu
Reformation (Protestant)
Reformation, Catholic, or Counter
    Reformation
Reformed Church in America
Regane™ gas treatment
Regency style
Regent's Park (Lon.)
Reggie Jackson
Regina, Saskatchewan, Can.
Reginald Gardiner
Regis Philbin
Regis Toomey
Regular Army
Rehnquist, Ch. Justice Wm. H.
Reichstag (German parliament)
Reid, Daphne Maxwell
Reid, Tim
Reign of Terror
Reilly, Charles Nelson
Reims Cathedral
Reims, France
Reiner, Carl
Reiner, Rob
Reinhardt, Max
Religious Society of Friends, or
    Quakers
Rembrandt van Rijn, or Ryn
'Remember the Maine'
Remick, Lee
Remington™ rifle
Remington, Frederic
Remus, Uncle
Remy Martin™ cognac
Renaissance man
Renaissance, the
Renata Tebaldi
Renault™ car
René Auberjonois

René Descartes
Rene Enriquez
René Magritte
Renfrew of the Mounted
Renfrew, Scotland
Reni Santoni
Rennes, Fr.
Reno Gazette Journal
Reno, NV
Renoir, Pierre Auguste
Renta, Oscar de la
Rent-A-Wreck™
Renuzit™ air freshener
REO Speedwagon
Republic (Plato's)
Republic of South Africa
Republican party
Requiem (mass for souls)
Respighi, Ottorino
Reston, VA
Restoration, English
Retin-A™
Retton, Mary Lou
Reunion in Vienna
Reuters Press
Reuther, Walter P.
Revere, Paul
Revereware™ cookware
Revlon™ cosmetics
Revlon Incorporated
Revolutionary War
Rex cat
Rex Harrison
Reykjavik, Iceland
Reynard the Fox
Reynolds Metals Corp.
Reynolds™ Wrap
Reynolds, Debbie
Reynolds, Frank
Reynolds, Sir Joshua
Rh (chem. sym. rhodium)
Rh factor
Rh-negative
Rh-positive
Rhea (Gr. myth)
Rhea (Saturn moon)
Rhea Perlman
Rheaban™

Rhee, Syngman, Pres.
Rheem™ water heater
Rheims Cathedral
Rheims, Fr.
Rhine river
Rhine wine
Rhineland region, W. Ger.
Rhode Island (RI)
Rhode Island Red
Rhodes, Greece
Rhodes scholar
Rhodesia (now Zimbabwe)
Rhodesian man
Rhodesian Ridgeback
Rhonda Fleming
Rhône river
Rhône-Alpes, Fr.
Ric Ocasek
Ricardo Montalban
Riccardo Muti
Riccardo Zandonai
Ricci, Nina
Rice Chex™
Rice Krispies™
Rice, Donna
Rice, Elmer
Rice-A-Roni™
Rich n' Chips™
Rich 'N Ready™
Rich, Buddy
Rich's Department Stores
Richard Aldington
Richard Dean Anderson
Richard Arkwright, Sir
Richard Arlen
Richard Attenborough, Sir
Richard Avedon
Richard Bach
Richard Basehart
Richard Boone
Richard Bradford
Richard Burbage
Richard 'Dick' Button
Richard E. Byrd
Richard Chamberlain
Richard Conte
Richard Crenna
Richard D'Oyly Carte

Richard Daley, Mayor
Richard Dawson
Richard Diebenkorn
Richard Dreyfuss
Richard Dysart
Richard Feynman
Richard Gatling (Gatling gun)
Richard A. Gephardt
Richard Gere
Richard Grenville, Sir
Richard Helms
Richard M. Johnson, V.P.
Richard Jordan
Richard Kiley
Richard Lion-Heart, or Richard
    Cœur de Lion
Richard Lovelace
Richard Marx
Richard Milhous Nixon, Pres.
    (resigned)
Richard Mulligan
Richard Neutra
Richard Plantagenet, Duke of York
Richard Pryor
Richard Rogers
Richard Sheridan
Richard Simmons
Richard Simmons Salad Spray™
Richard Strauss
Richard Henry Tawney
Richard Wagner
Richard Widmark
Richard, Maurice 'The Rocket'
Richards-Gebaur Air Force Base, MO
Richelieu, Cardinal Armand Jean, or
    Duc de Richelieu
Richie, Lionel
Richmond Times-Dispatch
Richmond, VA
Richter scale
Rick Moranis
Rickenbacker Air Force Base, OH
Rickenbacker, Edward 'Eddie', Capt.
Rickey, Branch
Rickles, Don
Rickover, Hyman George, Adm.
Ricky Schroder
Ricoh Co. Ltd.

Ricoh™ copier
Riddle, Nelson
Ride, Sally K, Astronaut
Ridgway, Matthew, Gen.
Ridiklis of Racketty Paketty House
Ridley Scott (director)
Riemann, Bernhard
Riemannian geometry
Riesling wine
Riga, Latvia
Rigby, Cathy
Rigg, Diana
Right Guard™ deoderant
Right, Petition of
Righteous Brothers
Rigoletto
Rijks Museum, or Ryks
Rijn, Rembrandt van, also Ryn
Riken™ tires
Riker, William, Cmdr. (on *Star Trek*)
Riki Turofsky
Riley, James Whitcomb
Riley, Jeannie C.
Rilian, Prince
Rimini, Italy
Rimsky-Korsakov, Nicolai
Rin Tin Tin
Rinehart, Mary Roberts
Ring of Kerry
Ring Lardner
Ring of the Nibelung
Ringer's solution
Ringling Brothers and Barnum &
    Bailey Circus
Ringo Starr
Ringwald, Molly
Rinkitink of Oz
Rio de Janeiro, Brazil
Rio Grande river
Riot Act (Eng. law)
Rip Van Winkle
Ripley's Believe It or Not
Ripplin's™ pot. chips
Risë Stevens
Rislone™ oil treatment
Rit™ dye
Rita Hayworth
Rita Moreno

Ritchard, Cyril
Ritchie Valens
Rittenhouse, David
Ritter, John
Ritter, Tex
Ritz™ crackers
Ritz-Carlton, The
River Jordan
River Ob
River Styx
River Thames
Rivera, Chita
Rivera, Diego
Rivera, Geraldo
Rivers, Joan
Riverside Church, NY
Riverside, CA
Riviera (Fr./Italy)
Riyadh, Saudi Arabia
Rizzoli International Bookstores
Rn (chem. sym. radon)
Roach Motel™
Roach, Hal
Road & Track magazine
Roald Dahl
Roanoke Island, NC
Roanoke River
Roanoke Times & World-News
Roanoke, VA
Roanoke Is., NC
Roaring '20s
Rob Lowe
Rob Reiner
Rob Roy (novel)
Rob Roy (Scot. outlaw)
Robards, Jason
Robb, Mrs. Charles (b. Lynda Bird
    Johnson)
Robbie Knievel
Robbin, Cock
Robbins, Harold
Robbins, Jerome
Robbins, Marty
Robert Alda
Robert Altman
Robert Armbruster
Robert Baden-Powell, Sir (Boy Scouts)
Robert Benchley

Robert Blake, Admiral
Robert Boyle
Robert Brakenbury, Sir
Robert Browning
Robert W. Bunsen (burner)
Robert Burns
Robert Carlyle Byrd, Sen.
Robert Conrad
Robert of Courtenay
Robert Crippen (1st Space Shuttle flight)
Robert Culp
Robert De Niro
Robert Duvall
Robert Essex, Earl of
Robert Frost
Robert Goulet
Robert Guillaume
Robert Heinlein
Robert Hooke
Robert Joffrey Ballet
Robert John McClure, Sir
Robert Francis Kennedy, Sen.
Robert Cavelier La Salle
Robert Lansing
Robert E. Lee, General
Robert Todd Lincoln
Robert Loggia
Robert Ludlum
Robert McNamara, Secy. Def.
Robert Millikan
Robert Mitchum
Robert Mondavi™ wines
Robert Montgomery
Robert Morley
Robert Motherwell
Robert Muldoon, P.M.
Robert J. Oppenheimer
Robert E. Peary
Robert Peele, Sir, P.M.
Robert Penn Warren
Robert Plant
Robert Redfield (anthropologist)
Robert Redford (actor)
Robert Schumann
Robert Wm. Service
Robert Sherwood
Robert Louis Stevenson
Robert Trout

Robert Urich
Robert Vaughn
Robert Vesco
Robert Wagner (actor)
Robert F. Wagner, Jr., Mayor
Robert F. Wagner, Sen.
Roberta Flack
Roberto Rossellini
Robert's Rules of Order
Roberts, Pernell
Robeson, Paul
Robespierre, Maximilien, `the
    Incorruptible´
Robie chair
Robin Cook
Robin Givens
Robin Goodfellow, or Puck
    (*A Midsummer Night's Dream*)
Robin Hood of Nottingham
Robin Hood's Merry Men
Robin Leach
Robin Piccone
Robin Strasser
Robin Williams
Robin, Christopher
Robinson Crusoe
Robinson, Bill 'Bojangles'
Robinson, Edward G.
Robinson, John 'Jackie'
Robinson, Ray 'Sugar Ray'
Robinson, Smokey
Robinson's Department Stores
Robitussin™
RoboCop
Robusti, Jacopo (aka Tintoretto)
Rocco 'Rocky' Marciano
Roche limit
Rochelle salt
Rochester Democrat-Chronicle
Rochester Times-Union
Rochester, NY
Rock Cornish (hen)
Rock Hudson
Rock Island Arsenal, IL
Rock of Gibralter
Rockefeller Center
Rockefeller Foundation
Rockefeller, oysters

Rockefeller, David
Rockefeller, John D., Jr.
Rockefeller, John D., III
Rockefeller, John D., IV, Gov.
Rockefeller, Laurance S.
Rockefeller, Nelson A., V.P.
Rockefeller, William
Rockefeller, Winthrop, Gov.
Rocket J. 'Rocky' Squirrel
Rockettes, the
Rockford Files
Rockford, IL
Rockies, or Rocky Mts.
Rockne, Knute, Coach
Rockwell International Corp.
Rockwell, Norman
Rocky Graziano
Rocky Marciano
Rocky Mountain Arsenal, CO
Rocky Mountain goat
Rocky Mountain Nat. Park
Rocky Mountain sheep, or bighorn
   sheep
Rocky Mountain spotted fever
Rocky Mts., or Rockies
Rod Carew
Rod Laver
Rod McKuen
Rod Serling
Rod Serling's Twilight Zone
Rod Steiger
Roddenberry, Gene
Roddy McDowall
Rodenstock™ lens
Rodeo Drive (in Bev. Hills)
Rodgers & Hart
Rodgers, Richard
Rodia, Simon, or Rodilla (*Watts
   Towers*)
Rodin, Auguste
Rodney Dangerfield
Rodrigo Carazo Odio, Pres.
Roe vs. Wade
Roehm, Carolyne
Roemer, Olaus, or Ole
Roentgen ray, or X-ray
Roentgen, Wilhelm, or Röntgen
Rogaine™ baldness treatment

Roger Bannister
Roger Brooke Taney, Ch. Justice
Roger Ebert
Roger Maris
Roger Moore
Roger Mudd
Roger Rabbit
Roger Sessions
Roger Staubach
Roger Vadim
Roger van der Weyden
Roger Whittaker
Rogers Dry Lake, CA
Rogers Hornsby
Rogers, Buck
Rogers, Fred (TV's Mr. Rogers)
Rogers, Kenny
Rogers, Roy
Rogers, W., Capt. (*USS Vincennes*)
Rogers, Will
Roget's Thesaurus (Peter Roget)
Rogue's Gallery
Roh Tae Woo, Pres.
Rokina™ lens
Rolaids™
Roland Barthes
Roland Kibbee
Roland Petit
Rold Gold™ pretzels
Rolex™ watch
Rolfing massage
Rolle, Esther
Rollei™ photo equip.
Roller, Gravella
Rolling Stone magazine
Rolling Stones, the
Rollins, Sonny
Rolls-Royce™ car
Rolls-Royce™ Corniche
Rolls-Royce Ltd.
Rolo™ candy
Rolodex™
Roman alphabet
Roman arch
Roman calendar
Roman candle
Roman Catholic
Roman Empire

Roman Holiday
Roman law
Roman nose
Roman numerals
Roman Polanski
Roman senate
Romania, or Rumania
Romanoff™ caviar
Romanoff, noodles
Romberg, Sigmund
Rome, Italy
Romeo Montague (*Romeo & Juliet*)
Romeo and Juliet
Romero, Cesar
Rommel, Erwin, Gen., 'the desert
    fox'
Romney, George
Romulan (of *Star Trek*)
Romulus & Remus
Ron Glass
Ron Howard
Ron Leibman
Ron Perlman
Ron Ziegler
Rona Barrett
Ronald Colman
Ronald McDonald
Ronald McDonald house
Ronald Wilson Reagan, Pres.
Rondos™ ice cream
Ronnie Milsap
Ronrico™ Rum
Ronstadt, Linda
Röntgen, Wilhelm, or Roentgen
Ronzoni™ pasta
Roone Arledge
Rooney, Andy
Rooney, Mickey
Roosevelt, Franklin Delano, Pres.
    (FDR)
Roosevelt, Theodore, Pres.
Roosevelt's Rough Riders
Roots
Roper Poll
Roquefort™ cheese
Rorschach test
Rosa, Julius La
Rosalind Russell

Rosalynn Carter
Rosalynn Sumners
Rosanna Arquette
Rosanne Cash
Rosarita™ Mex. foods
Roscoe Tanner
Rose Bowl (CA)
Rose Marie
Rose Marie Reid™ swimwear
Rose Parade, or Pasadena
    Tournament of Roses
Rose Schneiderman
Rose, Axl
Rose, Billy
Rose, Pete 'Charlie Hustle'
Roseanne Barr
Roseanne Roseannadanna
Roseau, Dominica
Rosemary Casals
Rosemary Clooney
Rosemary De Camp
Rosenberg (spy) Case
Rosenberg, Julius & Ethel
Rosencrantz & Guildenstern
Roses, War of the
Rosetta Stone
Rosey Grier
Rosh Hashanah
Rosi Mittermaier
Rosie the Riveter
Rosicrucian Order
Ross Macdonald (pseud. Kenneth
    Millar)
Ross, Betsy
Ross, Diana
Ross, Marion
Rossano Brazzi
Rossellini, Isabella
Rossellini, Roberto
Rossi™ rifle
Rossi, Leo
Rossignol™ skis
Rossini, Gioacchino
Rostand, Edmond
Rosten, Leo
Rostock, E. Ger.
Roswell, NM
Rotarian

Rotarian magazine
Rotary Club
Roth, David Lee
Roth, Philip
Rothschild family
Rothschild, Baron Lionel de
Roto-Rooter™
Rotterdam, Netherlands
Rottweiler (dog)
Rouault, Georges
Rouen Cathedral (Monet)
Rouen, France
Rough Riders, Roosevelt's
Round Table, Knights of the
Round The Clock™ hose
Roundheads, or Puritan Party
Rousseau, Henri
Rousseau, Jean Jacques
Rousseau, Théodore
Roy Bean, Judge
Roy Campanella
Roy Lichtenstein
Roy Orbison
Roy Rogers
Roy Scheider
Roy Wilkins
Royal Ballet (Lon.)
Royal Canadian Mounted Police
Royal Caribbean Cruise Line
Royal Copenhagen™ china
Royal Danish Ballet
Royal Discount Bookstores
Royal Doulton™ china
Royal Dutch/Shell Group of
    Companies
Royal Highlanders, or Black Watch
Royal Jordanian Airlines
Royal Oak (in Eng.-Charles II)
Royal Oak, MI
Royal Shakespeare Co.
Royal Victoria Hall, or Old Vic
Rozsa, Miklos
R2D2 & C3P0
Ru (chem. sym. ruthenium)
Rubáiyát of Omar Khayyam
Rubbermaid™
Rube Goldberg (cartoonist)
Rube Goldberg invention

Rubens, Peter Paul
Rubicon (imposed limit, as in 'crossing
    the')
Rubicon river (J. Caesar crossed)
Rubik's Cube
Rubinstein, Anton (Rus. pianist)
Rubinstein, Arthur (Pol.-Am. pianist)
Rubinstein, Helena
Ruby Dandridge
Ruby Keeler
Rudd Weatherwax (Lassie's trainer)
Rudolf Hess
Rudolf Nureyev
Rudolf Serkin
Rudolph Bing, Sir
Rudolph W. Giuliani
Rudolph Valentino
Rudy Vallee
Rudyard Kipling
Rue McClanahan
Rue Morgue
Ruehl, Mercedes
Ruffles™ Potato Chips
Rufino Tamayo
Rufus King
Rugby, Eng.
Rugby football
Rugby school
Ruggiero Leoncavallo
Ruggles, Charlie
Ruidoso Downs racetrack
Ruidoso, NM
Ruiz, Tracie
Rukeyser, Muriel
Ruler of Heaven and Earth (God)
Rumania, or Romania
Rumba
Rumpelstiltskin
Run - D.M.C.
Runner's World
Runnymede, or Runnimede
Runyon, Damon
Rupert Brooke
Rupert Murdoch
Rupert's Land (Can.)
R.U.R.
Rush, Benjamin
Rushdie, Salman

Rusk, Dean, Secy. State
Russ Taff
Russel Crouse
Russell, Bertrand
Russell, Jane
Russell, Lillian
Russell, Rosalind
Russell's viper
Russia
Russia Co., or Muscovy Co.
Russian blue cat
Russian Revolution
Russian Roulette
Russian Soviet Federated Socialist
  Republic
Russian Steppes, the
Russian wolfhound (now Borzoi)
Russo-Japanese War
Russo-Turkish Wars
Rust-Oleum™
Rutger Hauer
Rutgers University
Ruth Buzzi
Ruth Draper
Ruth Etting
Ruth Gordon
Ruth Hussey
Ruth Montgomery
Ruth St. Denis
Ruth Warrick
Ruth Westheimer, Dr.
Ruth, Babe (b. George Herman Ruth)
Rutherford atom
Rutherford B. Hayes, Pres.
Rutherford, Ernest, Baron
Rutherford, Margaret
Rutledge, Ann
Ruttan, Susan
Rwanda republic
Ry-Krisp™
Ryan O'Neal
Ryan, Meg
Ryan, Nolan
Ryder™ Trucks
Rye House Plot (Eng.)
Ryks Museum, or Rijks
Ryman Auditorium (home, Grand Ole
  Opry)

Ryshkov, Nikolai I., Prem.

S (chem. sym. sulfur)
S & W™ foods
S. E. Hinton
S. I. Hayakawa (Samuel Ichiye)
S. J. Perelman
S. N. Behrman
S. Pearson & Son plc
S. S. *Lusitania*
S. S. *Titanic*
S.W. Graham™ cereal
S.W.A.T. team
Saab™ car
Saadia ben Joseph al-Fayumi
Saarinen, Eero
Saarland
Saavedra, Miguel de Cervantes
Sabatini, Gabriela
Sabbatai Zevi
Sabbath
Sabin, Albert Bruce
Sabines
Sac and Fox Indians
Sacajawea, or Sacagawea, or
  Sakakawea
Sacco & Vanzetti Case (Nicola &
  Bartolomeo)
Sacher torte, or Sachertorte
Sacheverell Sitwell
Sachs, Hans
Sachs, Nelly
Sackville-West, Victoria
Sacramento Bee
Sacramento River
Sacramento, CA
Sacre-Coeur church

Sacred College, or College of
Cardinals
Sadat, Anwar, Pres., or Anwar al
Saddam Hussein, Pres.
Sadducees
Sade, Marquis Donatien de
Sadler's Wells Ballet
Safeco™ Insurance
Safer, Morley
Safeway stores
Sag Harbor™
Sagan, Carl
Sagan, Françoise
Saginaw, MI
Sagittarius (zodiac sign)
Sagittarius (Archer) constellation
Sahadi™ salad dressing
Sahara desert
Sahara Hotel
Sahel region, Africa
Sahl, Mort
Saigon (now Ho Chi Minh City)
Saint, Eva Marie
St. Agnes's Eve
St. Albans, Eng.
St. Ambrose
St. Andrew's cross
St. Anselm
St. Anthony's fire (skin condition)
St. Athanasius
St. Augustine, FL
St. Barnabas
St. Bartholomew
St. Bartholomew's Day massacre
St. Bede, or the Venerable Bede
St. Bernadette (Lourdes)
St. Benedict
St. Bernard dog
St. Bonaventura, or Bonaventure
St. Boniface
St. Calixtus tombs
St. Catharines, Ont., Can.
St. Catherine of Siena
St. Celestine I
St. Celestine V
St.-Chapelle chapel
St. Christopher
St. Clair, Arthur, Gen.

St. Clair, Lake
St. Croix, V.I.
St. Cyprian
St. Denis, Ruth
St. Dominic
St. Elizabeth Ann Seton, or Mother
Seton
St. Elmo's fire (visible electric discharge)
St. Frances Cabrini, also Mother
Cabrini
St. Francis of Assisi
St. Francis Xavier
St.-Gaudens, Augustus
St. George's, Grenada
St. Gotthard, Mt.
St. Helens, Mt.
St.-Hubert, Québec, Can.
Saint George (Donatello)
St. James the Greater
St. John the Baptist
St. John the Divine, Cathedral of
St. John, Jill
St. John's, Newfoundland, Can.
St. John's, Antigua
St. Jude
St. Jude Children's Research Hosp.
St. Justin Martyr
St. Kitts-Nevis
St. Laurent, Louis S., P.M.
St.-Laurent, Québec, Can.
St.-Laurent, Yves
St. Lawrence River
St. Lawrence Seaway
St.-Léonard, Québec, Can.
St. Louis Browns
St. Louis Cardinals
St. Louis Coast Guard Base, MO
St. Louis Post-Dispatch
St. Louis, MO
St. Loyola
St. Lucia
St. Mark's Basilica
St. Martin Island
St. Martin's Press publisher
St. Mary-le-Bow church (Bow Bells)
St. Mathew
St. Matthias

St. Moritz, Switz.
St. Nicholas, or Santa Claus, or Kriss
   Kringle
St. Patrick
St. Patrick's Cathedral, NYC
St. Paul Pioneer Press & Dispatch
St. Paul, MN
St. Paul, or Saul of Tarsus
St. Peter (at Heaven's Gate)
St. Peter Damian (Pope Gregory VII)
St. Peter's Church (Rome)
St. Petersburg Times
St. Petersburg, FL
St. Pierre and Miquelon (Fr. Overseas
   Dept.)
St. Polycarp
St. Regis-Sheraton hotel (NYC)
St.-Saëns, Camille (Charles)
St. Simon
St.-Simon, Claude Henri
St. Theresa, or Teresa
St. Thomas Aquinas
St. Thomas Becket, or Thomas à
   Becket
St. Thomas, Virgin Is.
St.-Tropez, Fr.
St. Valentine
St. Valentine's Day
St. Vincent and the Grenadines
St. Vincent de Paul
St. Vitus' dance
St. Wenceslaus, or 'good King'
   Wenceslaus
Ste.-Foy, Québec, Can.
Saipan island
Sajak, Pat
Sakharov, Andrei Dmitriyevich
Sakrete™ cement mix
Saks Fifth Avenue
Sal Mineo
Salamanca, Spain
Salamis Island
Salem witchcraft trials
Salem, MA, OR
Salerno, Italy
Sales, Soupy
Salic law
Salieri, Antonio

Salinan Indians
Salinas, CA
Salinger, J. D.
Salinger, Pierre
Salisbury Cathedral
Salisbury Plain, Eng. (Stonehenge)
Salisbury steak
Salisbury, Eng.
Salish Indians
Salk vaccine
Salk, Dr. Jonas Edward
Sally Field
Sally Hansen™ cosmetics
Sally Jessy Raphael
Sally K. Ride, Astronaut
Sally Lunn tea cake
Sally Struthers
Salman Rushdie
Salome & dance of 7 veils
Salon Selectives™ haircare
Salonen, Esa-Pekka
Salt Lake City, UT
Salt Lake Tribune
Salt, Veruca
Salton Sea, CA
Saluki (dog)
Salvador, Brazil, or Bahia
Salvadore Dali (artist)
Salvadore Dali™ perfume
Salvation Army
Salvatore Ferragamo
Salvatore Quasimodo
Salween River
Salyut space vehicle
Salzburg, Austria
Sam Browne belt (military)
Sam Donaldson
Sam Giancana
Sam Jaffe
Sam Moore Walton
Sam Peckinpah
Sam Rayburn, Speaker of House
Sam Shepard
Sam Slick (pseud. Thomas Haliburton)
Sam Snead ('Slamming Sammy')
Sam Spade
Sam Spiegel
Sam Wanamaker

Sam Waterston
Sam Wiesenthal
Samaras, Lucas
Samaria
Samaritan
Samarkand, USSR
Samarra, Great Mosque of
Sambuca Romana™ liqueur
Samms, Emma
Sammy Baugh
Sammy Davis, Jr.
Samoa Standard Time
Samoa, American
Samoa, Western
Samoyed people
Samoyed dog
Samson & Delilah
Samson Agonistes
Samsung™ electronics
Samuel Adams
Samuel Barber
Samuel Beckett
Samuel Butler
Samuel Clemens (Mark Twain)
Samuel Colt
Samuel de Champlain
Samuel Goldwyn
Samuel Gompers
Samuel Houston, Gen.
Samuel I. Newhouse, Jr.
Samuel Johnson
Samuel Morse
Samuel Pepys
Samuel Sewall (witch trials judge)
Samuel Taylor Coleridge
Samuelson, Paul A.
San Andreas fault
San Angelo, TX
San Antonio Express News
San Antonio Light
San Antonio, TX
San Bernardino, CA
San Clemente, CA
San Diego, CA
San Diego Chargers
San Diego Padres
San Diego Tribune
San Diego Union

San Fernando Valley, CA
San Francisco, CA
San Francisco Chronicle
San Francisco Examiner
San Francisco 49ers
San Francisco Giants
San Jacinto River
San Joaquin River
San Joaquin Valley
San Jose, CA
San José, Costa Rica
San Juan, Puerto Rico
San Juan Capistrano, CA
San Juan Hill, Cuba
San Leandro, CA
San Luis Obispo, CA
San Marino, CA
San Marino republic
San Mateo, CA
San Miguel™ beer
San Pedro Sula, Honduras
San Quentin State Prison
San Remo, Italy
San Salvador, El Salvador
San Simeon, Hearst's castle at
Sana, Yemen
Sanchez, Oscar Arias, Pres.
Sancho Panza
Sanctus (part of Mass)
Sanctus bell (rung during Mass)
Sand, George (pseud. Amadine Dupin)
Sandburg, Carl
Sander Vanocur
Sandia Base, NM
Sandinistas
Sandra Boynton
Sandra Day O'Connor, Justice
Sandrich, Jay
Sandro Botticelli
Sands Hotel (Las Vegas)
Sandusky, OH
Sandwich, Earl of, John Montagu
Sanford 'Sandy' Koufax
Sanford B. Dole, Gov.
Sanford, Isabel
Sanger, Margaret
Sangre de Cristo Mts. (NM)
Sanhedrin

Sanibel Island, FL
Sanka™ coffee
Sanskrit
Sansui™ electronics
Sant'Angelo, Giorgio
Sant'Elia, Antonio
Santa Ana, CA
Santa Ana winds, or Santa Anas
Santa Anita racetrack
Santa Anna, Antonio de, Gen.
Santa Barbara, CA
Santa Barbara Islands, CA
Santa Clara, CA
Santa Claus, or St. Nicholas, or Kriss
   Kringle
Santa Cruz, Bolivia
Santa Cruz, CA
Santa Fe, NM
Santa Fe Opera
Santa Fe Springs, CA
Santa Fe Trail
Santa Marta, Columbia
Santa Monica, CA
Santa Rosa, CA
Santa Sophia, or Hagia Sophia
Santana
Santayana, George
Santeria
Santiago, Chile
Santo Domingo, Dominican Republic
Santoni, Reni
Santos-Dumont, Alberto
Sanwa Bank™
Sanyo Electric Co. Ltd.
Sanyo™ electronics
São Paulo, Brazil
Sao Tome and Principe, Afr. nation
Sappho
Sapporo™ beer
Sapporo, Japan
Sara Lee ™ pastries
Sara Teasdale
Saracens
Sarah 'Fergie' Ferguson, Duchess of
   York
Sarah Bernhardt (actress)
Sarah Caldwell
Sarah Churchill

Sarah Kemble Siddons
Sarah Lawrence College
Sarah Vaughan
Sarajevo, Yugoslavia
Saranac Lake (NY)
Sarandon, Susan
Saran™ Wrap
Sarasota, FL
Saratoga, CA
Saratoga campaign
Saratoga Springs, NY
Saratoga Trunk
Sardi's restaurant
Sardinia, Italy
Sargasso Sea
Sgt. Bilko TV show
Sargent, Dick
Sargent, John Singer
Sgt. York (Alvin Cullum York)
Sargento™ cheese
Sarkis, Elias, Pres.
Sarnath site
Sarnoff, David, 'Gen.´
Saroyan, William
Sarrazin, Michael
Sarsi Indians
Sartre, Jean-Paul
Saskatchewan, Can.
Saskatoon, Saskatchewan, Can.
Sasquatch, also 'Big Foot'
SAS™ Scandinavian Airlines
Sassoon, Vidal
Satan
Satanic Verses, The
Sathanas (the Devil)
Sato, Eisaku, P.M.
Saturday Evening Post
Saturn
Sau-Sea™ sauce
Saucony™ shoes
Saudi Arabia
Saul Baizerman
Saul Bellow
Saul of Tarsus, or St. Paul
Saul, King
Sault Sainte Marie Canals, or Soo
   Canals
Sault Ste. Marie Coast Grd. Base, MI

Sault Sainte Marie, Ontario, Can.
Sausalito, CA
Saussure, Ferdinand de
Sauvignon Blanc wine
Sav-on drugs™
Savage, Fred
Savage's Station
Savalas, Telly
Savannah, GA
Savile Row, Lon.
Savin™ copier
Savitch, Jessica
Savonarola, Girolamo
Savoy Hotel
Savvy
Sawyer, Diane
Sawyer, Tom
Saxons
Saxony
Sayers, Dorothy
Sayles, John
Sb (chem. sym. antimony)
Sc (chem. sym. scandium)
Scaasi, Arnold
Scaggs, Boz
Scalawags
Scandinavia
Scandinavian Airlines-SAS
Scandinavian Peninsula
Scanpan™ cookware
Scaramouche
Scarborough, Chuck
Scarborough, Eng.
Scarborough, Ont., Can.
Scarlatti, Alessandro
Scarlatti, Domenico
Scarlet Letter, The
Scarlet Pimpernel (Sir Percival
    Blakeney)
Scarlet Pimpernel, The
Scarlett O'Hara
Scarsdale Diet
Scatman Crothers
Schaap, Dick
Schaeffer, George
Schapiro, Meyer
Schary, Dore
Scheduled Castes (India)

Scheherazade
Scheider, Roy
Schell, Maria
Schelling, Friedrich Wilhelm von
Schenectady, NY
Schenkel, Chris
Schering-Plough Corp.
Schiaparelli, Elsa
Schiaparelli, Giovanni
Schick test
Schickele, Peter (aka P.D.Q. Bach)
Schick™ razors
Schiele, Egon
Schiff's reagent
Schildkraut, Joseph
Schiller, Friedrich von
Schilling™ seasoning
Schipperke (dog), or schipperke
Schirra, Walter 'Wally', astronaut
Schism of the West, or the Great
    Schism
Schlafly, Phyllis
Schlage lock
Schlatter, George
Schlesinger, Arthur M.
Schliemann, Heinrich
Schlossberg, Caroline Kennedy
Schmeling, Max
Schmidt system
Schmidt, Helmut, Chanc.
Schnauzer (dog), or schnauzer
Schneider, John
Schneiderman, Rose
Schoenberg, Arnold
Schofield Barracks, HI
School of Athens (Raphael)
school of Paris (art)
Schopenhauer, Arthur
Schorr, Daniel
Schreiner, Olive (aka Ralph Iron)
Schroder, Ricky
Schrödinger, Erwin
Schrödinger's cat
Schubert Franz
Schubert Theatre
Schulz, Charles M.
Schuman, William
Schumann, Robert

Schumann-Heink, Ernestine
Schuschnigg, Kurt von, Chanc.
Schuyler Colfax, V.P.
Schuyler, Philip John, Gen.
Schwab's drugstore (old Hollywood)
Schwann cell
Schwarzenegger, Arnold
Schwarzkopf, Elizabeth
Schweitzer, Dr. Albert
Schwenkfeld, Kaspar von
Schwenkfeldians, or Schwenkfelders
Schweppes™ mixers
Schwinger, Julian
Schwinn™ bike
Schwitters, Kurt
Scientific American magazine
Scientologist
Scientology, Church of
Scobee, Francis 'Dick' (*Challenger*
    commander)
Scofield, Paul
Scoggins, Tracy
Scone, Scotland
Scooby Doo
Scooby Doo™ vitamins
Scopas (sculptor)
Scope™ mouthwash
Scopes monkey trial (John T.)
Scoresby, William
Scorpio (zodiac sign)
Scorpius (Scorpion) constellation
Scorsese, Martin
Scotch pine
Scotch™ Tape
Scotch whiskey
Scotch-gard™
Scotland
Scotland Yard (officially New Scotland
    Yard)
Scotland, Church of
Scots Guards
Scotsman
Scott Bakula
Scott Glenn
Scott Hamilton
Scott Joplin
Scott Paper Co.
Scott, David, Astronaut

Scott, George C.
Scott, Lizabeth
Scott, Montgomery 'Scotty' (*Star
    Trek*)
Scott, Ridley
Scott, Sir Walter
Scott, Willard
Scott, Winfield, Gen.
Scott, Zachary
Scotties™ tissues
Scottish Rite Bodies
Scottish terrier (dog)
Scotts™ turf builder
Scottsboro Case
Scottsdale, AZ
ScottTowels™
Scrabble™
Scranton, PA
Scratch (the Devil)
Scream, The (Munch)
Scriabin, Aleksandr
Scribe, Augustin Eugène
Scriblerus Club
Scribner Book Co., Inc.
Scribner Bookstores
Scripps College
Scripps Institution of Oceanography
    (CA)
Scripto™
Scripture
Scrooge (tightfisted person)
Scrooge McDuck
Scrooge, Ebenezer
Scrubb, Eustace Clarence
Scruff Rafferty
Scruggs, Earl
Scully, Vin
Scutum (Shield) constellation
Scylla and Charybdis
Scylla rock
Scythia
Se (chem. sym. selenium)
Sea Breeze™ skincare
Sea Islands (Atlantic coast)
Sea of Galilee
Sea of Okhotsk
Sea of Tranquility, Moon
Sea World

Seaborg, Dr. Glenn T.
Seagate Technology
Seagram Co. Ltd., The
Seagram's™ whisky
Seagram's™ wine coolers
Seagull, The
Seal Beach Naval Weapons Station,
    CA
Seale, Bobby
Sealtest™ ice cream
Sealy™ mattress
Sealy™ Posturepedic™
Sealyham terrier (dog)
Sean Connery
Sean O'Casey
Sean Penn
Sears, Roebuck & Co.
Sears Tower (Chicago)
Sears Weatherbeater™ paint
Seattle, Chief (Indian leader)
Seattle, WA
Seattle Mariners
Seattle Post-Intelligencer
Seattle Seahawks
Seattle Slew (racehorse)
Seattle Times
Sebastian Cabot
Seberg, Jean
Secaucus, NJ
Secession, War of, or Civil War, or
    War between the States, or War of
    the States
Seconal™
Second Sino-Japanese War
Second Triumvirate
Secret Service, U. S.
Secretariat (racehorse)
Secretariat, UN
Section Eight
Securities & Exchange Comm.
Security Council, UN
Security Pacific Bank
Sedaka, Neil
See's™ candy
Seelie Court (vs. Unseelie Court)
Segal, Erich
Segovia, Andres
Seiji Ozawa

Seiko™ watch
Seine River
Selassie, Haile, Emperor
Selkirk, Alexander (real Crusoe)
Sellecca, Connie
Selleck, Tom
Selma Diamond
Selma, AL
Selsun blue™
Selznick, David O.
Seminole Indians
Semites people
Semolina Silkpaws
Sendai, Japan
Sendak, Maurice
Seneca (Roman statesman)
Seneca Army Depot, NY
Seneca Falls, NY
Seneca Indians
Senegal republic
Sennett, Mack
Seoul, S. Korea
Sephardim
Sepoy Rebellion
Sequoia Nat. Park (CA)
Sequoyah, Chief
Serafin, Barry
Serbo-Croatian language
Serengeti Plain (Afr.)
Serge Koussevitzky (Sergel)
Sergei Diaghilev
Sergeant's™ flea collar
Sergei Prokofiev, or Sergey
Sergei V. Rachmaninoff
Sergio Mendes
Serkin, Rudolf
Serling, Rod
Sermon on the Mount
Serpico
Serra, Father Junipero
Serta™ mattress
Service, Robert William
Servile Wars
Sesame Street
Sesame Street™ vitamins
Sessions, Roger
Seton, Mother, or St. Elizabeth Ann
    Seton

Seurat, Georges
Sevareid, Eric
Sevastopol (Crimea)
7-Eleven store
Seven against Thebes
Seven Hills of Rome
Seven Sisters (7 colleges)
7-Up™
Seven Wonders of the World
Seven Years War
Seventeen
Seventh-Day Adventists
Severinsen, Doc
Seville, Spain
Sevres china
Sewall, Samuel (witch trials judge)
Seward, William Henry, Sen.
Seward's folly, or Alaskan purchase
Sewell, Anna
Sextans constellation
Sexton, Anne
Seychelles republic
Seymour, Jane (actress)
Seymour, Jane, Queen Consort
Sforza, ruling family of Italy
Shackleton, Sir Ernest
Shadoe Stevens
Shafites
Shafto, Bobby
Shagari, Ahaji, Pres.
Shah of Iran
Shahn, Ben (Benjamin)
Shakers, or Shaking Quakers
Shakespeare, William, or Shakespear,
    or Shakespere, or Shakspere
Shakespearean sonnet
Shalimar™ perfume
Shalit, Gene
Shalom Rubinowitz (aka Sholom
    Aleichem)
Shaman, or shaman
Shamir, Yitzhak, P.M., or Yitzak
Shamitoff's™ iced dessert
Shamu, the killer whale
Shandling, Garry
Shandong Peninsula
Shandong province, China
Shang dynasty, or Yin

Shanghai chicken
Shanghai, China
Shangri-La
Shankar, Ravi
Shanker, Uday
Shannon Inter. Airport
Shannon River, or the River Shannon
Shantung silk
Shaolin Temple
Shapiro, Karl
Shapley, Harlow
Shar Pei (dog)
Shari Lewis (& Lambchop)
Sharif, Omar
Sharkey, Jack
Sharon Gless
Sharon Tate
Sharon Tate murders (Charles Manson)
Sharon, Ariel
Sharp Corp.
Sharp™ electronics
Shasta™ cola
Shasta daisy
Shastri, Shri Lal Bahadur, P.M.
Shatner, William
Shatt al Arab river
Shavuot (Jew. feast)
Shaw, Artie
Shaw, Bernard (journalist)
Shaw, George Bernard (playwright)
Shaw, Henry Wheeler (aka Josh
    Billings)
Shawnee Indians, or Shawano
Shays, Daniel
Shays's Rebellion
Shazam
Shea Stadium
Shearer, Moira
Shearson Lehman Hutton
Sheba, Queen of
Shecky Greene
Shedd's Spread ™
Sheedy, Ally
Sheeler, Charles
Sheen, Bishop Fulton J.
Sheen, Charlie
Sheen, Martin
Sheetrock™

Sheffield, Eng.
Sheffield plate
Sheik™ condoms
Sheldon Leonard
Shelley Duvall
Shelley Long
Shelley Winters
Shelley, Mary
Shelley, Percy Bysshe
Shelly Manne
Shenandoah Mts.
Shenandoah Nat. Park
Shenandoah Valley
Shenandoah, VA
Shepard, Alan, Astronaut
Shepard, Sam
Shepherd, Cybill
Sheraton style furniture
Sheraton Hotel
Sheraton, Thomas
Sherbrooke, Québec, Can.
Sheridan, Philip Henry, Gen.
Sheridan, Richard
Sherlock Holmes
Sherman Antitrust Act
Sherman Hemsley
Sherman Silver Purchase Act
Sherman, James S., V.P.
Sherman, Wm. Tecumseh, Gen.
Sherrington, Sir Charles
Sherry Lansing
Sherry-Netherland hotel
Sherwin-Williams Co., The
Sherwood Anderson
Sherwood Forest
Sherwood, Robert
Shetland Islands
Shetland Pony
Shetland sheepdog
Shetland wool/sweater
Shevardnadze, Eduard, Foreign Min.
Shevat (Jew. month)
Shield™ soap
Shields, Brooke
Shih Tzu (dog)
Shiite Muslim
Shikoku Isl., Jap.
Shillito-Rike's Department Store

Shiloh (Biblical Palestine)
Shiloh, battle of
Shimon Peres
Shinto religion
Shire (draft horse)
Shirley Booth
Shirley Chisholm
Shirley MacLaine
Shirley Temple Black
Shiseido™ cosmetics
Shiva (Hindu god)
Shmuel Agnon
Shockley, Dr. William B.
Shoemaker, Willie 'the Shoe'
Shofar™ kosher franks
Shogun
Sholokhov, Mikhail Aleksandrovich
Sholom Aleichem (pseud. Shalom
  Rabinowitz)
Shoo-fly Pie
Shoo-Fly Pie & Apple Pan Dowdy
Shooting of Dan McGrew, The
Shopko Stores
Shor, Bernard 'Toots'
Shore, Dinah
Shorr, Lonnie
Shoshone Falls, ID
Shoshone Indians
Shoshone Nat. Forest
Shostakovich, Dmitri, or Dimitri
Shotwell, James Johnson
Shredded Wheat™
Shree Rajneesh, Bhagwan (now Osho)
Shreveport, LA
Shri Lal Bahadur Shastri, P.M.
Shriner, Herb
Shriner, Wil
Shriver, Eunice Kennedy
Shriver, Maria
Shriver, Pam
Shropshire Co., Eng.
Shroud of Turin
Shubert Alley
Shubert Brothers
Shubert Theater
Shulman, Max
Shultz, George P., Secy. State
Shute, Nevil

Shuttle, Old Mother
Shylock
Si (chem. sym. silicon)
Siam (now Thailand)
Siamese cat
Siamese twins
Sibelius, Jean
Siberia (mostly in the USSR)
Siberian husky
Sichuan cuisine
Sichuan province, China
Sicilian Vespers rebellion
Sicily, Italy
Sickert, Walter Richard
Sid & Marty Krofft
Sid Caesar
Sid Vicious
Siddhartha, or Siddhartha Gautama
   (Buddha)
Siddons, Sarah Kemble
Sidney Bechet
Sidney Guilaroff
Sidney Lumet
Sidney Poitier
Sidon, Lebanon
Sidonie Gabrielle Claudine (aka
   Colette)
Siege Perilous (Arthurian)
Siegel, Benjamin 'Bugsie'
Siegel, Joel
Siegel, Sol
Siegfried, or Sigurd (Ger. myth)
Siemaszko, Casey
Siemens Company
Siena, Italy
Sierra Club
Sierra Club Bulletin
Sierra Leone, republic
Sierra Madre, CA
Sierra Madre Mts. (Mexico)
Sierra Nevada Mountains (CA)
Sigismund (Roman emperor/Polish
   kings)
Sigmund Freud
Sigmund Romberg
Signac, Paul
Signal™ mouthwash
Signe Hasso

Signed English
Signoret, Simone
Sigourney Weaver
Sikh (Hindi disciple)
Sikh Wars
Sikkim, state
Sikking, James
Silas Marner
Silent Spring
Silesia, region, Europe
Silivas, Daniela
Silkience™ haircare
Silkpaws, Semolina
Silky terrier
Sills, Beverly
Silstar™ fishing rod
Silurian period
Silver (Lone Ranger's horse)
Silver Star medal
Silverheels, Jay (played Tonto)
Silverman, Fred
SilverStone™ cookware
Simi Valley, CA
Simitomo Bank
Simmons™ Beautyrest™
Simmons, Richard
Simon & Garfunkel
Simon & Schuster Inc.
Simon Bolivar
Simon Legree
Simon Rodia's *Watts Towers*, or
   Rodilla
Simon Templar
Simon Wiesenthal
Simon, Carly
Simon, Neil
Simon, Norton
Simon, Paul (musician)
Simon, Paul, Sen.
Simon, St.
Simone de Beauvoir
Simone Signoret
Simoniz™ car wax
Simple Simon
Simplesse™ fat substitute
Simplon pass, Swiss Alps
Simpson Department Stores
Simpson, O. J.

Sims, Zoot
Sinai Peninsula, or peninsula
Sinai, Mt.
Sinanthropus, or Peking man
Sinatra, Frank (Francis Albert)
Sinbad the Sailor
Sinclair Lewis
Sinclair, Upton
Sine-Off™
Sinéad O'Connor
Singapore
Singapore Airlines™
Singapore, Singapore (city, country)
Singer Sewing Machine Co.
Singer, Isaac B. (author)
Singer, Isaac M. (inventor)
Singhalese language
Singleton, Penny (played Blondie)
Singleton, Zutty
Sinhalese radical group
Sinn Fein movement
Sino-Japanese War, Second
Sino-Soviet
Sinutab™
Sioux City, IA
Sioux Falls, SD
Sioux Indians, or Dakota In.
Sippie Wallace
Sir Andrew Aguecheek
Sir Bedivere
Sir Bors (Arthurian)
Sir Francis Drake hotel
Sir John Falstaff
Sir Speedy™ Printing
Sir Toby Belch
Sirhan B. Sirhan
Sirimavo Bandaranaike, P.M.
Sirus, or Dog Star
Sisiutl™ kayak
Siskel & Ebert
Siskel, Gene
Sisley, Alfred
Sisophon, Cambodia
Sissy Spacek
Sistine Chapel (Vatican)
Sisyphus, king of Corinth (myth)
Sitka, AK
Sitka Coast Guard Air Station, AK

Sitkovetsky, Dmitry
Sitting Bull, Chief
Sitwell, Dame Edith
Sitwell, Sacheverell
Sitwell, Sir Osbert
Siuslaw Nat. Forest
Sivan (Jew. mo.)
Six-Day War, Arab-Israeli
Sixx, Nikki
Sizzler™ restaurant
Skeeter Davis
Skelton, Red
Skerritt, Tom
Skid Row
Skil™ power saw
Skinner, B. F.
Skinner, Cornelia Otis
Skinner, Otis
Skippy Homeir
Skippy™ Peanut Butter
Skiros Island (Greek)
Skittle Chips™
Skittles™ candy
Skokie, IL
Skol vodka
Skor™
Skouras, Spyros
Skowron, Bill 'Moose'
Skye Terrier
Skye, Scot.
Skylab space vehicle
Skywalker, Luke
Skywest™ Airlines
Slam Stewart
Slaney, Mary Decker
Slatkin, Leonard
Slaughter, Frank
Slave Coast of Africa
Slavs ethnic group
Sleep-eze™
Sleepinal™
Sleeping Gypsy, The (Rousseau)
Slezak, Walter
Slice™ soft drink
Slick, Sam (pseud. Thomas Haliburton)
Slidell, John, Sen.
Slik™ photo. equip.
Slim Gaillard

Sloan, Alfred Pritchard
Sloan-Kettering Institute
Slovenia rep, Yugoslavia
Slovo, Joe
Sm (chem. sym. samarium)
Smart Yellow Pages™
Smart, Maxwell
Smarte Carte™ luggage carrier
Smaug the dragon
Smetana, Bedrich
Smirnoff™ vodka
Smirnoff, Yakov
Smith & Kerns cocktail
Smith & Wesson gun
Smith Barney stock broker
Smith College (MA)
Smith Corona™
Smith, Bessie
Smith, Dean Wesley
Smith, Howard K.
Smith, Jaclyn
Smith, John (& Pocahontas)
Smith, Joseph (Mormon leader)
Smith, Kate (Kathryn)
Smith, Lane
Smith, Margaret Chase, Sen.
Smith, Snuffy
Smith, Thorne
Smithereens, The
SmithKline Beckman Corp.
Smithsonian Institution
Smithsonian magazine
Smits, Jimmy
Smokey Robinson & the Miracles
Smoky Mts. (ID)
Smoot, Reed, Sen.
Smothers Brothers Comedy Hour
Smucker's™ jams/jellies
Smurfs
Smyth, Dame Ethel
Sn (chem. sym. tin)
Snap-E-Tom™ tomato juice
Snead, Sam 'Slamming Sammy'
Sneaker Tamers™ insoles
Snell's law of refraction
Snickers™ candy
Snell, Willebrord
Snider, Duke

Snodgress, Carrie
Snooks, Baby
Snooky Lanson
Snooper™ radar detector
Snoopy (of *Peanuts*)
Snoqualmie, WA
Snoqualmie Falls, WA
Snoqualmie Pass
Snorkel™ Stove
Snow, Hank
Snowden, Eric
Snowy™ bleach
Snowy Mts. (Austl. Alps)
Snuffy Jenkins
Snuffy Smith
Snyder, Jimmy 'The Greek'
Snyder, Tom
Snyders, Frans
Soap Opera Digest
Soapbox Derby
Soave™ wines
Social Darwinism
Social Democratic party (Brit.)
Social Gospel movement
Socialist Labor party (U.S.)
Socialist Revolutionary party (Rus.)
Society of Friends, or Quakers
Socorro, NM
Socrates
Soddy, Frederick
Sodom and Gomorrah
Sofia, Bulgaria
Sofkins™ cloths
Soft & Dri™ anti-perspirant
Soft Logik™ software
Soft Scrub™ cleaner
Soft Spots™ shoes
Softique™
Softklon E ™ software
SoHo (NYC)
Soho (London)
Sokoloff, Nikolay
Sokolova, Lydia
Sokolow Dance Company
Sol Siegel
Solander™ kayak
Solarcaine™ ointment
Soleri, Paolo (Arcosanti)

Solidarity
Soligor™ lens
Solo, Han
Solomon Islands
Solomon R. Guggenheim Museum
Solomon, King
Solomon's seal
Solstice™ kayak
Solti, Sir Georg
Solvang, CA
Solvay process
Solzhenitsyn, Aleksandr
Solzhenitsyn, Ignat
Somalia, country, Afr.
Somaliland, region, Afr.
Somers, Suzanne
Somerset Co., Eng.
Somerset Maugham, W.
Somerset, FitzRoy, 1st Baron Raglan
   (raglan coat)
Somoza, Anastasio, Pres.
Sondheim, Stephen
Song of Solomon, Song of Songs, or
   Canticles
Sonja Henie
Sonny Bono
Sonny Liston
Sonny Rollins
Sonora, state, Mexico
Sons of Liberty (Stamp Act)
Sons of the Pioneers (music group)
Sontag, Susan
Sony Corp.
Sony™ electronics
Sony Walkman™
Sophia Loren
Sophie Tucker
Sophie's Choice
Sophists
Sophocles
Sopwith Camel
Sorbonne, or Univ. of Paris
Sören Kierkegaard, or Søren
Sorrento, Italy
Sosuke Uno, P.M.
Sotheby's auction house
Soto, Hernando De
Soundesign™ radio

Soupy Sales
Sousa, John Philip
South Africa, Republic of
South African Airways
South African War, or Boer War
South America
South American Indians
South Australia
South Bend Tribune
South Carolina (SC)
South China Sea
South Dakota (SD)
South Dartmouth, MA
South Korea
South Lake Tahoe, CA
South Orkney Is.
South Platte River
South Pole
South Sea Bubble (South Sea Co.)
South Seas
South West Africa
South Weymouth Naval Air Station,
   MA
South, the (U.S. region)
Southeast Asia
Southeast Asia Treaty Organization,
   SEATO
Southern Alps (New Zealand)
Southern Comfort™ liqueur
Southern Hemisphere
Southern Rhodesia (now Zimbabwe)
Southern Triangle (Triangulum
   Australe) constellation
Southern Yemen (now Yemen)
Southerner
Southhampton, Earl of, Henry
   Wriothesley
Southwest Airlines
Southwestern Indians
Soutine, Chaim
Sovereign of the Universe (God)
Soviet Far East
Soviet Politburo
Soweto (Africa)
Soyuz space vehicle
Soyuz T space vehicle
Space Age
Space Shuttle *Atlantis*

Space Shuttle *Challenger*
Space Shuttle *Columbia*
Space Shuttle *Discovery*
Spacek, Sissy
Spacelab
Spade Cooley
Spade, Sam
Spader, James
Spaghetti Os™
Spahn, Warren
Spain
Spaniard
Spalding™ sports equip.
Spam™
Spanish Armada
Spanish civil war
Spanish Inquisition
Spanish Main
Spanish moss
Spanish onion
Spanish paprika
Spanish rice
Spanish Steps (Rome)
Spanish Town, Jamaica
Spanish-American War
Spano, Vincent
Spansule™
Spar, or SPAR
Sparkletts™ Seltzer
Sparta (ancient Greece)
Spartacus (a gladiator)
Spartacus party, also Spartacists
Speaker, Tristram 'Tris'
Special Astrophysical Observatory
    (USSR)
Special K™ cereal
Specs McCann
Speed Stick™ deoderant
Speedo™ sportswear
Speer, Albert
Speke, John Hanning
Spelling, Aaron
Spencer Tracy
Spenser, Edmund
Sperry Corp.
Sperry, Elmer Ambrose
Sperry-Rand Corp.
Sphinx, the Great

Spic & Span™ cleaner
Spice Islands, or Moluccas
Spiegel catalog
Spiegel, Der
Spiegel, Sam
Spielberg, Steven
Spiffits™ cleaning towels
Spike Jones Band
Spike Lee
Spillane, Mickey
Spinks, Leon
Spinks, Michael
Spinoza, Baruch, or Benedict
Spirit of Evil (the Devil)
Spirit of St. Louis
Spiritus sanctus , or Holy Ghost
Spiro T. Agnew, V.P.
Spitalny, Phil, and his All Girl
    Orchestra
Spitz, Mark
Spivak, Charlie
Spivey, Victoria
Spock, Dr. Benjamin
Spock, Mr. (of *Star Trek*)
Spode china
Spode, Josiah
Spokane, WA
Spokesman-Review/Chronicle
Spoleto Festival, It., or Festival of the
    Two Worlds
Spoon River Anthology
Spoon Size Shredded Wheat™
Spooner, Wm. Archibald, Rev.
    (spoonerism)
Sports Illustrated
SportsChannel
SportsMate™ watch
Spray'n Wash™
Spring Air™ mattress
Spring Byington
Springfield Union News
Springfield, IL, MA, MO
Springsteen, Bruce
Sprouse Reitz store
Spruce Goose plane
Spuds McKenzie
SPY Magazine
Spyri, Johanna

Spyros Skouras
Squaw Valley, CA
Squeezit™ fruit drink
'Squeaky' (Lynette) Fromme
Squibb Corp.
Squirrel Nutkin
Squirt™ soft drink
Sr (chem. sym. strontium)
Sri Lanka (formerly Ceylon)
Stacy Keach
Stafford Co., Eng.
Stafford Cripps, Sir
Stafford, Jim
Stafford, Jo
Stafford, Thomas, Astronaut
Stahl, Leslie
StairMaster™
Stalin, Joseph Vissarionovich
Stalin's Five-Year Plan
Stalingrad, USSR (now Volgograd)
Stalker A/P™ tire
Stallone, Sylvester 'Sly'
Stamford, CT
Stamp Act (law)
Stamp Act Congress (met to repeal Act)
Stan Freberg
Stan Getz
Stan Lee (Marvel Comics)
Stan Laurel
Standard & Poor's
Standard Oil Co.
Standard Oil Co. of California
Standardbred horse
Standish, Miles, or Myles
Stanford Linear Accelerator
Stanford Univ., CA
Stang, Arnold
Stanislaus Nat. Forest
Stanislavsky, Constantin
Stanislaw Lem
Stanley & Livingstone (Sir Henry & Dr. David)
Stanley Cup
Stanley Kramer
Stanley Kubrick
Stanley, Sir Henry M.
Stanton, Edwin
Stanton, Elizabeth Cady

Stanwyck, Barbara
Stapleton, Jean
Stapleton, Maureen
Star Chamber
Star-Kist™ tuna
Star Micronics™ printer
Star of Bethlehem
Star of David, or Magen David
Star Spangled Banner, or *Star-spangled*
Star Trek
Star Trek: The Next Generation
Starburst™ fruit chews
Stark, Koo
Starker exchange
Starr, Belle (b. Myra Belle Shirley)
Starr, Ringo
Starry Night, The (van Gogh)
Stars and Bars (lst U.S. flag)
Stars and Stripes (current U.S. flag)
Stash™ tea
State, U.S. Dept. of
Stateline, NV (now Lake Tahoe)
Staten Island Advance
Staten Island, NY
Stater Bros. stores
Stations of the Cross, or Way of the Cross
Statler Brothers, The
Statler Hotel
Statue of Liberty
Staubach, Roger
Stay Trim™ diet gum
Stay-Puft Marshmallow Man
Stayfree™ maxi pads
Steadicam™
steak Diane
Steamboat Springs, CO
Steed, John
Steel, Danielle
Steelcase™ office furn.
Steen, Jan
Steenburgen, Mary
Steerforth, James
Steero™ bullion cubes
Stefan Edberg
Stefan Milenkovic
Stefan Wyszynski, Cardinal

Steffi Graf
Stegner, Wallace
Steichen, Edward
Steiger, Rod
Stein, Gertrude
Steinbeck, John
Steinbrenner, George
Steinem, Gloria
Steinway piano
Steinway, Henry
Stella Adler
Stendhal (pseud. Marie Henri Beyle)
Stengel, Charles 'Casey'
Step Saver™ floor cleaner
Stepford Wives
Stephan Austin
Stephanie Zimbalist
Stephen A. Douglas
Stephen Biko
Stephen Coonts
Stephen Crane
Stephen Decatur
Stephen Foster
Stephen Hawking
Stephen King
Stephen Sondheim
Stephen Vincent Benét
Stephens, Darrin (*Bewitched*)
Sterling Hayden
Sterling Heights, MI
Stern, Isaac
Sterne, Laurence
Stetson™ cologne
Stetson™ hat
Steuben glass
Steuben saddle
Steuben, Baron Friedrich von
Steve Carlton
Steve Garvey
Steve Guttenberg
Steve Lawrence
Steve Kroft
Steve Mahre
Steve Martin
Steve McGarrett of Five-O
Steve McQueen
Steve Winwood
Steven Bochco

Steven Halpern
Steven Spielberg
Stevens, Cat
Stevens, Justice John Paul
Stevens, Risë
Stevens, Shadoe
Stevenson, Adlai E., Jr., Gov.
Stevenson, Adlai E., Sr., V.P.
Stevenson, Adlai E. III, Sen.
Stevenson, McLean
Stevenson, Parker
Stevenson, Robert Louis
Stevie Nicks
Stevie Wonder
Stewart Granger
Stewart royal family, or Stuart
Stewart, James
Stewart, Slam
Stick Ups™ air freshner
Stillwater, OK
Stilton cheese
Stilwell, Joseph, Gen.
Stimson Doctrine
Stimson, Henry Lewis, Secy. War
Stockard Channing
Stockholm, Sweden
Stockton, CA
Stockton, Frank R.
Stockwell, Dean
Stoicism
Stoke-on-Trent, Eng.
Stokely-Van Camp™ foods
Stokowski, Leopold
Stolichnaya™ vodka ('Stoli´)
Stolz, Mary
Stone Age, Middle, or Mesolithic
    period
Stone Age, New, or Neolithic period
Stone Age, Old, or Paleolithic period
Stone Age (all inclusive)
Stone Mountain Memorial (GA)
Stone of Scone
Stone, Justice Harlan Fiske
Stone, Lucy
Stonehenge (Salisbury Plain)
Stonewall Jackson (pop singer)
Stonewall Jackson, Gen.
Stony Point, NY

Stoopnagle, Colonel
Stoppard, Tom
Stordahl, Axel
Storey, David Malcolm
Storm, Gale
StormShield™ tent
Story, Justice Joseph
Stossel, John
Stouffer Hotel
Stouffer's™ frozen foods
Stouffer's™ Lean Cuisine
Stove Top™ stuffing mix
Stowaway™ battery
Stowe, Harriet Beecher
STP™ Oil Treatment
Strabo (historian)
Stradivari, Antonio, or Antonius
    Stradivarius
Stradivarius violin, or 'Strad'
Strait of Hormuz, or Ormuz
Strait of Juan de Fuca
Strait of Mackinac
Strait of Magellan
Strait of Malacca
Strait of Messina
Straits Settlements (Brit.)
Strand Book Stores
Strange, Curtis
Strasberg, Lee
Strasberg, Susan
Strasbourg, Fr.
Strasser, Robin
Stratford, CT
Stratford-on-Avon, Eng., or
    Stratford-Upon-Avon
Strathclyde (Celtic Kingdom)
Stratolounger™ chair
Straub, Peter
Strauss, Franz Joseph
Strauss, Johann, Jr.
Strauss, Johann, Sr.
Strauss, Josef
Strauss, Richard
Stravinsky, Igor
Strawberry Newtons™
Streep, Meryl
Streicher, Julius
Streisand, Barbra

Stresstabs™ vitamins
Stride Rite™ shoes
Stri-Dex™ skincare
Strieber, Whitley
Strindberg, August
Stritch, Elaine
Stroessner, Alfredo, Pres.
Stroh's™ beer
Stroheim, Erich von
Stromboli Island
Struthers, Sally
Stuart Hall stationery
Stuart Little
Stuart royal family, or Stewart
Stuart, Gilbert
Stuart, Mary, or Mary Queen of Scots
Stubbs, George
Stubby Kaye
Studebaker™ car
Studs Terkel
Sturgeon, Theodore
Sturges, John
Sturges, Preston
Sturm und Drang (Storm and Stress)
Stuttgart, W. Ger.
Stuttgart Ballet
Stutz Bearcat (car)
Stuyvesant, Peter
Styrofoam™
Styron, William
Styx (rock group)
Styx River, or River Styx
Suave ™ haircare
Subaru™ car
Subaru™ Legacy
Success™ boil-in-bag rice
Success! magazine
Suckling, Sir John
Sucre, Bolivia
Sudafed™ decongestant
Sudan, country, Afr.
Sudbury, Ont., Can.
Suddenly Salad™
Suez Canal (Egypt)
Suez, Gulf of (Egypt)
Suffolk Co., Eng.
Suffolk draft horse
Suffolk sheep

Suffolk, VA
Sufism (Muslim movement)
Sugar Daddy (slang, rich man)
Sugar Daddy™ candy
Sugar Loaf Mountain (Rio)
Sugar Moma™ candy
Sugar Ray Leonard
Sugar Ray Robinson
Sui dynasty
Suisse (French for Switzerland)
Suk, Josef
Sukkoth (Jew. holiday)
Sulayman the Magnificent, or
    Sulayman I
Sullivan, Ed
Sullivan, Harry Stack
Sullivan, John L.
Sullivan, Kathleen
Sullivan, Margaret
Sullivan, Sir Arthur
Sullivan, Susan
Sully, Thomas
Sultan of Brunei
Sulu Archipelago
Sulu Sea
Sumac, Yma
Sumatra, Indonesia
Sumerian civilization
Summer, Donna
Summer's Eve™ douche
Summerall, Pat
Sumner Locke Elliott
Sumner, Charles, Sen.
Sumners, Rosalynn
Sumter, Fort (NC)
Sun Belt (SW U.S.), or Sunbelt
Sun Company Inc.
Sun Light™ detergent
Sun Maid™ raisins
Sun Microsystems™
Sun Myung Moon, Rev. (& the
    Unification Church)
Sun Yat-sen, Pres.
Sunbeam™ appliances
Sun Belt, or Sunbelt
Suncheros™ chips
Sunco™ gas
Sundance™ Sparklers

*Sunday Afternoon on the Island of La
    Grande Jatte* (Seurat)
Sunday best (good clothes)
Sunday punch (effective measure)
Sunday school
Sunday, Billy (Wm. Ashley)
Sunday-go-to-meeting clothes
Sundown™ sun screen
Sundrivers™ glasses
Sunflower State (Kansas)
Sung, Kim Il, Prem.
Sung dynasty
Sungari River
Sunkist™
Sunni (85% of all Muslims)
Sunny Delight™ drink
Sunnyvale, CA
Sunpak™ photo. flash
Sunshine Krispy™ crackers
Sunsweet™ prunes
Sununu, John H., Chief of Staff
Super Fix-a-Flat™
Superboy
Supercuts™
Superdome, the
Superfund (US govt.)
Superior, Lake
Superman
Superpretzel™
Supra™ cookware
Supra™ modem
Suprematism art, or suprematism
Supreme Being (God)
Supreme Court, U.S.
Supreme Goodness (God)
Supreme Soviet (parliament)
Supremes, The
Sur, Lebanon, or Tyre
Sure & Natural™
Surgeon General
Suriname (formerly Dutch Guiana)
Surrealism movement, or surrealism
Surrey County, Eng.
Surveyor space probe
Susan Anton
Susan Anspach
Susan B. Anthony
Susan Cheever

Susan Dey
Susan Hayward
Susan Isaacs
Susan Lucci
Susan Palwick
Susan Ruttan
Susan Sarandon
Susan Sontag
Susan Strasberg
Susan Sullivan
Susquehanna, PA
Susquehanna River
Susquehanna University
Sussex chicken
Sussex spaniel
Sussex, East, Eng.
Sussex, West, Eng.
Susskind, David
Susuki, Midori
Sutherland, Donald
Sutherland, Graham
Sutherland, Joan
Sutherland, Kiefer
Sutter, John A.
Sutter's Fort, CA
Sutter's Mill, CA
Sutton, Willie
Suva, Fiji
Suvero, Mark di
Suwannee River, or Swanee
Suzanne Pleshette
Suzanne Somers
Suzanne Vega
Suzi Wan™ Dinners
Suzman, Janet
Suzuki Harunobu ('Harunobo')
Suzuki Samurai
Suzuki Swift™
Suzuki Zenko, P.M.
Suzy Wong
Svengali
Sverdlovsk, Sov. Un.
Svetlana Alliluyeva
Swabia, region, W. Ger.
Swabian League
Swaggart, Jimmy, Rev.
Swahili language
Swammerdam, Jan

'Swamp Fox, the´ (Marion Francis)
Swann vs. Charlotte-Mecklenburg
    County Bd. of Education
Swansea, Wales
Swanson™ frozen foods
Swanson, Gloria
Swarthout, Gladys
Swastika
Swatch™ watch
Swayze, John Cameron
Swayze, Patrick
Swaziland (Africa)
Swede
Sweden
Swedenborg, Emanuel
Swedish turnip
Sweeney Todd
Sweet Home, OR
Sweet One™ sweetener
Sweet'N Low™
Sweetwater, TX
Swift, Jonathan
Swinburne, Algernon
Swing Out Sister
Swingline™ stapler
Swintec™ bus. equip.
Swish™ toilet bowl cleanser
Swiss Alps
Swiss Family Robinson
Swiss Guards
Swiss Kriss™ laxative
Swiss Miss™ puddings
Swissair™
Swit, Loretta
Switzerland, also Swiss
    Confederation
Swoosie Kurtz
Sword of Damocles
Sybarite people
Sybil Thorndike, Dame
Sydenham, Thomas
Sydenham's chorea
Sydney Biddle Barrows
Sydney Boehm
Sydney Greenstreet
Sydney Omarr
Sydney, Australia
Sydow, Max von

Sylvania™ light blulbs
Sylvester 'Sly' Stallone
Sylvester the Cat
Sylvia Plath
Symbionese Liberation Army
Symphonie Fantastique
Synanon (place + the therapy)
Synge, John M.
Syngman Rhee, Pres.
Synoptic Gospels
Syr Darya river
Syracuse (ancient place)
Syracuse, Italy
Syracuse, NY
Syracuse Herald-Journal
Syracuse Post Standard
Syracuse University
Syria, Arab republic
Szczecin, Poland
Szechwan (now Sichuan)
Szechwan cuisine
Szell, George
Szilard, Leo

T square
T-bar
T-Bird™ car, or Thunderbird™
T-bone steak
T-shirt, or tee shirt
T-strap
T. Boone Pickens, Jr.
T. J. Hooker
T. S. Eliot
T. Texas Tyler
Ta (chem. sym. tantalum)
Tabasco™ sauce
Tabasco, state, Mexico

Tabby cat
Tabriz, Iran
Tacitus (Publius Cornelius)
Taco Bell™ restaurant
Tacoma News Tribune
Tacoma, WA
TacoTime™ restaurant
Tadeusz Mazowiecki, P.M.
Tadzhikistan, or Tadzhik Soviet
    Socialist Republic
Tae Kwon Do
Taegu, S. Korea
Taejon, S. Korea
Taff, Russ
Taft, Lorado
Taft, William Howard, Pres.
Taft-Hartley Labor Act
Taglioni, Maria
Tagore, Sir Rabindranath
Tahiti
Tahoe, Lake
Tai Chi, or Tai Chi Chuan
Taine, Hippolyte
Taipei, Taiwan
Taiping Rebellion
Taittinger™ champagne
Taiwan (formerly Formosa)
Taiyuan, China
Taj Mahal
Takei, George (Sulu on *Star Trek*)
Talbot, J. Thomas
Talbot, Wm. Henry Fox
Talbot's™ clothes
Tales of Hoffmann
Taliesen West (F. L. Wright)
Talking Heads (rock group)
Talladega Nat. Forest
Tallahassee, FL
Tallchief, Maria
Talleyrand, Charles de
Tallinn, USSR
Tallis, Thomas, or Tallys
Tallulah Bankhead
Talmadge, Constance
Talmadge, Norma
Talmud, the
Tamara Karsavina
Tamayo, Rufino

Taming of the Shrew, The
Tamiroff, Akim
Tammany bosses
Tammany Hall
Tammany Society
Tammuz (Jew. mo.)
Tammy Faye Bakker
Tammy Grimes
Tammy Wynette
Tampa Bay Buccaneers
Tampa, FL
Tampa Tribune
Tampax™ tampons
Tampico, Mex.
Tanaka Kakuei, P.M.
Tandem™ Computers
Tandy™ computer
Taney, Ch. Justice Roger Brooke
Tang™ breakfast drink
T'ang dynasty
Tanganyika, Lake
Tangier, Morocco, or Tanger
Tangier, VA
Tanglewood Festival (in'Music Shed')
Tango dance
Tangshan, China
Tanguay, Eva
Tanguy, Yves
Tanita Tikaram
Tank McNamara
Tanner, Roscoe
Tannhauser
Tanqueray™ gin/vodka
Tantalus (Gr. myth)
Tantra ritual
Tanya Tucker
Tanzania
Taoism religion
Taos, NM
Tappan™ stove
Tar-Baby
Tarascan Indians
Tarawa atoll (Pacfic Ocean)
Tarbell, Ida Minerva
Targa™ car radio
Target stores
Tarkenton, Fran
Tarkett™ flooring

Tarkington, Booth
Tarnower, Dr. Herman
Tarpon Springs, FL
Tarrytown, NY
Tarsus, Turkey
Tartarus (lowest region Hades)
Tartikoff, Brandon
Tartuffe
Tarzan of the Apes
Tashkent, Uzbekistan
Tasman Sea
Tasman, Abel Janszoon
Tasmania
Tasmanian devil
Tass (USSR)
Tasso, Torquato
Taster's Choice™ coffee
Tate Gallery (was Nat'l Gallery Brit.
    Art)
Tate, Sharon (Manson murders)
Tatiana™ perfume
Tatum, Art
Tatum, Edward Lawrie
Tatum, Goose
Tatung™ computer
Taurus (Bull) constellation
Taurus (zodiac sign)
Tavern on the Green, The (NYC)
Tawney, Richard Henry
Taxco, Mex.
Tay-Sachs disease
Tayback, Vic
Taylor, Bayard (James)
Taylor, Elizabeth
Taylor, Frederick Winslow
Taylor, Maxwell Davenport, Gen.
Taylor, Zachary, Pres.
Taystee™ bread
Tb (chem. sym. terbium)
Tbilisi, USSR, or Tiflis
Tc (chem. sym. technetium)
Tchaikovsky, Peter Ilyich
Te (chem. sym. tellurium)
Teach, Edward (aka Blackbeard)
Teagarden, Jack
Teamsters Union
Teaneck, NJ
Teapot Dome scandal

Teasdale, Sara
Tebaldi, Renata
Tecate™ beer
Technicolor™
Technics™ stereo
Tecumseh, Chief
Ted Bundy
Ted Danson
Ted DeCorsia
Ted Knight
Ted Koppel
Ted Turner
Ted Williams (the 'Splendid Splinter')
Teddy Grahams™ snacks
Teddy Ruxpin™
Teenage Mutant Ninja Turtles
Teevee, Mike
Teflon™
Tegrin™
Tegucigalpa, Honduras
Tehachapi Mts.
Tehachapi, CA
Teheran Conference
Teheran, Iran, or Tehran
Tel Aviv, Israel
Telemann, Georg Philipp
TelePrompTer™
Teletype™
Telex Corp.
Tell, William
Teller, Dr. Edward
Telluride, CO
Telly Savalas
Tempe, AZ
Temperance movement
Tempest, The
Templar, Simon
Temple of Athena Nike (Acropolis)
Temple Black, Shirley
Temptations, The
TempTee™ cheese
Tempter (the Devil)
Ten Commandments, or Decalogue
Ten Years War (Cuba)
Ten-O-Six™ skincare
Tender Chops™ dog food
Tenderloin District (in S.F.)
Tennessee (TN)

Tennessee Ernie Ford
Tennessee River
Tennessee Valley Authority
Tennessee Walking Horse
Tennessee Williams
Tenniel, Sir John
Tennille, Toni
Tennyson, Lord Alfred
Tenure of Office Act (U.S.)
Teotihuacán (ancient city)
Terbrugghen, Hendrick
Terence Rattigan
Teresa Brewer
Teresa, Mother
Tereshkova, Valentina, Cosmonaut
Teri Garr
Terkel, Studs
Termagant (Muslim deity)
Terminal Island Coast Guard Base,
  CA
Terminix International Inc.
Terpsichore (muse)
Terre Haute, IN
Terry Drinkwater
Terry Melcher
Terry Waite
Terry, Dame Ellen
Terylene™ polyester
Tesh, John
Tesla coil/induction motor
Tesla, Nikola
Tess of the D'Urbervilles
Tethys (Saturn moon)
Tetilla cheese
Teton Range
Teutonic Order, or Teutonic Knights
Tevet (Jew. mo.)
Tex Ritter
Tex-Mex food
Texaco Incorporated
Texarkana, AR, TX
Texarkana Gazette
Texas (TX)
Texas Instruments Inc.
Texas Ranger (peace officer)
Texas Rangers (team)
Texas Ware™ dinnerware
Texsport™

Texsun™ juice
Textra™ hair care
Th (chem. sym. thorium)
Thackeray, Wm. Makepeace
Thai Airways International Ltd.
Thai cuisine
Thailand (formerly Siam)
Thalberg, Irving
Thalidomide, or thalidomide
Thames River, or the Thames
Thang, Ton Duc, Pres.
Thanksgiving Day
Thant, U, UN Secy. Gen.
Tharp, Twyla
Thatcher, Margaret, P.M.
The Congressional Record
The Dalles, OR
The Hague, Netherlands
Thebes (ancient Greece, also ancient
    Egypt)
Themistocles (Gr. statesman)
Theo van Doesburg
Theocritus (Gr. poet)
Theodor Geisel (Dr. Seuss)
Theodore Dreiser
Theodore Roosevelt Nat. Pk. (ND)
Theodore Roosevelt, Pres.
Théodore Rousseau
Theodore Sturgeon
Theognis (Gr. poet)
Theory of Relativity (Einstein's)
Theosophical Society
Theosophy
Theresa, Maria, of Austria
Theresa, Saint, or Teresa
Thermador™ stove
Thermo-Grip™ glue gun
Thermos™
Theseus (myth. hero)
Thespis (Gr. dramatist)
Thessalonians
Thessaly, reg., Gr.
Thicke, Alan
Thieu, Nguyen Van, Pres.
Thimbu, Bhutan
Thinsulate™ ski wear
Thiokol™
Third of May, 1808 (Goya)

Third Reich
Third Republic
Third World, or 'developing nations'
Thirteen Colonies
Thirty Years War (Europe)
thirtysomething
Thisbe, Pyramus &
Thívai, Greece
Tho, Le Duc
Thomas Bailey Aldrich
Thomas Aquinas, Saint
Thomas à Becket, or St. Thomas
    Becket
Thomas Beecham, Sir
Thomas Hart Benton (artist)
Thomas Hart Benton, Sen.
Thomas Bowdler (bowdlerize)
Thomas Carew
Thomas Chatterton
Thomas Chippendale
Thomas Cook (Cook's Tours)
Thomas Dekker
Thomas E. Dewey
Thomas A. Dooley, Dr.
Thomas Eakins
Thomas Alva Edison
Thomas'™ English Muffins
Thomas Gage, Gen./Gov.
Thomas Gainsborough
Thomas Gresham, Sir
Thomas Haliburton (aka Sam Slick)
Thomas Hardy
Thomas Hearns
Thomas A. Hendricks, V.P.
Thomas A. Heppenheimer
Thomas Hobbes
Thomas Jefferson, Pres.
Thomas Kyd, or Kid
Thomas Malory, Sir
Thomas Mann
Thomas R. Marshall, V.P.
Thomas Moore (Ir. poet)
Thomas More, Sir (*Utopia*)
Thomas Nast
Thomas 'Tip' O'Neill, Speaker of
    House
Thomas Paine
Thomas Sheraton

Thomas Stafford, Astronaut
Thomas Sully
Thomas Sydenham
Thomas Wolfe
Thomas Wolsey, Cardinal
Thomas, Debi
Thomas, Dylan
Thomas Aquinas, Saint
Thomasville™ furniture
Thompson seedless grapes
Thompson submachine gun, or
    'Tommy gun'
Thompson, Lea
Thomson Newspapers Ltd. (Can.)
Thomson, Joseph J., Sir
Thomson, Kenneth Roy
Thor Heyerdahl (Kon Tiki raft)
Thor, the Thunder God
Thorazine™
Thoreau, Henry David
Thorn-EMI plc
Thorndike, Dame Sybil
Thorne Smith
Thoroughbred horse (a breed)
Thorpe, Jim
Thorton Wilder
Thousand and One Nights, or
    Arabian Nights, The
Thousand Island dressing
Thousand Islands (St. Lawrence River)
Thousand Oaks, CA
Thrace (region S.E. Europe)
3M, or Minnesota Mining and
    Manufacturing Co.
Three Emperors' League
Three Kingdoms dynasty
Three Kings, or Magi, or Three Wise
    Men
Three Marx Bros. (Groucho, Chico,
    Harpo)
Three Mile Island, PA
Three Musicians (Picasso)
Three Musketeers (Athos, Porthos,
    Aramis)
Three Musketeers™ candy bar
Three Stooges (Curly, Moe, Larry)
Three Suns, The
three R's, the

Thrifty Drug and Discount Stores
Thrifty Rent-A-Car™
Thrushbeard, King
Thucydides (Gr. historian)
Thugs (sect of murders)
Thule (ancient northern land)
Thumbelina
Thunder Bay, Ont., Can.
Thunderbird™ car, or T-Bird™
Thunderbird™ wine
Thundercats
Thurber, James
Thurgood Marshall, Justice
Thuy Thu Le
Ti (chem. sym. titanium)
Tian An Men Square, China
Tibbett, Lawrence
Tibbs, Casey
Tiber River
Tibet
Tibetan Buddhism
Tibetan language
Tibetan terrier
Ticketmaster Corp.
Ticonderoga, NY
Ticonderoga, Fort
Tiddly-Winks™
Tide™ detergent
Tidy Cat™ litter
Tiegs, Cheryl
Tiepolo, Giovanni
Tierney, Gene
Tierra del Fuego
Tiffany & Co.
Tiffany Chin
Tiffany lamp
Tiffany, Louis
Tiger Beat magazine
Tiger Moth airplanes
Tigger (*Winnie-the-Pooh*)
Tiggy-Winkle, Mrs.
Tigris Expedition (T. Heyerdahl)
Tigris River
Tijuana, Mex.
Tikaram, Tanita
Tilden, 'Big' Bill
Tillamook, OR
Tillamook cheese

Tillis, Mel
Tilly, Meg
Tilsit cheese
Tilton, Charlene
Tim Reid
Timberline Geodesics™ homes
Timbuktu ("to T_____ & back")
Time Incorporated
Time magazine
Time Warner Inc.
Time-Life Books
Times Square (Broadway)
Times Wire Services
Times-Picayne/States-Item
Timex™ watch
Timon of Athens
Timotei™ Shampoo
Timothy Hutton
Timothy Leary
Timurids dynasty
Tina Yothers
Tinker, Grant
Tintoretto (b. Jacopo Robusti)
Tiny Grimes
Tiny Tim (entertainer)
Tiny Tim Cratchit
Tiomkin, Dimitri
Tippecanoe (nick. for Wm. Henry Harrison)
Tippecanoe River
Tipperary, Ire.
Tippetarius, Queen of Oz
Tippett, Sir Michael
Tippi Hedren
Tissot, J. J.
Titan (Saturn moon)
Titania (Uranus moon)
Titania, Queen of the Fairies
Titanic, S.S.
Titian (painter)
Titicaca, Lake
Titius-Bode law
Tito, Marshal, P.M.
Tittlemouse, Mrs.
Titus Andronicus (play)
Titus, Emperor (Titus Flavius)
Tivoli Gardens
Tivoli, Italy

Tiwanaku, or Tiahuanacu
Tiy, Queen of Egypt
Tl (chem. sym. thallium)
Tlingit Indians
Tm (chem. sym. thulium)
TNT, or trinitrotoluene
Toad of Toad Hall
Toastettes™ tarts
Toastmaster™ toaster
Tobago Island
Tobruk, Libya
Toby Belch, Sir
Today™ sponge
Tofutti™
Togo Heihachiro, Adm.
Togo, Republic of
Tojo Hideki, Prem.
Tokay grapes
Tokay wine
Tokelau (formerly Union Islands)
Tokina™ lens
Toklas, Alice B.
Tokugawa regime (Shogun)
Tokyo, Jap.
Toledo Blade
Toledo, OH
Toledo, Spain
Tolkien, J. R. R.
Toll House cookies™
Tollen's reagent
Tolstoy, Leo, or Tolstoi
Toltec Indians
Tom and Jerry (cartoon)
Tom and Jerry (cocktail)
Tom Berenger
Tom Bosley
Tom Bradley, Mayor
Tom Brokaw
Tom Clancy
Tom Collins (drink)
Tom Conti
Tom Cruise
Tom Ewell
Tom T. Hall
Tom Hanks
Tom Hulce
Tom Jarriel
Tom Landry

Tom Mix
Tom Petty & The Heartbreakers
Tom Sawyer
Tom Selleck
Tom Skerritt
Tom Snyder
Tom Stoppard
Tom Thumb (Circus person)
Tom Thumb (Eng. folklore)
Tom Waits
Tom Wopat
Tom, Dick and Harry ('anybody' at random)
Tomato™ menswear
Tombouctou, Mali (was Timbuktu)
Tombstone, AZ
Tomlin, Lily
Tommaso Guidi (Masaccio)
Tommy (Br. slang)
Tommy Atkins (slang, Br. soldier)
Tommy Chong (Cheech &)
'Tommy Gun', or Thompson submachine gun
Tommy Lee Jones
Tommy Lasorda
Tommy Tune
Tompkins, Daniel D., V.P.
Ton Duc Thang, Pres.
Tone Loc
Tone, Franchot
Tonga, or, the Friendly Islands
Toni™ perm
Toni Tennille
Tonkin Gulf resolution
Tonkin Gulf, or Gulf of Tonkin
Tonto (Lone Ranger's sidekick)
Tony Awards
Tony Bennett
Tony Curtis
Tony Danza
Tony Orlando and Dawn
Tony Randall
Tony Roma's restaurant
Too Too the owl
Tooele Army Depot, UT
Took, Olly
Toomey, Regis
Tootsie Pop™

Tootsie Roll™
Top Forty, or Top 40
Top of the Mark (Mark Hopkins hotel)
Top Ramen™ noodles
Top Shelf™ entrees
Topeka, KS
Topol™ toothpaste
Topsiders
Torah, the
Torie Steele store
Torme, Mel
Toronto Blue Jays
Toronto Globe & Mail
Toronto Sun
Toronto, Ont., Can.
Toronto, Univ. of
Torquato Tasso
Torrance, CA
Torremolinos, Sp.
Torrens Act
Torrens, Sir Robert
Torres wine
Torrijos Herrera, Omar
Tors, Ivan
Tortilla Flat
Tortino's™ pizza
Tortoiseshell cat
Tortuga Island, Haiti
Tory party (vs. Whig)
Tosca
Toscanini, Arturo
Toshiba Corp.
Toshiba™ electronics
Toshiki Kaifu, P.M.
Toshiro, Mifune
Tostitos™ tortilla chips
Total™ cereal
Toto of Oz
Touchstone Pictures
Tough Act™ bathroom cleaner
Toughskins™ boyswear
Toulouse, France
Toulouse-Lautrec, Henri de
Tour de France bicycle race
Tourette's syndrome
Tours, France
Tower of Babel
Tower Books

Tower of London
Tower Records/Video
Towle™ silver
Town & Country magazine
Townes, Charles Hard
Townsend plan (social security)
Townsend, Francis E.
Townshend Acts (replace stamp acts)
Townshend, Charles, Viscount
Toynbee, Arnold
Toyobo Co. Ltd.
Toyota Motor Co. Ltd.
Toys "R" Us
Tracey Ullman
Traci Lords
Tracie Ruiz
Tracy Austin
Tracy Chapman
Tracy Scoggins
Tracy Keenen Wynn
Tracy, Dick
Tracy, Ellen
Tracy, Spencer
Trader Bay™
Trader Vic's Restaurant
Trafalgar Square, Lon.
Trafalgar, battle of
Trailblazer™ fat substitute
Trang Bang village, Vietnam
Trans World Airlines™, or TWA™
Transamerica Pyramid
Transcendental Meditation
Transcendentalist
Transjordan (now Jordan)
Transportation, U.S. Dept. of
Trans-Siberian Railroad
Transylvania region, Rumania
Transylvanian Alps
Trapp, Maria von
Trapper Keeper™ notebook
Trappist monk
Traubel, Helen
Travanti, Daniel J.
Travel and Leisure
Travel-Holiday
Traveler's Aid
Travelodge™ Motel, or TraveLodge
Travers, P. L. (*Mary Poppins*)

Travilla, Bill
Travis Air Force Base, CA
Travis, Merle
Travis, Randy
Travolta, John
Treacher, Arthur
Treasure Island, FL
Treasure Island Naval Station, CA
Treasury, U.S. Dept. of
Treaty of Cambrai
Treaty of Guadalupe Hidalgo
Treaty of Paris
Treaty of Versailles
Trebek, Alex
Trebizond, empire of (ancient)
Tree Top™ juice
Tree, Ellen
Tree, Sir Herbert
Treet™ canned meat
Trekkie (*Star Trek* fan)
Tremayne, Les
Trenary, Jill
Trendar™
Trent Affair (Civil War)
Trent, Council of (Catholic Church)
Trenton, NJ
Tretorn™ shoes
Trevi Fountain (Rome)
Trevino, Lee
Tri-Corder (*Star Trek*)
Tri-Star Pictures
Triangle Shirt Waist Co. fire
Triangulum Australe (Southern Triangle) constellation
Triassic period
Tribeca, or TriBeCa (NYC)
Tribes of Israel
Triborough Bridge (NYC)
Tricia Nixon
Trident™ gum
Trident 2 missile
Trieste, Fountain of (Italy)
Trieste, Italy
Trifari™ jewelry
Trigère, Pauline
Trigger (Roy Rogers' horse)
Trinidad and Tobago
Trinity College Library (Ire.)

Trinity, the
Trinity doctrine
Trinity Sunday
Triple Alliance (Europe)
Triple Crown
Triple Sec liqueur
Tripoli, Libya
Tripolitan War
Triscuit™ crackers
Tristan and Isolde, or Tristram and
   Isolde
Tristano, Lennie
Tristram 'Tris' Speaker
Tristram Shandy
Tritin™
Triton (Neptune moon)
Triton Fountain (Bernini)
Triumvirate, First
Triumvirate, Second
Trivial Pursuit™ game
Trix™ cereal
Troi, Deanna, Counselor (*Star Trek*)
Troilus and Cressida
Trois-Rivières, Québec, Can.
Trojan™ condom
Trojan horse
Trojan War
Trojan Women, The
Trollope, Anthony
Tropic of Cancer (N of equator)
Tropic of Cancer (novel)
Tropic of Capricorn (S of equator)
Tropic of Capricorn (novel)
Tropical Zone, or Torrid Zone
Tropicana™ juice
Tropicana Twister™
Trotsky, Leon, or Trotski
'Trotsky's Dilemma'
Trotter, John Scott
Trousdale Estates (in Bev. Hills)
Trout, Robert
Troy (ancient)
Troy Donahue
Troy, MI
Troy-Bilt™ tractor
Truckee, CA
Trudeau, Garry (*Doonesbury*)
Trudeau, Margaret

Trudeau, Pierre Elliott, P.M.
True Grit
Truex, Ernest
Truffaut, François
Truman Bradley
Truman Capote
Truman, Harry S., Pres.
Truman, Margaret
Trumbull, John (painter)
Trumbull, John (poet)
Trump the Game™
Trump, Donald J.
Trump, Ivana
Truth or Consequences radio/TV
   show
Truth or Consequences, NM
TRW credit rating
TRW Incorporated
Trygve H. Lie, Secy. Gen.
Tse-tung, Mao, Chairman, or Zedong
Tshombe, Moise, Pres.
Tsimshian Indians
Tsin dynasty, or Chin
Tu Fu (Chinese poet)
Tuaca liqueur
Tubb, Ernest
Tubby™ baby furn.
Tubman, Harriet
Tuborg™ beer
Tucana constellation
Tuchman, Barbara W.
Tucker, Michael
Tucker, Sophie
Tucker, Tanya
Tucson, AZ
Tucumcari, NM
Tucume pyramids, Peru
Tudor style
Tudor, royal house of
Tuff Shield™ car wax
Tuftex™ carpet
Tug-of-War
Tugboat Annie
Tuileries gardens
Tuileries, France
Tull, Jethro
Tulsa, OK
Tultex™ sweats

Tumbling Tumbleweeds
Tums™ antacid
Tums E-X™ antacid
Tumwater, WA
Tune, Tommy
Tunis, Tunisia
Tunisia (N. Afr.)
Tunney, Gene
Tupelo, MS
Turandot
Turin, Italy
Turin, Shroud of
Turk
Turkey
Turkish bath
Turkish delight
Turkish language
Turkish tobacco
Turkish towel
Turko-Persian war
Turks and Caicos Islands (Br. colony)
Turner Broadcasting System
Turner, Kathleen
Turner, Joseph Mallord
Turner, Lana
Turner, Nat
Turner, Ted
Turofsky, Riki
Turpin, Dick, the highwayman
Tuscaloosa, AL
Tuscany, region, Italy
Tuscarora Indians
Tuskegee Institute (AL)
Tuskegee Nat. Forest
Tussaud, Marie (waxworks)
Tutankhamen, or Tutenkhamon, or
   'King Tut'
Tutsi people, or Watutsi, or Batusi
Tuttle, Frank
Tutu, Desmond, Archbishop
Tuvalu, country, Oceania
TV Guide
TWA™ or Trans World Airlines™
Twain, Mark (pseud. Samuel Clemens)
Tweed Ring
Tweed, William Boss
Tweedledum & Tweedledee
Twelfth Day

Twelfth Night
Twelfth Night; Or What You Will
Twelve Apostles, or Disciples
20th Century Fox
Twentynine Palms, CA
Twiggy
Twilight of the Gods
Twin Cities, Minneapolis & St. Paul
Twin Falls, ID
Twin Peaks
Twinings™ Tea
Twinkies™
Twist, Oliver
Twisted Sister (rock group)
Twitchett, Mother
Twittering Machine, The (Klee)
Twitty, Conway
Twix™ candy
2 AM Publications
Two Gentlemen of Verona, The
Two Sicilies, kingdom of the
Twyla Tharp
Ty Cobb
Ty-D-Bol™ toilet cleaner
Tybalt Capulet (*Romeo & Juliet*)
Tyco™ toys
Tylenol™ pain reliver
Tyler, Anne
Tyler, John, Pres.
Tyler, Royall
Tyler, T. Texas
Tyler, TX
Tyne Daly
Type A personality
Type B personality
Typhoid Mary (Mary Mallon)
Tyre, Lebanon, or Sur
Tyrol, Austria
Tyrolian shorts
Tyrone Guthrie, Sir
Tyrrhenian Sea
Tyson, Cicely
Tyson, Mike
Tze, Lao, or Lao-tzu

U Thant, UN Secy. Gen.
U-2 spy plane
U-Can-Build™ power tool
U-Haul™
U-joint
U-turn
U-No™ candy
U. S. Air Force Academy
U. S. Coast Guard Academy
U. S. Dept. of Justice
U. S. Dept. of State
U. S. Dept. of Treasury
U. S. Marine Corps
U. S. Merchant Marine Academy
U. S. Military Academy at West Point
U. S. Naval Academy at Annapolis
U. S. News & World Report
U. S. Secret Service
U. S. Sprint™
U.S.S. Pueblo
U.S.S. Vincennes
Uccello, Paolo
Udall, Morris K., Rep.
Uday Shanker
Ueberroth, Peter
Uecker, Bob ('Mr. Baseball')
Uffize palace
Uffizi Gallery
Uganda
Ugarte Augusto Pinochet, Pres.
Uggams, Leslie
Uggug, son of sub-warden of Outland
Ugly Duckling™ Rent-A-Car
UKIRT Unit of the Royal
  Observatory (HI)
Ukraine, or Ukrainian Sov. Soc. Rep.

ul-Haq, Zia, Mohammad, Pres., or
  'Pres. Zia´
Ulan Bator, Mongolia
Ullman, Tracey
Ullmann, Liv
Ulster, Ireland
Ultra-Stereo™
Ulysses (novel)
Ulysses Simpson Grant, Pres.
Ulysses, king of Ithaca
Umberto Boccioni
Umberto Giordano
Umberto Mastroianni
Una Merkel
Uncle Remus
Uncle Sam
Uncle Tom's Cabin
Uncle Vanya
Underalls™ pantyhose
Underground Railroad
Underwood Deviled Ham™
Underwood, Blair
UNESCO
UNICEF
Ungaro™ designer wear
Uni-ball™ pen
Unicap™ vitamins
Unification Church (Sun Myung
  Moon's)
Union Bank
Union Islands (now Tokelau)
Union of South Africa
Union of Soviet Socialist Republics
Unisol Plus™ eye care
Unisom™ sleep aid
Unisys Corp.
Unitarianism
Unitas, Johnny
United Airlines
United Arab Emirates (federation)
United Arab Republic (political union,
  Egypt/Syria)
United Artists
United Church of Christ
United Colonies of New England
United Nations
United Negro College Fund
United Press International, or UPI

Univega™ bike
Universal Pictures
Universal Studio
Uno, Sosuke, P.M.
Unocal Corp.
Unseelie Court (vs. Seelie Court)
Unser, Al
Upanishads
Updike, John
UPI Cable News
UPI Radio Network
Upjohn Co., The
Upland, CA
Upper Eastside Manhattan
Upper Nile basin
Upper Volta (now Burkina Faso)
Uppsala, Sweden
Upton Sinclair
Ur (ancient city)
Urals, or Ural Mts.
Uran
Uranus
Uri Geller
Uriah Heep
Urich, Robert
Uris, Leon
Ursa Major (Big Dipper)
Ursa Minor (Little Dipper)
Ursula K. Le Guin
Uruguay
US Magazine
US News and World Report
USA Cable Network
USA Network
USA Today
USAir
Ustinov, Peter
Utah (UT)
Ute Indian
Uther Pendragon (Arthurian)
Utica (ancient Afr. city)
Utica, NY
Utley, Garrick
Utopia
Utrillo, Maurice
Uxmal (ancient city)
Uzbekistan, or Uzbek Soviet Socialist
    Republic

Uzi submachine gun

V (chem. sym. vanadium)
V-day
V-E Day
V-8™ juice
V-J Day
V-neck
V-2 rocket (WWII)
Vacaville, CA
Vaccaro, Brenda
Vadim Brodsky
Vadim Medvedev
Vadim, Roger
Vaduz, Liechtenstein
Vagisil™ medication
Vague, Vera
Vail, CO
Valdez, AK
Valencia, CA
Valencia oranges
Valencia, Spain
Valens, Ritchie
Valenti, Jack
Valentin Lebedev, Cosmonaut
Valentina Tereshkova, Cosmonaut
Valentine, Saint
Valentine's Day
Valentino™
Valentino Rudolph
Valenzuela, Fernando
Valeria Messalina, Empress
Valerie Bertinelli
Valerie Perrine
Valery Koubassov, Cosmonaut
Valhalla, also Walhalla
Valium™

Valjean, Jean
Valkyries
Vallee, Rudy
Vallejo, CA
Valletta, Malta
Valley Forge (PA)
Valli, June
Valparaíso, Chile
Valvoline™ motor oil
Van Allen radiation belts
Van Ark, Joan
Van Brocklin, Norm
van Beethoven, Ludwig
Van Buren, Abigail (aka 'Dear Abby')
Van Buren, Martin, Pres.
Van Camp's™ foods
Van Cleef & Arpels™
Van Cliburn
Van Damme, Jean-Claude
van de Graaf generator
Van de Kamp™ bakery/frozen foods
van der Rohe, Mies (Ludwig)
van der Weyden, Roger
van Doesburg, Theo
Van Doren, Charles (TV scandal)
Van Doren, Mamie
van Druten, John
Van Dyck, Sir Anthony, or Vandyke
Van Dyke, Dick
Van Dyke, Jerry
van Eyck, Hubert
van Eyck, Jan
Van Gogh, Vincent
Van Halen
Van Heflin
Van Heusen, James 'Jimmy'
Van Heusen™ shirts
Van Houten™ chocolate
Van Johnson
van Leeuwenhoek, Antony
van Ostade, Adriaen
van Rijn, Rembrandt, or Ryn
Van Thieu, Nguyen, Pres.
van Vogt, A. E.
Van Winkle, Rip
Vance Air Force Base, OK
Vance Brand, Astronaut
Vance, Cyrus R., Secy. State

Vancouver, B.C., Can.
Vancouver Island, B. C., Can.
Vancouver Province
Vancouver Sun
Vancouver, WA
Vandenberg Air Force Base, CA
Vanderbilt, Amy
Vanderbilt, Cornelius
Vanderbilt, Gloria
Vandross, Luther
Vandyke beard
Vandyke brown
Vandyke collar
Vanessa Harwood
Vanessa Redgrave
Vanessa Williams
Vanish™ toilet bowl cleaner
Vanna White
Vanocur, Sander
Vanuatu republic
Vargas, Virgilio Barco, Pres.
Varona, Donna De
Vasco da Gama
Vasco de Balboa
Vaseline™
Vaseline™ Lip Therapy
Vaslav Nijinsky
Vasquez Rocks (CA)
Vassar College
Vatican City, or the Vatican
Vatican Councils
Vatican Library (Rome)
Vaudeville, or vaudeville
Vaughan Williams, Ralph
Vaughan, Sarah
Vaughn, Robert
Vauxhall, Prince Henry
Vaxholm, Sweden
Veadar (Jewish mo.)
Vector Research™ VCR
Veda, the (sacred Hindu book)
Veep (slang, Vice President)
Vega, Suzanne
Vegit™ seasoning
Veg-O-Matic™
Velamints™
Velázquez, Diego
Velcro™

Velux™ windows
Velveeta™
Venera space probe
Venerable Bede, or St. Bede
Venezuela
Venice, CA
Venice, Italy, or Venezia
Ventarama™ windows
Ventura, CA
Venus (planet/myth. goddess)
Venus de Milo
Venus' flytrap
Venuta, Benay
Vera Vague
Vera-Ellen
Veracruz, state, Mexico
Verdi™ tote bag
Verdi, Giuseppe
Verdon, Gwen
Verdun, Québec, Can.
Vereen, Ben
Vergil (Publius Vergilius Maro), or
    Virgil
Vermeer, Jan, or Johannes
Vermont (VT)
Verne, Jules
Vernon Castle
Vero Beach, FL
Verona, Italy
Veronica Hamel
Veronica Lake
Verrazano-Narrows Bridge (NYC)
Verrocchio, Andrea
Versailles, France
Versailles, Palace of
Versailles, Treaty of
Veruca Salt
Vesco, Robert
Vespa™ motor scooter
Vespucci, Amerigo
Vesta (Rom. goddess)
Vestal Virgins
Vestron Inc.
Vesuvius, Mount (volcano)
Veteran's Day
Veterans Administration
Veterans of Foreign Wars
Vetii house (in Pompeii)

Viadent™ toothpaste
Vic Damone
Vic Tayback
Vicenza, Italy
Vichy government
Vichy™ water
Vichy, France
Vicious, Sid
Vicki Lawrence
Vicks VapoRub™
Vicksburg campaign
Vicksburg, MS
Victor Borge
Victor Herbert
Victor Hugo, Vicomte
Victor Jory
Victor Kiam
Victor Mature
Victor McLaglen
Victor Milan
Victor Moore
Victoria & Albert Museum (Lon.)
Victoria, B.C., Can.
Victoria Brucker
Victoria Cross
Victoria Falls (Africa)
Victoria Guadalupe, Pres.
Victoria Principal
Victoria Sackville-West
Victoria Spivey
Victoria Station restaurant
Victoria, Queen
Victoria's Secret store
Victorian style
Victorinox™ swiss army knife
Vidal Sassoon™ haircare
Vidal, Gore
Vidkun Quisling
Vidmar, Peter
Vidor, King
Vienna State Opera Orch.
Vienna, Austria
Vienna, Congress of
Viet Minh
Vietcong, or Viet Cong
Vietnam War
Vietnam
Vietnamese (native, Vietnam)

Vietnamize policy (military operation)
Viking Penguin Inc.
Viking space probe
Vikings
Villa, Pancho
Village Voice
Villanova, PA
Villanova University
Villechaize, Herve
Villeroy & Boch™ china
Villon, François
Villon, Jacques
Vilnius, Lithuania
Vin Scully
Vince Lombardi
Vincennes, U.S.S.
Vincent d'Indy
Vincent de Paul, Saint
Vincent Gardenia
Vincent Spano
Vincent Van Gogh
Vincent, Francis T. Jr.
Vincente Minnelli
Vincenzo Bellini
Vinci, Leonardo da
Vineland, NJ
Vinton, Bobby
Violet Beauregarde
Violeta de Chamorro, Pres.
Virgil (Publius Vergilius Maro), or
    Vergil
Virgilio Barco Vargas, Pres.
Virgin Islands Nat. Pk.
Virgin Islands of the U.S.
Virgin Islands, British
Virgin Mary
Virginia (VA)
Virginia Beach, VA
Virginia Company
Virginia creeper
Virginia Dare
Virginia deer
Virginia Egnor (aka Dagmar)
Virginia fence (rail fence)
Virginia E. Johnson, Dr.
Virginia Madsen
Virginia reel
Virginia Resolutions

Virginia Slims™
Virginia Woolf
Virgo (Virgin) constellation
Visa™ card
Visalia, CA
Vishnu (Hindu god)
Visigoths, or West Goths
Visine™
Vitale, Dick
Vitalis™ haircare
vitamin B-complex
Vitas Gerulaitis
Viterbo, Italy
Vittel™ water
Vittadini, Adrienne
Vittorio De Sica
Vittoro Gassman
Viva™ paper towels
Viva Zapata
Vivaldi, Antonio
Vivarin™ energy pills
Vivian Blaine
Vivien Leigh
Vivitar™ camera
Vizsla (dog), or vizsla
Vladimir Ashkenazy
Vladimir Feltsman
Vladimir Gelvan
Vladimir Horowitz
Vladimir Ilyich Lenin
Vladimir Zworykin
Vladivostok, USSR
Vlaminck, Maurice de
Vlasic™ Deli Dills
Vlasic™ pickles
VO5™ hair care
Vogue magazine
Voice of America
Voight, Jon
Voit™ sports equip.
Vogt, A. E. van
Vol, Frank De
Volans (Flying Fish) constellation
Volcker, Paul
Volga River
Volgograd, USSR (formerly Stalingrad)
Volkswagen™ car
Volkswagen™ 'Bug'

Volkswagen™ Rabbit
Volkswagenwerke
Volpone
Volstead, Andrew, Rep.
Volsted Act
Volta, Alessandro, Conte
Voltaire, François
von Anhalt, Prince Frederik
von Behring, Emil
von Bismarck, Prince Otto ('Iron Chancellor')
von Braun, Wernher
von Bülow, Claus
von Bülow, Martha 'Sunny'
von Dohnányi, Ernst
von Flotow, Friedrich
von Furstenberg, Diane
von Goethe, Johann Wolfgang
von Karajan, Herbert
von Schelling, Friedrich Wilhelm
von Schiller, Friedrich
von Schuschnigg, Kurt, Chancellor
von Schwenkfeld, Kaspar
von Steuben, Baron Friedrich,
von Stroheim, Erich
von Sydow, Max
von Trapp family
von Trapp, Maria
von Wassermann, August
von Weber, Carl Maria, also Karl
von Zeppelin, Ferdinand Graf, Count
Vonnegut, Kurt, Jr.
VonZell, Harry
Voskhod spacecraft
Vostok spacecraft
Voyager space probe
Voyageurs Nat. Pk.
Vreeland, Diana
Vries, Hugo De, or de Vries
Vuarnet™ sun glasses
Vuillard, Edouard
Vulcan (of *Star Trek*)
Vulcan (myth god of fire)
Vulgar Latin
Vyacheslav M. Molotov, Vice-Premier

W (chem. sym. tungsten)
W H Smith Bookstores
W. Averell Harriman
W. C. Fields
W. C. Handy
W. E. Du Bois (Wm. Edward - NAACP)
W. Somerset Maugham
W.A.S.P. (rock group)
Wabash Cannonball
Wabash, IN
Wacky Wallwalker
Waco, TX
Wade, Benjamin Franklin, Sen.
Wadi Qumran, Jordan (Dead Sea Scrolls site)
Wag, Charlcy
Wages and Hours Act
Waggoner, Lyle
Wagner, Lindsay
Wagner, Richard
Wagner, Robert (actor)
Wagner, Robert F., Sen.
Wagner, Robert F., Jr., Mayor
Wagnerian opera
Wahabi reform
Wahl™ hair appliances
Wahl, Ken
Waikiki, Honolulu, HI
Wailing Wall, or Western Wall
Waimea, HI
Wainwright, Jonathan, Gen.
Waipahu, HI
Waite, Terry
Waiting for Godot
Waits, Tom

Wake Forest, NC
Wake Island
Wakefield, MA
Walcott, Jersey Joe
Wald, Jerry
Walden Pond
Waldenbooks
Waldheim, Kurt, UN Secy. Gen./Pres.
  Austria
Waldo, Janet
Waldorf salad
Waldorf-Astoria hotel (NYC)
Wales
Walesa, Lech
Walgreen, Charles
Walgreen's Drug Stores
Walhalla, or Valhalla
Walkman, Sony™
Wall Street Journal
Wall Street (NYC)
Walla Walla, WA
Wallace Beery
Wallace Stegner
Wallace, George, Gov.
Wallace, Henry A., V.P.
Wallace, Mike
Wallace, Sippie
Wallach, Eli
Wallaroo™ drink
Wallenda, Karl
Waller, Fats
Wallis and Futuna Islands (S. Pacific)
Wallis Warfield, duchess of Windsor
Wallis, Hal B.
Wally Cox
Wally Westmore
Wal-Mart Stores
Walnut Creek, CA
Walpole, Horace
Walt Disney World
Walt Elias Disney
Walt Whitman
Walter Bagehot
Walter Brennan
Walter P. Chrysler
Walter Cronkite
Walter Huston
Walter 'Big Train' Johnson

Walter Kerr
Walter Koenig
Walter Lippmann
Walter Matthau
Walter Mitty
Walter F. Mondale, V.P.
Walter O'Keefe
Walter O'Malley
Walter Pidgeon
Walter Pitkin
Walter Raleigh, Sir, or Ralegh
Walter Reed, Dr.
Walter Reed Army Med. Cntr. (DC)
Walter P. Reuther
Walter 'Wally' Schirra, astronaut
Walter Scott, Sir
Walter Richard Sickert
Walter Slezak
Walter Wanger
Walter Winchell
Walters, Barbara
Walther gun
Walton, Sam Moore
Walton, William, Sir
Wambaugh, Joseph
Wanamaker, John
Wanamaker, Sam
Wanamaker's store
Wandering Jew plant
Wang Laboratories
Wang Wei
Wang, Lu
Wanger, Walter
Wapner, Judge Joseph (of *People's Court*)
War between the States, Civil War, or War of Secession, War of the Rebellion
War of 1812
War of Jenkin's Ear
War of the Pacific
War of the Roses
Warhol, Andy
Waring™ blender
Waring, Fred
Warner Bros.
Warner Communications Inc.
Warner, Jack L.

Warner, Malcolm-Jamal
Warren Beatty
Warren Earl Burger, Ch. Justice
Warren Commission
Warren G. Harding, Pres.
Warren Spahn
Warren, Lesley Ann
Warren, Robert Penn
Warrick, Ruth
Warsaw Treaty Organization
Warsaw, Poland
Warwick Co., Eng.
Warwick, Dionne
Warwickshire, Eng.
Wasatch Range
Wash a-bye Baby™
Washington International Report
Washington Irving
Washington Journalism Review
Washington Monument
Washington Post
Washington Post Book World
Washington Redskins
Washington Senators
Washington, Booker T.
Washington, DC
Washington, Denzel
Washington, George, Pres.
Washington's Birthday
Wasserman, Lew
Wassermann test
Wassermann, August von
Wassily Kandinsky
Water Pik™
Waterbury, CT
Waterford crystal
Waterford, Ireland
Watergate Hotel
Watergate scandal
Waterloo Bridge
Waterloo campaign
Waterloo, Belgium
Waterloo, IA
Waterman, Willard (played Great
    Gildersleeve)
Waterston, Sam
Watervliet Arsenal, NY
Watley, Jody

Watson, Dr. (& Sherlock Holmes)
Watson, James Dewey
Watson-Crick model
Watt, James G., Interior Secy.
Watteau, Jean-Antoine
Watts' riots
Watts Towers (Simon Rodia, or
    Rodilla)
Watutsi, or Tutsi, or Batusi people
Waugh, Evelyn
Waukegan, IL
Wausau, WI
Wauwatosa, WI
Wave (member of WAVES)
WAVES (women's reserve US Navy)
Waxman, Franz
Waxman, Phillip A.
Waxtex™ waxed paper
Way of the Cross, also Stations of the
    Cross
Waylon Jennings
Wayne Gretzky
Wayne, Anthony, Gen.
Wayne, Bruce (Batman)
Wayne, John, or 'the Duke'
Wealthy apple
Wear-Dated™ Carpet
Wear-Ever™ appliance
Wearever™ pens
WeatherAll™ paint
Weatherwax, Rudd (Lassie's trainer)
Weaver, Charlie (pseud. Cliff Arquette)
Weaver, Dennis
Weaver, Doodles
Weaver, Sigourney
Webb, Jack
Weber, Carl Maria von, also Karl
Weber, Max (artist)
Weber, Max (sociologist)
Weber's™ Bread
Webster, Daniel (politician)
Webster, Noah (Dictionary)
Webster's New World Dictionary
Weddell Sea
Wedgwood china
Wedgwood, Josiah
Wedtech scandal
Wee Willie Winkie

Weed, CA
Weed Eater™
Weejuns shoes
Weeki Wachee Spring
Wei, Wang
Weight Watchers™
Weill, Kurt
Weimar, E. Ger.
Weimaraner dog
Weinberger, Caspar
'Weird Al' Yankovic
Weissmuller, Johnny (played Tarzan)
Weitz, Bruce
Welch, Raquel
Welchade™ drink
Welcome Back Kotter
Weldwood™ glue
Welk, Lawrence
Well-Tempered Clavier (Bach's)
Wella Balsam™
Welland Ship Canal
Welles, Gideon
Welles, Orson
Wellesley College
Wellesley, MA
Wellington boots
Wellington, Duke of (wellington boots)
Wellington, New Zealand
Wells Fargo Bank
Wells Fargo Express
Wells, H.G.
Welsh cob
Welsh Corgi, or corgi
Welsh language
Welsh Pony
Welsh rabbit
Welsh springer spaniel
Welsh terrier
Weltschmerz (world pain)
Wembley district, Lon.
Wenatchee Nat. Forest
Wenceslaus, 'good King', or St.
   Wenceslaus
Wendell Corey
Wendell L. Willkie
Wendy's™ restaurant
Wente-Martini wine
Wenzel, Hanni

Werner Heisenberg
Werner Herzog
Werner, Oskar
Wernher von Braun
Wertheimer, Max
Wes Craven
Wesley Crusher, Ensign (of *Star Trek*)
Wesleyan College (GA)
Wesleyan University (CT)
Wessex, Eng.
Wesson™ Oil
West Bank (Israel/Jordan)
West Bank (Paris)
West Bend™ cookware
West Berlin, W. Ger.
West Bromwich, Eng.
West Chester, PA
West Germany, or Federal Republic
   of Germany
West Goths, or Visigoths
West Hartford, CT
West Haven, CT
West Highland white terrier
West Indies
West Orange, NJ
West Pakistan (now Pakistan)
West Palm Beach, FL
West Point, NY
West Point, U.S. Military Academy at
West Siberian Plain
West Sussex Co., Eng.
West Virginia (WV)
West, Mae
Westbrook Pegler
Westchester, NY
Westclox™ Baby Ben
Westclox™ clocks
Western Hemisphere
Western liberalism
Western saddle
Western Samoa
Westfalia (Volkswagen van)
Westheimer, Dr. Ruth
Westinghouse™ appliances
Westinghouse Electric Corp.
Westinghouse, George
Westlake, Donald E.
Westminster Abbey

Westminster Palace, or Houses of Parliament (Lon.)
Westminster, CO
Westmore, Bud
Westmore, Perc
Westmore, Wally
Westmoreland, Wm., Gen.
Westover Air Force Base, MA
Westphalia region, W. Ger.
Westways
Wet 'n Wild™ cosmetics
Wet Ones™
Wexford, Ireland
Weyden, Roger van der
Weyerhaeuser Co.
Weyerhaeuser™ lumber
Weymouth, MA
Wharton, Edith
Wheatena™ cereal
Wheaton, Wil
Wheel of Time, or Kalachakra
Wheeler Air Force Base, HI
Wheeler, William A., V.P.
Wheeling, WV
Whidbey Island Naval Air Station, WA
Whiffenpoof Song
Whig (member Whig party)
Whig party (vs. Tory)
Whirlpool Corp.
Whirlpool™
Whiskas™ cat food
Whiskey Rebellion
Whiskey Ring
Whistler, James McNeill
Whitchurch Stouffville, Ont., Can.
White Friar (Carmelite friar)
White Horse™ whiskey
White House (U.S. Pres. home)
White Oak Naval Surface Weapons Center, MD
White Plains, NY
White Rain™ haircare
White Russian (cocktail)
White Sands Missile Range, NM
White Sox (team)
White, Byron R., Justice
White, E. B.

White, Edward, astronaut
White, Vanna
White-Westinghouse™
Whitefriars district (Lon.)
Whitehall Palace (Lon.)
White Chapell district (Lon.)
Whitehorse, Yukon, Can.
Whiteman Air Force Base, MO
Whiteman, Paul
Whitesnake (rock group)
Whitey Ford (aka Duke of Paducah)
Whiting Field Naval Air Station, FL
Whiting, Margaret
Whitley Strieber
Whitman, Walt
Whitmore, James
Whitney Houston
Whitney Museum of American Art
Whitney, Eli
Whitney, Mt.
Whittaker, Roger
Whittier, CA
Whittier, John Greenleaf
Whoopi Goldberg
Wichita, KS
Wichita Eagle Beacon
Wichita Falls, TX
Wichita Indians
Wicked One (the Devil)
Wicked Witch of the West
Wicklow, Ireland
Widdle Waddle, Mother
Widmark, Richard
Wiener Schnitzel
Wienerschnitzel™ restaurant
Wiesbaden, W. Ger.
Wiesenthal, Sam
Wiesenthal, Simon
Wiest, Dianne
Wiggle-Bug of Oz
Wigglesworth, Michael
Wight, Isle of
Wigwam™ socks
Wil Shriner
Wil Wheaton
Wilander, Mats
Wilbur Wright (Wright Bros.)
Wild Bill Hickok (b. James Hickok)

Wild Eights, also Crazy Eights
Wild Kingdom
Wild West show
Wild West, or old West
Wilde, Brandon De
Wilde, Cornel
Wilde, Oscar
Wilder, Billy
Wilder, Douglas, Gov. (1st U.S. black governor)
Wilder, Gene
Wilder, Laura Ingalls
Wilder, Thornton
Wilder, William
Wilderness campaign
Wilderness of Zin
Wilderness Road
Wile E. Coyote, or Wylie, or Wiley
Wiley Post
Wilford Brimley
Wilhelm Friedemann Bach
Wilhelm Roentgen, or Röntgen
Wilhelmina, Queen of Netherlands
Wilkins, Roy
Will and Ariel Durant
Will Geer
Will Rogers
Willa Cather
Willamette Nat. Forest
Willard Scott
Willard Waterman (*Great Gildersleeve*)
Willebrord Snell
Willem Dafoe
Willem de Kooning
Willemstad, Netherlands Antilles
Willi Baumeister
William Albright
William Harrison Ainsworth
William and Mary, College of, VA
William Anders, astronaut
William Baffin
William Michael Balfe
William Baziotes
William Beaverbrook, Baron
William Beebe
William Bendix
William Blackstone, Sir
William Blake

William Bligh, Capt. (*Bounty*)
William H. Bonney (Billy the Kid)
William Booth
William Henry Bragg, Sir
William Lawrence Bragg
William J. Brennan, Justice
William Jennings Bryan
William Cullen Bryant
William F. Buckley Jr.
William Caslon
William Caxton
William Chambers, Sir
William 'Buffalo Bill´ Cody
William Congreve
William Conrad
William Cowper (jurist)
William Cowper (poet)
William Crookes, Sir
William Demarest
William Devane
William O. Douglas, Justice
William Faulkner
William Frawley
William Friedkin
William Gilbert, Sir
William Gladstone, P.M.
William Glakens
William Golding
William Henry Harrison, Pres.
William S. Hart
William Randolph Hearst
William R. Higgins, Lt.Col.
William Hogarth
William Howard Taft, Pres.
William Hurt
William Inge
William Katt
William Thomson Kelvin, Lord
William Kidd, Capt.
William R. King, V.P.
William H. Masters, Dr.
William 'Bill' Mauldin
William McKinley, Pres.
William Claire Menninger, Dr.
William Morris Agency
William of Orange, or 'William the Silent'
William S. Paley

William Edward Parry, Sir
William Penn
William Petrie, Sir
William H. Pickering
William Pitt, P.M.
William Sydney Porter (aka O. Henry)
William Powell
William Proxmire, Sen.
William Clarke Quantrill
William H. Rehnquist, Ch. Justice
William Riker, Cmdr. (*Star Trek*)
William Rockefeller
William Saroyan
William Schuman
William Scoresby
William Henry Seward, Sen.
William Shakespeare or Shakespear,
    or Shakespere, or Shakspere
William Shatner
William Tecumseh Sherman, Gen.
William B. Shockley, Dr.
William Archibald Spooner, Rev.
    (spoonerism)
William Styron
William Henry Fox Talbot
William Tell
William Tell Opera
William Makepeace Thackeray
William "Boss Tweed" Tweed
William Walton, Sir
William Westmoreland, Gen.
William A. Wheeler, V.P.
William Wilder
William Wordsworth
William Wrigley, Jr.
William Butler Yeats
Williams, Cootie
Williams, Esther
Williams, JoBeth
Williams, Hank
Williams, Hank, Jr.
Williams, Robin
Williams, Ted 'the Splendid Splinter'
Williams, Tennessee
Williams, Vanessa
Williamsburg, VA
Willie Bobo
Willie (Howard) Mays

Willie Nelson
Willie 'the Shoe' Shoemaker
Willie Sutton
Willis, Bruce
Willkie, Wendell L.
Willy Brandt, Chancellor
Willy Loman
Willy Messerschmitt
Willy Wonka
Wilmington, DE
Wilmington News Journal
Wilmot Proviso
Wilson™ tennis balls
Wilson, Sir Harold, P.M.
Wilson, Henry, V.P.
Wilson, Woodrow, Pres.
Wiltshire knives
Wimbledon Tennis Championships
Wimbledon, Eng.
Wimsey, Lord Peter
Winchell, Walter
Winchell's™ Donut House
Winchester House
Winchester™ rifle
Wind in the Willows, The
Wind Song™ perfume
Windex™ cleaner
Windmere™
Window Rock, AZ
Windsor Castle
Windsor, Edward, duke of
Windsor, Eng.
Windsor, Ont., Can.
Windsor, Wallis Warfield, duchess of
Windward Islands, W.I.
Windward Passage, W.I.
Windy City (Chicago)
Winesap apple
Winfield Scott, Gen.
Winfrey, Oprah
Winger, Debra
Winkle, Rip Van
Winkler, Henry
Winky Dink
Winnebago Indians
Winnebago™ RV
Winnemucca, NV
Winnetka, IL

Winnie Mandela
Winnie-the-Pooh
Winnipeg Free Press
Winnipeg, Man., Can.
Winslow, AZ
Winslow Homer
Winston Churchill, Sir
Winston-Salem Journal
Winston-Salem, NC
Winston, Harry
Winter of Our Discontent, The
Winter's Tale, The
Winters, Shelley
Winthrop Rockefeller, Gov.
Winthrop, John, Gov.
Winwood, Steve
Wirephoto™
Wisconsin (WI)
Wisconsin vs. Yoder
Wise Men of the East, or Magi, or
    Three Kings
Wish-Bone™ dressings
Wisk™ detergent
Wispride™ cheese
Witt, Katarina
Witt, Paul Junger
Witwatersrand, or the Rand (gold
    mining area S. Afr.)
Wizard of Id
Wizard of Oz, The
WKRP TV show
Wobblies (members Industrial Workers
    of the World)
Wodehouse, Sir P. G. (Pelham
    Grenville)
Woden, or Odin
Wojtyla, Karol (Pope John Paul II)
Wolf Man, the
Wolf Trap Farm
Wolf, Hugo
Wolfe, Nero
Wolfe, Thomas
Wolff™ Tanning System
Wolfgang Amadeus Mozart
Wolfgang Puck
Wolf-Ferrari, Ermanno
Wolper, David L.
Wolsey, Thomas, Cardinal

Woman's Christian Temperance
    Union
Woman's Day magazine
Women's Army Corps, or WAC
Women's Wear Daily
Wonder Woman
Wonder, Stevie
Wondra™ hand lotaion
Wong, Suzy
Wonka, Willy
Woo, Roh Tae, Pres.
Wood, Grant
Woodard, Alfre
Wooden Award, John R.
Woodhouse, Barbara
Woodiwiss, Kathleen
Woodrow Wilson, Pres.
Woods Hole Oceanographic Inst.
Woodsmith
Woodstock Festival, also Music &
    Art Fair (NY)
Woodward & Bernstein
Woodward Stores Ltd.
Woodward, Bob
Woodward, Edward
Woody Allen
Woody Guthrie
Woolco stores
Woolf, Virginia
Woolite™
Woollcott, Alexander
Woolley, Monty
Woolworth Building (NYC)
Woolworth, Frank W.
Woolworth's stores
Wopat, Tom
Worcester china
Worcester Evening Gazette
Worcester Telegram
Worcester, Eng.
Worcester, MA
Worcestershire sauce
Wordsworth, William
Worf, Lt. (*Star Trek*)
Work Projects Adm., or WPA
World Bank, or Internat'l Bank for
    Reconstruction & Development
World Council of Churches

World Court, or International Court of Justice
World Savings & Loan
World Series
World Trade Center (NYC)
World War I, or the Great War
World War I Central Powers
World War II
World War II Allies
Worldwatch Institute
Worley, Jo Anne
Worzel Gummidge
Wouk, Herman
Wounded Knee creek (SD)
Wrangler™ jeans
Wrather, Jack
Wreck of the Hesperus, The
Wren, Sir Christopher
Wright brothers (Wilbur & Orville)
Wright, Frank Lloyd
Wright, Orville
Wright, Wilbur
Wright-Patterson Air Force Base, OH
Wrigley Field
Wrigley, William, Jr.
Wrigley's™ gum
Wrinkle in Time, A
Wriothesley, Henry, Earl of Southampton
Writer, The magazine
Writer's Digest
Wunderkind
Wurlitzer™
Wurtsmith Air Force Base, MI
Wüsthof Knives™
Wuthering Heights
Wyatt Earp
Wyatt, Jane
Wyclif, John, or Wycliffe, or Wickliffe
Wyeth, Andrew N.
Wyeth, Newell Convers
Wyman, Jane
Wynette, Tammy
Wynken, Blynken & Nod
Wynn, Ed
Wynn, Keenan
Wynn, Tracy Keenan

Wynonna Judd
Wyoming (WY)
Wyss, Johann David (*The Swiss Family Robinson*)
Wyszynski, Stefan, Cardinal

X-ray, or X ray
X-ray therapy
X-ray tube
XX Dos Equis™ beer
XYZ Affair
Xanadu
Xavier Cougat
Xavier, Francis, St.
Xe (chem. sym. xenon)
Xenophanes
Xerox Corp.
Xerxes (2 kings of Persia)
Xi'a Xi'ang™ perfume
Xiaoping, Deng
Xinjiang, China, or Sinkiang

Y (chem. sym. yttrium)
Yablonski, Joseph A.
Yahoo (*Gulliver's T.*)
Yahweh
Yakima, WA

Yakov Smirnoff
Yakovlev, Alexander N.
Yakuza
Yale University
Yalta Conference
Yalu River
Yamaha™ motor bikes
Yamaha Motor Co. Ltd.
Yangtze River, or Chang
Yankee
Yankee Doodle
Yankovic, Frank
Yankovic, 'Weird Al'
Yaoundé, Cameroon
Yaqui Indians
Yarborough, Barton
Yarbro, Chelsea Quinn
Yasmin Khan, Princess
Yasser Arafat, or Yasir
Yasuhiro Nakasone, P.M.
Yat-sen, Sun, Pres.
Yb (chem. sym. ytterbium)
Yeager, Chuck, Col.
Yeats, William Butler
Yehudi Menuhin
Yeliseyev, Aleksei, Cosmonaut
Yellow Brick Road
Yellow Christ, The (Gauguin)
Yellow Pages™
Yellow Sea
Yellowknife, NW Territories, Can.
Yellowstone Falls
Yellowstone Lake
Yellowstone Nat. Pk.
Yellowstone River
Yemen
Yendi™ perfume
Yenisei River, or Yenisey
Yeoman of the Guard
Yerby, Frank
Yerevan, Armenia
YES™ Clothing Co.
Yevgeny Khrunov, Cosmonaut
Yiddish
Yitzhak Shamir, P.M., or Yitzak
Yma Sumac
Yo-Yo Ma
Yoakam, Dwight

Yogi Bear (cartoon)
Yogi Berra (sports figure)
Yogi, Maharishi Mahesh
Yoko Ono
Yokohama, Japan
Yom Kippur (Jew. holiday)
Yom Kippur War
Yom Tov
Yonkers, NY
Yoo-Hoo™ cola
Yoplait™ Yogurt
York, Dick
York, Eng.
York Peppermint Pattie™
York, Sgt. (Alvin Cullum York)
Yorkin, Bud
Yorkshire ham
Yorkshire pudding
Yorkshire terrier
Yorktown campaign
Yorktown Naval Weapons Station,
   VA
Yosemite Falls
Yosemite Nat. Park (CA)
Yothers, Tina
You Can't Go Home Again
Young & Rubicom adv. agency
Young, Andrew Jackson, Mayor
Young, Brigham
Young, Cy
Young, John (1st Space Shuttle flight)
Young, Karen
Young, Loretta
Younger, Cole
Youngstown Vindicator
Youngstown, OH
Your Cheatin' Heart
Yüan dynasty
Yuban™ coffee
Yucatán Peninsula
Yucatán, state, Mexico
Yugo™ car
Yugoslavia, also Jugoslavia
Yukio, Mishima
Yukon River
Yukon Territory
Yul Brynner
Yuma, AZ

Yuma Proving Ground, AZ
Yuri Andropov, Gen. Secy.
Yuri A. Gagarin, Cosmonaut
Yves Montand
Yves Saint-Laurent
Yves Tanguy
Yvonne DeCarlo

Zabar's deli (NYC)
Zachary Scott
Zachary Taylor, Pres.
Zacky Farms™ chicken
Zadora, Pia
Zagreb, Yugoslavia
Zagros Mts.
Zaharias, Mildred 'Babe' Didrikson
Zahn, Paula
Zaire
Zambezi River
Zambia (formerly Northern Rhodesia)
Zamboanga, Mindanao, Phil.
Zamfir (musician)
Zamora, Jaime Paz, Pres.
Zandonai, Riccardo
Zane Grey
Zanuck, Darryl F.
Zanzibar, Tanzania
Zapotec Indians
Zappa, Dweezil
Zappa, Frank
ZaSu Pitts
Zayak, Elaine
Zazee, Buell
ZCMI Department Stores
Zedekiah, king
Zedong, Mao, Chairman, or Mao Tse-
　　tung

Zee™ paper products
Zeebrugge, Belgium
Zeeland, Netherlands
Zeeman effect
Zeffirelli, Franco
Zeist, Netherlands
Zeitgeist (Ger. spirit)
Zemin, Jiang
Zen Buddhism
Zena™ Jeans
Zenith Laboratories
Zenith Radio Corp.
Zenith™ TV/electronics
Zenko, Suzuki, P.M.
Zeppelin, Ferdinand, Graf von, Count
Zeppo Marx (Herbert)
Zermatt, Switz.
Zero Mostel
ZERON Group
Zest™ soap
Zeus (Phidias)
Zeus (myth. chief god)
Zevi, Sabbatai
Zhangjiakou, China
Zhao Ziyang, Premier
Zhejiang province, China
Zhengzhou, China, or Chengchow
Zia-ul-Haq, Mohammad, Pres., or
　　'Pres. Zia'
Ziegfeld Follies
Ziegfeld, Florenz 'Flo'
Ziegler, Ron
Ziggy Elman
Zigong, China
Zimbabwe (formerly Rhodesia)
Zimbalist, Efrem, Jr. (actor)
Zimbalist, Efrem, Sr. (musician)
Zimbalist, Stephanie
Zimmer, Kim
Zin, Wilderness of
Zina Garrison
Zindcl, Paul
Zinka Milanov
Zinnermann, Fred
Zinsser, Hans
Zion Nat. Park (UT)
Zion, Mt.
Zion, or Sion ('City of David')

Zionism
ZIP Code™
Zip™ depilatory
Zip Wax™ car polish
Zip-a-dee-doo-dah
Ziploc™ Storage Bags
ZIV-TV
Ziyang, Zhao, Premier
Zn (chem. sym. zinc)
Zoeller, Fuzzy
Zog I (deposed Albanian king)
Zola Budd
Zola, Emile
Zoltán Kodály
Zomax™
Zona Gale
Zond space probe
Zoot Sims
Zoot suit
Zorba the Greek
Zorn, Anders
Zoroaster
Zoroastrianism
Zorro (Don Diego)
Zouave tribe
Zr (chem. sym. zirconium)
Zsa Zsa Gabor
Zubin Mehta
Zuckerboard™
Zuckerman Unbound
Zuckerman, George
Zuckerman, Mort
Zuckerman, Pinchas
Zuider Zee
Zukor, Adolph
Zulu, tribe
Zululand
Zumwalt III, Elmo, Admiral
Zuñi Indians
Zuñi pueblo
Zürich, Switz.
Zutty Singleton
Zvereva, Natasha
Zwickau, E. Ger.
Zwolle, Netherlands
Zworykin, Vladimir
ZZ Top

ACRONYMS

AA	Alcoholics Anonymous
AA	American Airlines
AA	Associate of Arts
AAA	American Automobile Association
AARP	American Assoc. of Retired Persons
AAU	Amateur Athletic Union
AAUW	American Association of University Women
ABA	American Bar Assoc.
ABA	American Booksellers Assoc.
ABC	Alcoholic Beverage Control Board
ABC	American Broadcasting Co.
ABM	antiballistic missile
A/C	air conditioning
AC	alternating current
AC	Athletic Club
ACLU	American Civil Liberties Union
ACS	American Cancer Society
ACV	Hovercraft
AD	active duty (military)
A.D.	*Anno Domini* - in the year of the Lord
ADC	aide-de-camp
ADP	automatic data processing
AF	Air Force
AF	audio frequency
AFA	Air Force Academy
AFB	Air Force Base
AFC	automatic frequency control
AFDC	Aid to Families with Dependent Children
AFL	American Federation of Labor
AFL-CIO	Am. Fed. of Labor & Congress of Industrial Organizations
AFTRA	American Federation of Television and Radio Artists
AG	Adjutant General
AG	Attorney General
AI	artificial intelligence
AIDS	Acquired Immune Deficiency Syndrome
AIM	American Indian Movement
AK	Alaska
AKA	also known as
AKC	American Kennel Club
AL	Alabama
AL	American Legion
ALA	American Library Association
AMA	American Medical Association
AMEX	American Stock Exchange
AMVETS	American Veterans of WW II, Korea, Vietnam
ANA	American Nurses' Association
ANTA	American National Theatre and Academy
AP	Associated Press
AP	Author's Proof
APA	American Pharmaceutical Association
APA	American Psychiatric Association
APA	American Psychological Association
APB	all-points bulletin
API	American Petroleum Institute
APO	Army and Air Force Post Office (overseas)
APV	All-Purpose Vehicle
AR	Arkansas
AR	Army Regulation
ARE	Arab Republic of Egypt
ARE	Association for Research & Enlightenment

ARM	adjustable-rate mortgage
ASAP	as soon as possible
ASCAP	American Society of Composers, Authors & Publishers
ASL	American sign Language
ASPCA	Am. Society for the Prevention of Cruelty to Animals
AST	Atlantic Standard Time
AT & T	American Telephone & Telegraph
ATM	Automatic Teller Machine
ATV	all-terrain vehicle
AV	audiovisual
AWOL	absent without leave, or awol
AZ	Arizona
B & B	bed and breakfast
B & E	breaking and entering
B & W	black-and-white, or b & w
BA	Bachelor of Arts
BBC	British Broadcasting Corporation
BC	before Christ
BC	British Columbia
BFA	Bachelor of Fine Arts
BHA	synthetic antioxidant preservative (foods, fat, oil)
BHT	synthetic antioxidant preservative (foods, oil, rubber)
BIA	Bureau of Indian Affairs
BIP	*Books In Print* (Bowker)
BLM	Bureau of Land Management
BLT	bacon, lettuce, and tomato sandwich
BMOC	Big Man on Campus
BO	box office
BO	branch office
BOMC	Book-of-the-Month Club
BOQ	bachelor officers' quarters, also base officers' quarters
B/P	blood pressure
BPD	barrels per day, or bpd
BPI	bytes per inch, or bpi
BPOE	Benevolent and Protective Order of Elks
BR	bedroom
BRE	business reply envelope
BS	Bachelor of Science, or Bsc
BSA	Boy Scouts of America
Btu	British thermal unit
BVM	Blessed Virgin Mary
BX	Base Exchange
BYO	bring your own (liquor)
C in C	Commander in Chief
C & W	Country and Western (music)
CA	California
CAB	Civil Aeronautics Board
CACM	Central American Common Market
CAP	Civil Air Patrol
CARE	Cooprative for American Relief Everywhere, Inc.
CBC	Canadian Broadcasting System
CCC	Civilian Conservation Corps
CCU	coronary care unit
CD	certificate of deposit
CD	Civil Defense
CD	compact disk
CDC	Centers for Disease Control
CE	Civil Engineer
CEO	Chief Executive Officer
CFI	cost, freight, and insurance
CFTC	Commodity Futures Trading Commission
CG	Coast Guard
CIA	Central Intelligence Agency
CITES	Convention on International Trade in Endangered Species

COD	cash, or collect, on delivery
COD	Certificate of Death
CORE	Congress of Racial Equality
COS	cash on shipment
CP	Command Post
CP	Communist Party
CPA	Certified Public Accountant
CPI	consumer price index
CPO	Chief Petty Officer
CPR	cardiopulmonary resuscitation
CRT	cathode-ray tube
CST	Central Standard Time
CT	Connecticut
CWO	cash with order
CWO	Chief Warrant Officer
D & B	Dun & Bradstreet financial rating
D & C	dilatation and curettage
DA	District Attorney
DAR	Daughters of the American Revolution
DBA	official business name - 'doing business as'
DC	direct current, or dc
DC	District of Columbia
DDC	Dewey Decimal Classification
DDS	Doctor of Dental Surgery
DDT	Dichlorodiphenyltrichloroethane
DE	Delaware
DE	football - defensive end
DEA	Drug Enforcement Administration
DFC	Distinguished Flying Cross
DI	drill instructor
DJ	disc jockey
DJI	Dow-Jones Industrials
DL	football - defensive lineman
DLO	Dead Letter Office (US Postal Service)
DMSO	colorless liquid used as solvent and in experimental medicine
DMZ	demilitarized zone
DNA	deoxyribonucleic acid
DO	Doctor of Osteopathy
DOA	dead on arrival
DOB	Date of Birth
DOD	Department of Defense
DOS	disk operating system
DP	baseball - double play
DP	dew point
DSC	Distinguished Service Cross
DSM	Distinguished Service Medal
DSO	Distinguished Service Order
DST	daylight saving time
DT	football - defensive tackle
DT's	Delirium Tremens
DVM	Doctor of Veterinary Medicine
DWI	driving while intoxicated
ECG	electrocardiogram
EDA	Economic Development Administration
EDT	Eastern Daylight Time
EDTA	crystalline solid used as food preservative
EEG	electroencephalogram
EEOC	Equal Employment Opportunity Commission
EFT	electronic fund transfer through computer database
EKG	electrocardiogram
EMS	European Monetary System
EPA	Environmental Protection Agency
ERA	Equal Rights Amendment
ESP	extrasensory perception

ETA	estimated time of arrival
ETD	estimated time of departure
FAA	Federal Aviation Administration
FAX	facsimile
FB	football - fullback
FBI	Federal Bureau of Investigation
FCC	Federal Communications Commission
FDA	Food and Drug Administration
FDIC	Federal Deposit Insurance Corp.
FFA	Future Farmers of America
FG	basketball, football - field goal
FHA	Farmers Home Administration
FHA	Federal Housing Administration
FHMA	Federal Home Mortgage Corp. (Freddie Mac)
FICA	Federal Insurance Contributions Act
FIFO	accounting method of first in, first out
FL	Florida
FLSA	Fair Labor Standards Act
FNMA	Federal National Mortgage Assn. (Fannie Mae, or May)
FO	Foreign Office
FOE	Fraternal Order of Eagles
FPC	Federal Power Commission
FPO	U.S. Navy Fleet Post Office
FRS	Federal Reserve System
FS	Forest Service
FSLIC	Federal Savings & Loan Insurance Corp. (defunct)
FT	basketball - free throw
FTC	Federal Trade Commission
FTD	Florists' Transworld Delivery
FYA	for your attention
FYI	for your information
GA	Georgia
GAO	General Accounting Office (U.S. govt.)
GB	Great Britain
GCT	Greenwich Conservatory Time
GDR	German Democratic Republic (East Germany)
GED	general equivalency diploma (high school)
GESTAPO	*Geheime Staats Polizei* - Secret State Police Nazi Ger.
GI	gastrointestinal
GIGO	Garbage In, Garbage Out
GM	General Manager
GMT	Greenwich Mean Time
GNP	gross national product
GOP	Grand Old Party (Republican Party)
GPO	General Post Office
GSA	General Services Administration
GSA	Girl Scouts of America
GST	Greenwich Sidereal Time
HB	football - halfback
HDL	high-density lipoprotein
HEW	Dept. of Health, Education and Welfare
HF	high frequency
HH	Her (or His) Highness
HH	His Holiness
HHS	Dept. of Health and Human Services
HI	Hawaii
HM	Her (or His) Majesty
HMO	Health Maintenance Organization
HMS	Her (or His) Majesty's Service, Ship, or Steamer
HP	horsepower
HQ	headquarters
HR	baseball - home run
HS	High School
HTLV	human T-cell leukemia virus

HUAC	House Un-American Activities Committee
HUD	Department of Housing and Urban Development
IA	Iowa
IAS	indicated airspeed
IBM	International Business Machines Corp.
ICAO	International Civil Aviation Organization
ICBM	intercontinental ballistic missile
ICC	Interstate Commerce Commission
ICU	intensive care unit
ID	Idaho
ID	identity document (card, driver's license)
IFR	Instrument Flight Rules
IG	Inspector General
IGY	International Geophysical Year
ILGWU	International Ladies' Garment Workers' Union
ILO	International Labor Organization
IMF	International Monetary Fund
IN	Indiana
INC	Incorporated
Interpol	International Criminal Police Organization
IOOF	Independent Order of Goodfellows
IOU	for 'I owe you' - signed pledge of debt
IQ	Intelligence Quotient
IRA	Individual Retirement Account
IRA	Irish Republican Army
IRBM	intermediate range ballistic missile
IRS	Internal Revenue Service
ISBN	International Standard Book Number
ITO	International Trade Organization
IUD	intrauterine device
IWW	Industrial Workers of the World
JA	Judge Advocate
JAG	Judge Advocate General
JAP	Jewish American Princess
JC	Jesus Christ
JC	Julius Caesar
JD	Justice Department
JD	juvenile delinquent
JDL	Jewish Defense League
JP	Justice of the Peace
JPL	Jet Propulsion Laboratory
JWB	Jewish Welfare Board
JWV	Jewish War Veterans
KGB	*Komityet Gosudarstvyennoj Byezopasnosti* - security police and intelligence agency of Soviet Union
KKK	Ku Klux Klan
KO	boxing - to knock out
KP	kitchen police (duty)
KS	Kansas
KY	Kentucky
LA	Los Angeles
LA	Louisiana
LB	football - linebacker
LC	Library of Congress
LC	U.S. Navy prefix for landing craft
LCD	liquid crystal display
LCV	landing craft vehicle
LDL	low-density lipoprotein
LED	light-emitting diode
LEM	lunar excursion module
LM	Lord Mayor
LOX	liquid oxygen
LPN	Licensed Practical Nurse
LSD	lysergic acid diethylamide

LTC	Lieutenant Colonel, or Lt Col
LTD	Limited
LTG	Lieutenant General, or Lt Gen
MA	Massachusetts
MA	Master of Arts
MAD	Mutually Assured Destruction theory
MADD	Mothers Against Drunk Driving
MB	megabyte
MBA	Master of Business Administration
MC	Master of Ceremonies
MC	Medical Corps
MD	Doctor of Medicine
MD	Maryland
MF	Microfiche
MFA	Master of Fine Arts
MFH	Master of Foxhounds
MG	football - middle guard
MH	Medal of Honor
MH	Most Honorable
MI	Michigan
MI	Military Intelligence
MIA	missing in action
MIRV	multiple independently targeted reentry vehicle
MISC	miscellaneous
MN	Minnesota
MO	money order
MP	Military Police
MP	Mounted Police
MPV	Multi-Purpose Vehicle
MS	Mississippi
MS	multiple sclerosis
MSG	monosodium glutamate
MST	Mountain Standard Time
MT	Montana
N/A	not applicable
NAACP	National Assoc. for the Advancement of Colored People
NAB	naval air base
NABISCO	National Biscuit Co.
NASA	National Aeronautics and Space Administration
NATO	North Atlantic Treaty Organization
NDE	near death experience
NGC	New General Catalog (astronomy)
NLRB	National Labor Relations Board
NOW	National Organization for Women
NPV	no par value
NQB	no qualified bidders
NRA	National Rifle Assoc.
NRC	Nuclear Regulatory Commission
NSC	National Security Council
NSF	non, or not-sufficient funds
NTP	normal temperature and air pressure
NV	Nevada
NY	New York
NYC	New York City
NYSE	New York Stock Exchange
OAS	Organization of American States
OBE	out of body experience
OC	Officer Commanding
OCD	Office of Civil Defense
OCS	Officer Candidate School
OD	Officer of the Day
OD	overdose of narcotic substance
OE	Old English
OECD	Organization for Economic Cooperation & Development

OH	Ohio
OK	Oklahoma
OK	*oll korrect* - all right
OMB	Office of Management and Budget
OPEC	Organization of Petroleum Exporting Countries
OR	operating room
OR	Oregon
ORC	Officers' Reserve Corps
OSG	Office of Secretary General (UN)
OSHA	Occupational Safety and Health Administration
OTB	off-track betting
OTC	over-the-counter (stock sale)
OTEC	ocean thermal energy conversion
P & L	profit and loss
PA	Pennyslvania
PA	Post Adjutant
PA	power of attorney
PA	public address system
PABA	para-aminobenzoic acid
PAC	political action committee
PBS	Public Broadcasting Service
PBX	private branch exchange
C	Post Commander
PCB	polychlorinated biphenyl
PCP	phenylcyclohexylpiperidine
PCV	positive crankcase ventilation (valve)
PD	per diem
PD	Police Department
PD	postal district
PDQ	pretty damn quick
PE	Physical Education
PETA	People for the Ethical Treatment of Animals
PFC	Private First Class, or Pfc
PGA	Professional Golfers Association
PIB	person(s) in black
PKU	phenylketonuria
PLO	Palestine Liberation Organization
PM	Paymaster
PM	*post meridiem* - from noon to midnight
PM	Postmaster
PM	Prime Minister
PM	Provost Marshal
PMG	Paymaster General
PMG	Postmaster General
PMS	premenstrual syndrome
PO	Petty Officer
PO	Post Office, or post office box
POB	Post Office box
POW	Prisoner(s) of War, or PW
PP	parcel post
PR	Public Relations
PROM	programmable read-only memory (chip)
PS	postscript
PSRO	Professional Standards Review Organ.
PST	Pacific Standard Time
PTA	Parent-Teacher Association
PTL	Praise The Lord Club
PVC	polyvinyl chloride
PWA	Public Works Administration
PX	Post Exchange
Q & A	question and answer
QB	football - quarterback
QB	qualified bidders
QC	quality control

QM	Quartermaster
QT	keep secret, as 'on the QT'
R & B	rhythm and blues
R & D	research and development
RADAR	Radio Detection and Ranging
RAM	random-access memory (chip)
RCAF	Royal Canadian Air Force
RCMP	Royal Canadian Mounted Police
RCP	Royal College of Physicians
RCS	Royal College of Surgeons
R/D	Rural Delivery
RDA	recommended daily (or dietary) allowance
RDD	Research and Development Division
RE	football - right end
REM	rapid eye movement
RFD	Rural Free Delivery
RI	Rhode Island
RIP	*requiescat in pace* - rest in peace
RMA	Royal Military Academy
RMC	Royal Military College
RMS	Royal Mail Service
RMS	Royal Mail Ship
RN	Registered Nurse
RN	Royal Navy
RNA	ribonucleic acid
RNR	Royal Naval Reserve
ROM	read-only memory (chip)
ROTC	Reserve Officers' Training Corps
RR	railroad
RSVP	*répondez s'il vous plaît* - please reply
RV	recreation vehicle
SA	Salvation Army
SAC	Strategic Air Command
SADD	Students Against Drunk Driving
SAE	self-addressed envelope
SANKA	sans caffeine (brand name)
SAP	soon as possible
SART	Strategic Arms Reduction Talks
SASE	self-addressed stamped envelope
SAT	Scholastic Apitude Test
SBA	Small Business Administration
SC	Security Council (of the UN)
SC	Signal Corps
SC	South Carolina
SCLC	Southern Christian Leadership Conference
SCORE	Service Corps of Retired Executives
SDI	Strategic Defense Initiative
SDR	Special Drawing Rights (international monetary reserves)
SEATO	Southeast Asia Treaty Organ. (1955-76)
SEC	Securities & Exchange Commission
SIDS	sudden infant death syndrome, or crib death
SITCOM	situation comedy
SMOG	smoke and fog (now for any poor air quality)
SNAFU	situation normal, all fouled (f——d) up
SOB	son of a bitch, or sob
SOP	standard operating procedure
SOS	Save Our Ship, Souls
SPAR	woman member of U.S. Coast Guard
SPCA	Society for the Prevention of Cruelty to Animals
SPCC	Society for the Prevention of Cruelty to Children
SRO	standing room only
SS	*Schutzstaffel* - quasi-military unit of Nazi party
SS	Social Security
SSA	Social Security Administration

SSR	Soviet Socialist Republic
SSS	Selective Service System
SST	supersonic transport
ST	Saint
START	Strategic Arms Reduction Talks
STD	sexually transmitted disease
STP	standard temperature and pressure
SWAK	sealed with a kiss, or swak
SWAT	Special Weapons and Tactics, as in 'SWAT team'
SYD	Scotland Yard
TA	Teaching Assistant
TARMAC	tar macadam
TARP	tarpaulin
TB	Tuberculosis
TBA	to be announced
TD	football - touchdown
TGIF	Thank God It's Friday
TLC	tender, loving care
TM	trademark
TM	Transcendental Meditation
TN	Tennessee
TNT	trinitrotoluene
TVA	Tennessee Valley Authority
TWA	Trans World Airlines
TWX	Teletypewriter Exchange Service
TX	Texas
UAE	United Arab Emirates
UAW	United Automobile Workers (of America)
UCC	Uniform Commerical Code
UFO	unidentified flying object
UHF	ultrahigh frequency
UN	United Nations
UNESCO	United Nations Educational, Scientific, & Cultural Organ.
UPC	Universal Product Code
UPI	United Press International
UPS	United Parcel Service
US	United States
USA	United States of America
USAF	United States Air Force
USCG	United States Coast Guard
USDA	United States Department of Agriculture
USES	United States Employment Service
USGS	United States Geological Survey
USJCC	United States Junior Chamber of Commerce
USIA	United States Information Agency
USM	United States Mail
USM	United States Mint
USMC	United States Marine Corps
USN	United States Navy
USNG	United States National Guard
USO	United Service Organization
USP	United States Pharmacopeia
USPS	United States Postal Service
USS	United States Senate
USS	United States Ship
USSR	Union of Soviet Republics
USTA	United States Tennis Association
UT	Universal time
UT	Utah
UV	ultraviolet
V.R.	*Victoria Regina* - Queen Victoria
VAR	visual-aural (radio) range
VC	Vice-Chairman
VC	Vice-Consul

VC	Victoria Cross
VC	Viet Cong
VCR	videocassette recorder
VD	veneral disease
VDT	video display terminal
VDU	visual display unit
VET	veteran
VFR	Visual Flight Rules
VFW	Veterans of Foreign Wars
VHF	very high frequency
VHS	video home system
VISTA	Volunteers in Service to America
VLF	very low frequency
VLSI	very-large scale integration (chip)
VMD	Doctor of Veterinary Medicine
VP	Vice-President
VS	versus (against), or vs., v.
VS	Veterinary Surgeon
VT	variable time
VT	Vermont
VTR	video tape recorder
WA	Washington
WAC	Women's Army Corps
WAF	Women in the Air Force
WASP	white Anglo-Saxon Protestant
WATS	wide area telecommunications service
WAVES	Women Accepted for Volunteer Emergency Service
WC	water closet (Br. colloq. for toilet)
WCA	Workmen's Compensation Act
WCC	World Council of Churches
WCTU	Woman's Christian Temperance Union
WHO	World Health Organization (UN)
WI	West Indies
WI	Wisconsin
WO	Warrant Officer
WPA	Works Projects Administration
WPM	words per minute
WPS	words per second
WR	football - wide receiver
WRAC	Women's Royal Army Corps
WRAF	Women's Royal Air Force
Wren	member of Women's Royal Naval Service
WSJ	Wall Street Journal
WV	West Virginia
WW I	World War I
WW II	World War II
WY	Wyoming
XL	extra large
XL	extra long
XS	extra small
YAR	Yemen Arab Republic
YMCA	Young Men's Christian Assoc.
YMHA	Young Men's Hebrew Assoc.
YWCA	Young Women's Christian Assoc.
YWHA	Young Women's Hebrew Assoc.
ZPG	Zero Population Growth